Christian Souls and Chinese Spirits

Christian Souls
and Chinese Spirits

A Hakka Community in Hong Kong

NICOLE CONSTABLE

University of California Press

BERKELEY   LOS ANGELES   LONDON

University of California Press
Berkeley and Los Angeles, California

University of California Press, Ltd.
London, England

© 1994 by
The Regents of the University of California

Constable, Nicole.
    Christian souls and Chinese spirits: A Hakka community in Hong Kong / Nicole Constable.
        p.   cm.
    Includes bibliographical references.
    ISBN 0-520-08384-9 (alk. paper)
    1. Hakka (Chinese people)—Hong Kong—Ethnic identity.   2. Hakka (Chinese people)—
Hong Kong—Religion.   3. Lutherans—Hong Kong.   I. Title.
    DS796.H79H353   1994
    305.895'1—dc20   93-24006
                                                                                                          CIP

Printed in the United States of America

9 8 7 6 5 4 3 2 1

For three teachers
Andrew Y. L. Cheung
Antoinette Constable
William A. Shack

Contents

List of Tables and Illustrations

Acknowledgments

I am grateful to a number of institutions and individuals for the support they have given to this project. Preliminary research funding was provided by a Humanities Graduate Research Grant and the Robert H. Lowie Fund at the University of California at Berkeley. Generous funding for a year of research in Hong Kong was provided by a grant from the Joint Committee on Chinese Studies of the American Council of Learned Societies and the Social Science Research Council. A grant from the Mabelle McLeod Lewis Memorial Fund contributed to the first stage of writing. A summer stipend from the National Endowment for the Humanities and a grant from the Faculty Research and Creative Activities Support Fund of Western Michigan University provided funds for research at the Basel Mission Archives in Switzerland.

I can never adequately express my appreciation to all the individuals in Hong Kong who have contributed to my research in some way. This book is especially dedicated to the women and men of Shung Him Tong village who were at once gracious hosts, kind friends, and wise teachers. In particular I must thank Cheung Yan Lun (Andrew), who always exhibits the best of "Hakka qualities," and who was kind enough to read and comment on a draft of this book. Without his helpful comments, and those of Rev. Tong Siu Ling, Pang Chui On, Cheung Sui Wing, Tsui Pui Tin, Leung Pui Tong, Esther Chang, Lam Wai Tak, Li Chiu Lai, Lin Yat San, Lin Yan San, and the many Tsuis, Cheungs, Pangs, Chans, Lings, Lins, Lams, Lungs, Tongs, and Yaos of Shung Him Tong, as well as the Wans of Ma Wat village, I could not have written this book. I am also indebted to several of the members and leaders of the Shung Him Tong youth group, especially my good friends and companions Pang Wai Ying (Mildred) and Fu Yan Ho. There are many others whose names I have left out, not by design or lack of appreciation, but because they were so numerous.

Several people from the Tsung Tsin and Basel missions deserve to be acknowledged here: Rev. Chow Tin Wo, Rev. Yu Wai Hong, Mr. Simon P. K. Sit, Rev. and Mrs. Richard Deutsch, and Rev. Hans Lutz. Paul Jenkins and his staff at the Basel Mission Archives were most generous with their time and assistance. Rev. Carl Smith, Bart Tsui, Louise Ho, Daniel and Grace Lin, Sr. Ann Gray, Anita Weiss, and Jash and Elisabeth Dahele were consultants, advisors, and friends. David Faure and Nicholas Tapp of the Chinese University of Hong Kong provided me with important references and useful suggestions. Thanks also to Rev. Kong Bou-ling of the YMCA, Fr. Harold Naylor of Wah Yan College, Esther Ng of the China Graduate School of Theology, John Dolfin of the Universities Service Centre, and Cora Man of the Yale in China Language School. I am grateful to the Hong Kong government for its cooperation and particularly for the help of Sir David Akers-Jones, Paul Tsui, James Hayes, Raymond Pang, Matthew K. C. Cheung, and the staffs at the Fanling District Office, the Lands Office, the Public Records Office, and the Government Secretariat Library. Kwong Lai King (Rica), Poon Lai Ying (Cecilia), Liang Shuk Fan (Estella), Cheung Man Hon (Michael), and Chung Yuet Fong provided valuable assistance with translations of written Chinese materials. Peter Haenger and Nicholas Schaffner have earned my gratitude for their painstaking work translating Basel mission archival materials from German handwritten in Gothic script.

A number of teachers and colleagues have earned my respect and gratitude. The help and encouragement of William A. Shack, friend and advisor at the University of California at Berkeley, have been invaluable. I have benefited from his meticulous editing of my research proposals, his careful responses to my field notes, and his continued generous and critical attention to my written work. I am also grateful to James Anderson, Burton Benedict, Stanley Brandes, Alan Dundes, Thomas Gold, Nelson Graburn, and Joyce Kallgren, also at the University of California. Nancy Abelmann, Jeanne Bergman, Pamela Myers Moro, Lesley Sharp, Jacqueline Urla, and members of the dissertation writing group at Berkeley also deserve thanks for their suggestions. Donald Brown and Edwin Clausen, my teachers at the University of California at Santa Barbara, and the late Barbara E. Ward, my teacher at the Chinese University of Hong Kong, helped to spark my early interest in Asia and anthropology. I am also grateful to my friends at Western Michigan University, especially to Lee Ann Claussen and Victor Cunrui Xiong, and to Robert Sundick for helping me to secure the time and facilities to finish this book.

My work has benefited significantly from the meticulous reading and critical comments of James L. Watson and Myron L. Cohen. I also appreciate the help and support I received from Sheila Levine, Monica McCormick, and the anonymous reviewers for the University of California Press.

Finally, many Constables, Alters, and Constable-Alters have contributed directly or more subtly to this project. My deepest, most heartfelt appreciation is to Joseph S. Alter, who in his roles as anthropologist, editor, baby-sitter, cook, housekeeper, companion, and spouse, has contributed immeasurably every step of the way.

Note on Romanization

In romanizing Chinese words, I have used the following conventions: Chinese place names outside of Hong Kong, and common terms or concepts (e.g., Qing dynasty, *feng-shui*, Guangdong province) are in pinyin. Place names within the territory of Hong Kong are romanized according to the system found in *A Gazetteer of Place Names in Hong Kong, Kowloon and the New Territories* (Hong Kong Government 1960) or *Hong Kong Streets and Places* (Hong Kong Government 1983, 1985). Where it is important to convey the language in which certain words or phrases were spoken, I have romanized Cantonese terms according to the Yale system as found in Huang's *Cantonese Dictionary* (1970).

With the exception of a few individuals who are known to follow a different convention, Chinese names are given in the traditional Chinese order: surname followed by given name. Personal names presented the most difficulty in romanization. Whenever possible, a name follows the English spelling preferred by the individual (e.g., "Pang Lok Sam") or as found in such written sources as family, church, or government records in Hong Kong. These generally do not follow any one style of romanization. The names of more widely known individuals have been written in pinyin (e.g., Deng Xiaoping). Personal names in the appendices follow the system of romanization used in the archival material in which they were written, unless they could be identified with names appearing elsewhere in the text (e.g., "Hung Syu Tschen" is changed to "Hong Xiuquan"). All surnames and names used repeatedly in the text are included in the glossary.

Chinese terms in quotations that use other recognizable systems of romanization have not been adjusted. Where confusion may arise, an additional transliteration appears in brackets, or in a footnote when some explanation is required. Terms such as Hakka and Punti are given in their most common English spellings. A glossary of Chinese terms is provided at the end of the text.

1 Who Are the Hakka?

Hong Kong is not, as many people envision it, all high-rises and urban sprawl. In the approximately 350 square miles of the New Territories there are several New Towns with high-rise housing estates erected on the sites of old market towns and surrounded by hundreds of smaller villages nestled in farmland among rolling hills and open spaces. Nor is the population of Hong Kong homogeneous. The dominant language is Cantonese, and Chinese of Cantonese origin are in the majority, but the Chinese population also comprises Hakka, Hokkien, Chaozhou, Shanghai, and Mandarin speakers.

In the northeastern sector of the New Territories, less than one mile from the Fanling train station and the Fanling New Town housing estate, is one small village that stands out visually from the rest mainly because of the church on its main road, a modern blue and gray structure that contrasts abruptly with the surrounding stone houses and vegetable gardens. The village is named Shung Him Tong—"the village of the Hall of Humble Worship" or "Humble Worship Village"—and well over 90 percent of its residents are Hakka and Christian.[1]

The village was established by Hakka Christians at the turn of this century in an area of the New Territories that was the ancestral land of the dominant Cantonese-speaking, higher order Teng lineage for over five hundred years. The region, comprising five walled and six unwalled villages and bordered on the west by the Phoenix River, takes its name of Lung Shan or "Dragon Mountain" from the summit looming auspiciously to the southeast. The area is also known as Lung Yeuk Tau or the "Land of Jumping Dragons" (see maps 1, 2). According to local legends, the dragon holds a pearl in his mouth, and it is there on top of the pearl, in a place with powerful geomantic features (*fengshui*) at the heart of Teng ancestral lands, that Hakka Christians founded their village in 1903.

1

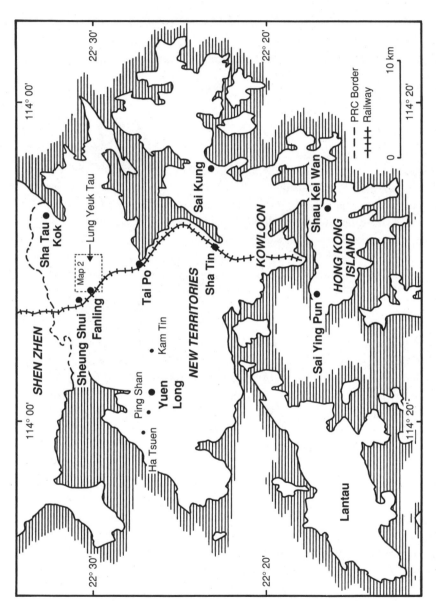

Map 1. Hong Kong, Kowloon, and the New Territories. Adapted from Hong Kong Government, Lands Department, Survey Division Map (1985).

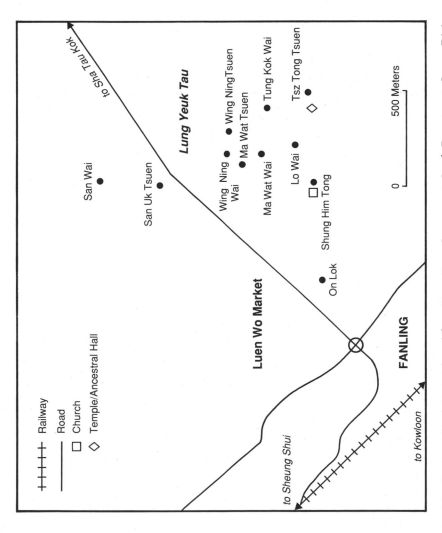

Map 2. Lung Yeuk Tau. Adapted from Hong Kong Government, Lands Department, Survey Division Map (1985).

As Christians, the current residents claim that it was certainly not the *feng-shui* that attracted their ancestors to the region but its beauty and a host of other practical considerations, including potential escape from the hardships and discrimination faced by earlier generations in Guangdong province. Rarely was I taken for a walk through the village without hearing mention of both the difficulties faced by the early settlers and the geomantic features of the region. Such was the case when, on my first Sunday in the village, as I embarked on a year's study in this Hakka community, I was conducted by a respected elderly man on a tour of the places where the villagers lived, worshiped, studied, played, and were buried.

Our walk led uphill from the church to the school and playground, with a brief reprieve from the summer heat in the shade of some old trees. On our way down the narrow pathways he pointed out houses, gardens, and other landmarks, each evoking stories of the Second World War, when the Japanese used the school as their headquarters, women denuded the hillsides of vegetation in search of fuel, and a church-organized group marched all the way back to Meixian, the region of Guangdong province that many Hakka claim as their homeland. Empty houses evoked stories of families who had moved overseas and who still came back to visit every Christmas or at the Chinese New Year. Traditional horseshoe-shaped graves reminded my guide of wealthy movie stars and overseas Chinese millionaires who had arranged to be buried in auspicious locations along the flanks of the dragon. Fences and bridges suggested alliances or feuds with non-Hakka non-Christians from the neighboring communities. At the village cemetery, rectangular "European" grave markers—with their inscriptions and black-and-white photographs—served as genealogies of the "church family" and elicited from my guide names of many famous Hakka people. The tour ended, appropriately, where it had begun, at the church, the center and focus of the community.

A composite of this walk—repeated many times with numerous companions—is etched in my mind. Each guide related distinct yet similar reflections on the community, its history, and his or her place in it. The villagers' dual Hakka and Christian identity is inscribed in the physical construction of the community and also in their day-to-day lives, which in turn project this identity to the outside world. The main focus of this study is how the people of Shung Him Tong conceive of their Hakka identity, and how they express it through their voices, their daily lives, their construction of the village, and their conceptions of the way their local history links with broader Hakka and Chinese history. A particular focus is on how Christianity has influenced their Hakka identity and how these Hakka Christians have attempted to reconcile their Chinese and Christian identities and maintain—despite accusations to the contrary—that although they are Christian they are still Chinese. Significantly, images of Christmas and the lunar new year in Shung Him Tong, of Christian and Chinese graves, of the modern architecture of the church juxtaposed with attention to *feng-shui,* produce an uneasy fusion of Christian and Chinese elements. Similarly, the various aspects of their identity—Chinese, Hakka, and Christian—are easily rationalized by members of the community, but they are not so easily reconciled in terms of experience.

THE ORIGIN OF THE RESEARCH PROBLEM

Although the bulk of my research was carried out during twelve months in 1986 and 1987, the project had its roots in my earlier experiences in Hong Kong. It was during my first visit there as an undergraduate studying anthropology at the Chinese University of Hong Kong in 1979–80 that the Hakka first captured my interest. It was then that I first learned from a teacher, the late Barbara E. Ward, about what she called "conscious models" and about occupational specialization among Chinese "sub-ethnic" groups (1965, 1966). I was particularly interested in the women I saw wearing flat circular straw hats with black fringe while they carried heavy loads, worked on construction sites, tended vegetable plots, and hawked their wares in rural markets. These women, I was told, were Hakka. In contrast to the stereotype of Chinese women as delicate and frail, the reputation of Hakka women was one of exceptional strength, both mental and physical—they were known to be surefooted, hardworking, and proud.

On my second visit to Hong Kong in 1984, I intended to conduct a pilot study of Hakka market women and to learn about the relevance of Hakka identity to their work. But after numerous attempts to interview "Hakka" women in the marketplaces with the help of my assistant, it became less and less clear who actually was Hakka. We found candidates extremely reluctant to discuss Hakka identity. The main problem, we discovered, aside from suspicions that we might be there to discover unlicensed hawkers, was that the term "Hakka" had various, and sometimes negative, connotations. Some who spoke Hakka, and whom others in the market readily identified as Hakka, refused to label themselves as such. As one market woman put it, "My ancestors were Hakka, but I am not." Another told us, "You are more *hakka* than I am! Compared with you, I am *punti!*" She was referring to the literal translation of Hakka (*kejia*) as "stranger," "newcomer," "settler," or "guest," and Punti (*bendi*) as "indigenous," "local," or "native inhabitant."

Most of the Hakka people I met during that summer seemed ambivalent toward their Hakka identity until I met a man in his early seventies, whom I will call "Mr. C.," from Shung Him Tong.[2] Mr. C. began our conversation by listing all the famous Hakka he could think of, including Deng Xiaoping, Sun Yat-sen, Singapore's president Lee Kwan Yew, Taiwan's president Lee

Teng-hui, the famous Taiping Rebellion leader Hong Xiuquan, Chinese generals, and many others. He talked for hours about the Hakka people of Shung Him Tong village, Hakka history, and his beloved Hakka church. Only months later did it dawn on me that the questions I ought to address involved the reasons why the Hakka Protestants of Shung Him Tong appeared far more willing to acknowledge and discuss their Hakka identity with me, and far more reflexive about their Hakka identity, than the other Hakka people I had met in Hong Kong. What social and historical factors underlay Hakka conversion to Christianity? How did the change in religious orientation influence the social organization, the belief system, and the ethnic identity of the people of Shung Him Tong? And what advantages and difficulties were associated with maintaining both Hakka and Christian identities?

FIELDWORK AND METHODS

When I returned to Shung Him Tong in 1986 to conduct a year of anthropological research, Mr. C. became my entrée into the community and introduced me to members of his family, his village, and his church, most of whom were Hakka and eager to discuss that fact. Our first Sunday there, after providing a tour through the village and attending the church service, the church board members held a special meeting and within an hour found my husband and me a place to stay on the edge of the village with a non-Christian Hakka family. Although I had hoped to live in the heart of the village with a Christian family, I was less than five minutes' walk from the church—a situation that allowed me to learn more about the relationship between Hakka and non-Hakka in the adjacent village and between Christians and non-Christians.

From the start, the friendliness and hospitality of the congregation was overwhelming. Their attitude toward us was due in part to the assumption that, like other occasional white visitors to the church, we must be missionaries or somehow associated with the Basel mission or the Lutheran church. Despite many explanations, my role as an anthropologist was never entirely clear to some people. The word "anthropology" has the same unfortunate connotations for many people in Hong Kong as it has for some people in the United States. To those who were familiar with the Cantonese translation (*yahn leuih hohk*) it suggested the study of "primitive," "exotic," or "backward" societies. After the first few negative reactions—"Then why study *us*?"—I began to describe my research as the "history and customs" (*lihksi jaahpgwaan*) of the community, a topic that was far more acceptable.

It was mistakenly taken for granted by members of the local community that, since I regularly attended church services and activities, I must share their religious beliefs. From the start there existed an unquestioned assumption of a common religious bond between myself and the members of the congregation, because my interests and activities centered on the church as much as theirs. At times I wondered whether this explained their many attempts to rationalize or justify to me certain seemingly non-Christian beliefs and practices, and to present themselves as unquestionably pious Christians. It was also apparent, however, that they felt the need to justify their behavior not only to me but also to one another.

By the end of the year, it had become obvious to my closest informants and friends that I came from a religious background very different from their own, and that I was far more sympathetic and tolerant of non-Christian beliefs and practices than they were. Some were even comfortable questioning or criticizing my lack of Christian commitment. In practice, however, I believe they treated me—as much as possible—as one of them.

Twice a week I taught small informal English conversation classes. This was a way to meet more people, learn more about the community, and reciprocate the village's hospitality. It soon became clear to me that the church leaders hoped the English class would be a way to attract non-Christians to the church. To their disappointment, those students who were not already Christian did not convert—nor did my landlady's family. Inevitable though it is that an anthropologist leave certain marks in the community, I did not wish to leave behind a trail of Christian converts. My main influence was more likely to cause an increase in the levels of reflexivity and discourse surrounding the issue of Hakka identity, and perhaps also to inspire a more conscious rationalization of some of the contradictions and ambiguities regarding that identity. Those who had previously taken the meaning of "Hakka" for granted were forced to articulate their views in our interactions. It is also likely that those who were already interested in issues pertaining to Christianity and Hakka identity, those (such as Mr. C.) whose "narrative structure" coincided with mine, were the ones most eager to work with me (see Bruner 1986). As a result, this study may convey a far more "Hakka-centric" community than would have been the case had I not selected Hakka identity as a research topic. That is not to say that my influence makes my representation of the Hakka any less valid than studies that approach anthropology as an "objective science." As numerous anthropologists have expressed in recent works (e.g., Clifford and Marcus 1986; Marcus and Fischer 1986; Rabinow 1977; Rosaldo 1986), ethnography is not an objective collection of "facts" but rather a highly subjective endeavor for both the anthropologist and the people among whom he or she studies.

Like other anthropologists, I found that gender can pose certain problems for conducting fieldwork, but these problems can also reveal important cultural patterns. During the first five months of fieldwork, I was fortunate to have been accompanied by my spouse, Joseph Alter, also an anthropologist. His presence facilitated contacts with younger men that might otherwise have been

difficult for me to make. Men in the community found it less awkward to approach him to chat or to offer to help with "his" research. Joe and I quickly
discovered that most men—including those who had married into the village—reflected on the history and social organization of the village and church
far more than did the women. Women, on the other hand, taught me more
about Hakka and Christian customs and rituals and spoke to me more about
their religious beliefs and personal concerns than did the men. The relevance
of these and other important gendered patterns is discussed in more detail in
Chapter 6. By the time Joe left to begin his own research in India, I had earned
the reputation of a respectable married woman and was able to continue my
contact with both male and female informants.

I participated in and observed church activities such as youth group meetings, worship services, and field trips; life-cycle rituals such as weddings, birthdays, and funerals; and daily activities such as excursions to the market and the
teahouse. In addition to these observations, I conducted informal interviews
with a small, unobtrusive notebook in hand, which most of my informants preferred to a tape recorder. These interviews were conducted with residents of
Shung Him Tong and the neighboring village and with members of the
church, the mission, and the theological seminary affiliated with the church.
In more formally arranged meetings, and when doing one-time interviews
with church and government officials, I was more likely to use a tape recorder
as much for convenience as because they seemed to expect it. Several times I
met with people who had once lived in the village and had since moved away,
among them people who came to visit from overseas at Christmas or the Chinese New Year. My main informants from Shung Him Tong were men and
women ranging in age from their late teens to their seventies. I either approached them at random at church or in the village or was introduced through
interpersonal networks. On numerous occasions I was invited to people's
homes for delicious meals and to pore over old photo albums, books, and genealogies. Such informal settings proved ideal for collecting field data that
would not have lent itself to a formal interview approach.

My research was conducted in both Cantonese and English. Although I do
not speak Hakka and my Cantonese was at first rudimentary, this did not present any insurmountable difficulties. Some people of Shung Him Tong speak
four or more languages, including Hakka, Cantonese, Mandarin, and English.
Cantonese is spoken by all but the oldest women in the village. Older men,
and young men and women under thirty, speak at least some English since
many were required to study it in Hong Kong schools. Most people of all ages
understand at least some Mandarin—and point out how similar it is to
Hakka—but do not speak it. Although by the end of the year I could understand some Hakka, I did not learn to speak more than a few simple words and

phrases. My early interviews were most often conducted in English because at first the English of my informants was far better than my Cantonese, and because many informants requested the opportunity to practice their English by way of an interview. As my Cantonese improved, more conversations and interviews were conducted in Cantonese. When someone I wanted to talk to did not speak Cantonese or English, I preferred to rely on friends and relatives as translators rather than bring in an assistant whose ethnic or religious identity might make the situation less comfortable.

Most informants held a typically Chinese high regard for written materials, and several suggested that, as a scholar, perhaps I should spend less time chatting with people about the Hakka and more time reading books. As a result, I was presented with numerous genealogies, church documents, and books on the history of the village and the church. I was repeatedly referred to an important volume of village and family histories compiled by Pang Lok Sam, and to the books of the famous Hakka historian Luo Xianglin, who had been a respected elder and church member. Such sources have proven to be invaluable. As I discovered, many people knew these sources and their contents but had not read them. These written materials are of key importance to the people of Shung Him Tong both as symbols of legitimacy and for their content. The written word, as they know, is more authoritative than the spoken word and serves to reinforce and legitimize certain privileged viewpoints. That, in part, is why they were supportive of the idea that I write a book on Hakka identity.

WHO ARE THE HAKKA?

As the following chapters demonstrate, "Hakka" defies any attempt to arrive at a single, simple definition. To some, including many in Shung Him Tong, the name "Hakka" evokes pride and patriotism and connotes Chinese origins of high status dating back to when Henan province was the "cradle of Chinese civilization" in the fourth century A.D. To others the term can evoke shame and embarrassment. Spoken by a non-Hakka, it can suggest poor, uneducated country bumpkins—connotations similar to those of "Oakie" and "hillbilly" in the United States.

Today, the name "Hakka" is commonly used in Guangdong, Hong Kong, Taiwan, Southeast Asia, North America, and other regions throughout the world to refer to the approximately seventy-five million members of this Chinese ethnic or subethnic group. "Hakka" is the Cantonese (or Yue) pronunciation of a term that translates literally as "guests" or "stranger families," or less literally as "settlers," "sojourners," "immigrants," or "newcomers." Scholars speculate that the name originated in the descriptive term used before the seventeenth century in Chinese population registers to distinguish recent immigrants from earlier Yue inhabitants (Leong 1980). The label "Hakka" indicated the relatively recent arrival of a group of people in Guangdong as compared with the longer tenure of the Cantonese-speaking inhabitants. The word "Hakka" also connotes a transitory or temporary social status; indeed, many people, including members of some of the oldest lineages in the New Territories, are thought to have once been Hakka who crossed the "ethnic boundary" and assimilated into the larger, dominant Cantonese-speaking group for a variety of political and economic reasons (Baker 1966; Faure 1986; J. Watson 1983).

When the term became fixed as a group label is a debated issue (M. Cohen 1968; T. Hsieh 1929; Leong 1985; see chap. 2), but by the nineteenth century it clearly distinguished a group of people who were not Punti, that is, not "indigenous" or "native inhabitants" of Guangdong province in southeastern China. By the early 1920s, due in large part to the establishment of the Tsung Tsin (Chongzheng) Association in Hong Kong, and the United Hakka Association (Kexi Datonghui) in Shanghai and Canton, the name became more widely accepted as an ethnic label. These two associations, founded by Hakka elites and intellectuals, were highly successful in their goals to unify Hakka organizations worldwide and to promote Hakka solidarity, but perhaps somewhat less so in their attempt to foster a public understanding of Hakka culture and identity (T. Hsieh 1929; Leong 1985). In 1921, in response to a Shanghai Commercial Press publication of *The Geography of the World* that erroneously described the Hakka as non-Chinese, the United Hakka Association held a conference in Canton attended by over a thousand angry delegates representing Hakka organizations worldwide (ibid.). The result was a forced retraction of the offending phrases. Since then Hakka associations continue to regularly publish and assert their views regarding Hakka identity, which are discussed in the following chapter.

In the People's Republic of China today, the Hakka are officially recognized as members of the Han Chinese *minzu* or nationality, but in nineteenth- and early twentieth-century China their Han status was debated and not widely acknowledged. At that time violence often broke out between Hakka and non-Hakka (cf. M. Cohen 1968; Leong 1985; W. Lo 1965), and Hakka, with their different language, clothing, and cultural practices, were often accused of being non-Chinese barbarians of lowly tribal origin. Although this accusation is now uncommon, and linguists and Hakka historians have demonstrated that it has little basis in fact, it still underlies the gravest insults that are directed toward the Hakka in Hong Kong today.

Anthropologists have used many different approaches to analyze or attempt to "define" ethnic groups and their identities. One older approach that has been aptly criticized tries to demarcate an ethnic group on the basis of a distinct culture or a list of distinguishing cultural traits or markers. Language, place of origin, clothing, food, religion, and numerous other cultural criteria have all been used to define ethnic groups. The case of the Hakka demonstrates the problem with such an essentialist approach.

No single cultural trait or group of traits can determine who is Hakka and who is not. Some Hakka may suggest that all Hakka speak the language, come from Meixian, or cook stuffed tofu. Non-Hakka might suggest that all Hakka are poor and darker skinned and wear circular black-brimmed hats. However, many of those who are considered Hakka, or who consider themselves Hakka, do not fit these criteria. In Hong Kong today, "Hakka" refers sometimes to people who speak or whose ancestors spoke Hakka language, yet not all of these would identify themselves or be identified by others as Hakka. Conversely, many who no longer speak Hakka still consider themselves to be Hakka; the young people of Shung Him Tong are a case in point.

Place of origin presents a problem in defining the Hakka because although some proud Hakka say their people originated in north central China as early as the fourth century A.D., this is where all Chinese claim their origin. As Skinner (1977) and Leong (1980) have pointed out, the Hakka are the only Chinese "ethnic group" not to be named after a single place of origin or native place they can call their own. The Cantonese come from the area around Canton; the Chaozhou from the synonymous region, and likewise for the Shanghainese.

Although many Hakka identify Meixian or the wider region of Meizhou as the Hakka "heartland" or the core of Hakka culture, the areas that Hakka identify as their native places are as widely dispersed as is the Hakka population. Hakka are most densely concentrated in northeastern Guangdong, east of the North River, in the mountainous, less fertile region of Meizhou prefecture that includes seven predominantly Hakka counties surrounding Meixian. But sizable Hakka populations are also located in southwestern Fujian, southern Jiangxi, and eastern Guangxi, on Hainan Island, Hong Kong, and Taiwan, and in lesser numbers in Sichuan and Hunan. Overseas, Hakka can be found on virtually every continent, from South and Southeast Asia and the South Pacific to Europe, North and South America, Africa, and the Caribbean. This wide migration—discussed in the following chapter—makes it all the more impossible to identify any one set of cultural traits that can be labeled as Hakka.

Certain settlement patterns have been identified as typically Hakka, but these demand special qualification and contextualization. As relatively late arrivals in many of the regions of China where they settled, Hakka were generally forced into the more hilly, less productive, and less desirable lands. Such was the case in Guangdong, Guangxi, and the New Territories of Hong Kong, where the Punti or Cantonese had already settled the more fertile river valleys, and also in Taiwan where the Hokkien (Min speakers) owned the better land (cf. Lamley 1981; Pasternak 1983, 1972).

During the eighteenth and nineteenth centuries, Hakka settlements in some regions of Guangdong could be distinguished from those of the Punti. There the Hakka often lived in small numbers, sparsely dispersed throughout the hills on land that they often rented from Punti landlords. In contrast, Punti were more likely to live in densely populated towns or in large, single-surname villages surrounded by their fields. In other regions Hakka and Punti occupied separate villages in the same areas (M. Cohen 1968).

There are also certain architectural styles that appear to be uniquely Hakka, but again these point to strictly regional variations. In southwestern Fujian and northern Guangdong, Hakka built "roundhouses," circular, multistoried, fortresslike dwellings designed for defensive purposes with walls of adobe or tamped earth nearly a meter thick (Knapp 1986:45–49). At one time, in certain locations, Hakka communities might have been identified by their architectural styles (see Naquin and Rawski 1987:180), or by the fact that their villages were more dispersed than those of the Punti (M. Cohen 1968; Eitel 1867), but today in Hong Kong these are no longer valid distinctions and a Hakka house or village can generally not be distinguished from a Cantonese one. Hakka now reside in villages that were once Punti, people who were once Hakka are now identified as Punti, and members of both groups often live side by side in both urban and rural areas.

In many ways Hakka and non-Hakka Chinese in Hong Kong today are virtually indistinguishable. Most dress the same way, speak Cantonese, and eat virtually the same foods. Although some people say that the Hakka are shorter and darker skinned and have larger feet, it is impossible to distinguish them from other Chinese on this basis. In terms of clothing, a few older women still wear a black cloth draped over their heads (similar to a nun's wimple) and tied over the top and behind the ear with an embroidered band (Blake 1981, 105–10, 150–51; E. Johnson 1976a; see plate 3). Others wear what is called the "Hakka hat," a flat circular hat with a black cloth "curtain" around the brim; but as often as not these women either are not Hakka or do not identify themselves as such.

The "Hakka hat," the most public symbol associated with the Hakka, is worn by many Hakka and non-Hakka women who work outdoors. It serves, like the stereotypes of large feet, muscularity, and dark skin, as a class marker: those who do hard labor are naturally more tanned and more muscular and do not wear dainty shoes. Tourist brochures and postcards reinforce the stereotype of Hakka by labeling women farmers and construction workers wearing the "Hakka hat" as Hakka. In Shung Him Tong village, women are rarely seen wearing such a hat, although several older women wear the black head cloth with embroidered band that they say is the only "real" remaining clothing marker of Hakka identity.

In Hong Kong, there are few indicators of whether a person is Hakka, other than hearing him or her speak the Hakka language, which is increasingly rare since many Hakka speak Cantonese in public. When they are away from their village, the people of Shung Him Tong are no exception. The majority of their interactions with people outside of the community—with the exception of their association with members of other Hakka churches and the Hong Kong Hakka Association—are without reference to their Hakka or Christian identities. Only occasionally, I was told by several people under forty, does one discover that a coworker or classmate is also Hakka. For the teachers, politicians, and businesspeople I spoke to, the majority of their interactions outside of the village are with non-Hakka non-Christians, and they do not make it a point to let others know that they are Hakka. Most of the time they "pass" as Cantonese or Hong Kong Chinese. Christian identity may be more apparent because of such outward markers as jewelry and desktop decorations, and because it is a more common topic of conversation. As will become more apparent in the course of this book, the church is the main context in which Hakka identity is important for the people of Shung Him Tong.

Although there are few visible markers of ethnic identity in Hong Kong, in some specific locations or contexts ethnic identity may be presumed. Some villages, such as Shung Him Tong, are known to be Hakka by those who live in the vicinity. Certain prominent individuals are also known to be Hakka. The winners of the "Miss Hong Kong" competitions of 1986 and 1987, for example, were both reported in the local newspapers as being Hakka. This knowledge is often only noteworthy to other Hakka. Certain restaurants may be billed as Hakka restaurants—though these are not as popular or as conspicuous as the large, elaborate, popular Chaozhou restaurants that were established in the 1980s. As some Shung Him Tong villagers explained, Hakka restaurants are not tourist attractions, but Hakka people know where to find them. At Luen Wo and Cheung Wah, the two markets closest to Shung Him Tong, it does not appear that most people conduct business along ethnic lines (see also Blake 1975, 1981; cf. E. Anderson 1968). Most shoppers would rather look for the best bargain or the freshest products, or return to the same vendor whom they trust, regardless of ethnic identity.

Although some anthropologists, Hakka historians, and nineteenth-century missionaries have presented evidence of distinct Hakka religious practices, styles of clothing, foodways, and architecture, these are regionally or generationally specific and cannot distinguish Hakka from others except in a particular historical and cultural context. One of the objectives of this book in considering the many beliefs regarding Hakka cultural differences is to avoid an essentialist, reductionistic portrayal of the Hakka as much as possible. The case of the Hakka supports the view that "ethnic groups are categories of ascription and identification by the actors themselves" that cannot be reduced to a static list of traits (Barth 1969:10). Furthermore, ethnicity is situational, structural, and interactional. Dual Hakka and Christian identity takes on great relevance to residents while they are in Shung Him Tong, but with their classmates, coworkers, and colleagues outside of the village this identity is far less an issue.

Another general approach to the study of ethnicity has been labeled the "circumstantialist" or "instrumentalist" approach, in which ethnicity is viewed as primarily a manipulative or political strategy.[3] Typical of this genre is Abner Cohen's (1969) work on Hausa immigrants in Yoruba towns in Nigeria, in which he demonstrates how the Hausa use religion to strengthen the ethnic boundaries between themselves and the Yoruba in order to protect the political and economic interests of the Hausa community. Similarly, Barth has used an ecological analogy to suggest that different groups maintain structural boundaries in order to maintain their monopolies of particular occupational niches (1969).

Leong (1980, 1985) has illustrated how an instrumental approach is applicable to the Hakka, particularly during the nineteenth and early twentieth centuries when Hakka could perceive themselves as sharing an economic niche in competition with the Punti. Blake has also convincingly demonstrated the way in which, during the 1970s, political and economic distinctions in the Hong Kong market town of Sai Kung lined up along ethnic/linguistic lines that were "negotiable" and situational (1975, 1981). Today there is no question but that Hakka associations, including the Hakka church, continue to exist and thrive in vastly different settings, serving a variety of the political, economic, and other needs of their members. As I relate in Chapter 2, Hakka identity was the basis of a number of political and economic groupings during the nineteenth century. In Chapter 3 I show how ethnic and religious solidarity served Hakka interests in the establishment and foundation of Shung Him Tong.

However, today in Shung Him Tong, Hakka identity no longer serves the instrumental economic or political interests that it did in earlier decades. That is not to say that members of the community do not share certain political interests, but in Shung Him Tong, as in many parts of Hong Kong today, ethnicity has decreased in political relevance. Most occupations and economic interests no longer break down along ethnic lines to the extent that they once did, and there is little competition with other ethnic groups for economic resources. During the past twenty or thirty years, with the decline of ethnic tensions and of Hakka/Punti economic competition, one should expect, according to Barth, "either no interaction [between ethnic groups], or interaction without reference to ethnic identity" (1969:18). Neither has been the case for the Hakka of Shung Him Tong.

Regardless of how useful an instrumental approach may appear, it too often overlooks the less material, more subtle features of ethnic identity and ethnic groupings that help explain the recent "reemergence" of ethnic affiliations in places such as eastern Europe and the former Soviet Union. An instrumental focus does not help us understand periods during which ethnicity is not blatantly political. As I describe in Chapters 4 and 5, economic and political ethnic interests in Shung Him Tong wax and wane, and today they are not as clear, uniform, or crucial a concern as they were during the early decades of this century. But ethnic identity in Shung Him Tong persists—although not in a static and timeless way—because it is linked to the unique history of the community and the particular pairing of Hakka identity with Christianity.

Abner Cohen's (1969, 1974) and Barth's (1969) insights into how ethnic boundaries and interests are created and maintained through cultural symbols are nonetheless very pertinent to the case of Hakka Christians. If the Hakka of Shung Him Tong have a "political strategy," it is to maintain power and control over the meaning of their own identity. At present, that in itself is the goal, rather than the means to another more explicitly political or economic end. The "power" of Hakka Christians in Shung Him Tong is not merely over resources or politics in the narrow sense but over the symbols that define them as a group.

The church is what provides Hakka Christians with a context in which to construct Hakka history and, more importantly, the authority by which they can promulgate and take control of their own identity. The "resources" that they attempt to control are not primarily economic but cultural and religious— if saved souls can be counted as such. As discussed in Chapter 4, Hakka identity plays a central role in attracting converts to the congregation.

Another anthropological approach to ethnicity has been labeled the "primordialist" or "sentimentalist" approach (see Bentley 1981, 1983). The emphasis is not on ethnicity as a strategy but on the basis of the shared identity— on the idea of shared history or ancestry, whether real or imagined. The idea that Geertz called "primordial attachments" (1973a) is useful in an analysis of Hakka identity because it points to history, process, and cultural symbols. In contrast to the situation during the nineteenth and early twentieth centuries, when the instrumental aspect of Hakka ethnicity was most evident, the contemporary situation calls attention to the cultural and symbolic aspects of ethnicity (see chap. 6). Shared history and a common "primordial past" are the central themes of Hakka identity in Shung Him Tong today.

Keyes is one of several scholars who have taken the position that ethnicity should not be seen as either primordial or instrumental but entails both facets (Keyes 1981; see also Bentley 1981, 1983, 1987; Harrell 1990; Nagata 1981).

Focusing on the primordial aspect of ethnicity, Keyes argues that ethnicity "derives from a cultural interpretation of descent" (1981:5, 1976). While he views ethnicity as "a form of kinship reckoning," he stresses that "it is one in which connections with forbears or with those with whom one believes one shares descent are not traced along precisely genealogical lines" (1981:6). In the case of Hakka Christians this is an important point. Hakka pay particular attention to Hakka history—which serves as their "genealogy"—in order to reinforce their claims to Chinese identity.

HAKKA IDENTITY AND THE BASEL MISSION

The Basel Evangelical Missionary Society was founded in Basel, Switzerland, in 1815 with the support of members in Switzerland, Germany, Yugoslavia, and Austria. It is an international and interdenominational organization with its major constituents today among Reformed and Lutheran churches. It has "partnerships" with independent churches that trace their origins to the Basel mission in Hong Kong, Singapore, Sabah, Indonesia, Taiwan, India, and regions of Africa, South America, and the South Pacific.[4] Among these partner churches is the Tsung Tsin mission, better known in Hong Kong as the "Hakka church." Tsung Tsin mission is a Hong Kong organization that includes fifteen preaching stations and churches, of which Shung Him Tong is one; over twenty schools, nurseries, and kindergartens; and a hostel for the elderly.

The first Basel missionaries arrived in Hong Kong in 1847. As I was told by one Shung Him Tong villager, they were latecomers in China and other Protestant missions had already "claimed" the more accessible Cantonese-speaking regions of Guangdong. So after some initial work among the Chaozhou, they decided to focus their evangelizing efforts almost exclusively on the Hakka. Between the time of their arrival in Hong Kong in 1847 and 1850, they recorded fifty converts, and by 1855 the number rose to over two hundred (Yu 1987:65). In the period following the Taiping Rebellion (1851–64), and the Hakka-Punti wars (1850–67), the number of converts increased more dramatically. By 1909 the Basel mission recorded over ten thousand converts in Guangdong (Voskamp 1914; Yu 1987:65), and by 1948 the number reached close to twenty thousand (Yu 1987:64). Of these converts, the vast majority were Hakka.

After the defeat of the Taiping Rebellion, Taiping rebels and their friends and relatives were "under the threat of massacre" by Qing authorities (Tsang 1983:5). Many fled to Hong Kong or sought refuge with the Basel missionaries (see app. 1). Rudolf Lechler, who with Theodore Hamberg was one of the first Basel missionaries sent to China, was responsible for arranging the resettlement of hundreds of Hakka refugees overseas (Tsang 1983:5; Yu 1987; see also Smith 1976, 1985). Between 1860 and the turn of the century, entire

Hakka congregations emigrated from China to Hong Kong, British Guyana, Sabah, and elsewhere overseas. Among the early Basel mission converts were some of the parents and relatives of those who founded Shung Him Tong village in 1903 (see apps. 1, 2).

It is difficult to estimate the number of Hakka or the number of Hakka Christians in Hong Kong today. Government census figures do not differentiate the population by "ethnicity," and figures that indicate Guangdong as "place of origin" cannot accurately distinguish Cantonese from Hakka. However, Hakka are believed to be about 12 percent of the total Hong Kong population (Guldin 1977:127), the third largest Chinese group in Hong Kong after the Cantonese and the Hoklo (Min speakers), and they represent the largest proportion of the rural population. This suggests a Hakka population of around 600,000 in 1980.

The number of Chinese Christians in Hong Kong (Protestant and Catholic) was estimated at 10 percent of the population in 1980, with Protestants numbering slightly less than half (Law 1982:51). In 1985 the Tsung Tsin mission had approximately eight thousand members, and of these a conservative estimate of four thousand speak Hakka fluently (Yu Wai Hong, pers. comm., 1986). A much larger number speak some Hakka and consider themselves Hakka. Shung Him Tong itself has about two hundred regularly attending members, and over thirteen hundred if we include overseas members and those who only occasionally attend church. Of these, over 90 percent are Hakka.

Despite the fact that they represent a relatively small proportion of the total Hakka population, Hakka Christians, along with missionaries and scholars, commonly assert that Hakka "were more receptive to Christianity than any other group in China" (Bohr 1980:133). Hakka Christians often remain active in the wider Hakka community and, I argue, have been influential in formulating and defining Hakka identity. Several of the early members of Shung Him Tong helped to establish the international Hakka association in Hong Kong, and today a number of Shung Him Tong people still belong. Among the large numbers of Hakka Christian immigrants from Hong Kong in recent years, most have gone on to join related Hakka churches in Canada (mainly Vancouver and Toronto) and the United States.

There have undoubtedly been material advantages to be gained by becoming Christian in China and Hong Kong during the nineteenth and early twentieth centuries, and in the British colony of Hong Kong (see Smith 1985). But this explanation does not adequately explain the disproportionate attraction of Hakka to Christianity, or the question of why some Hakka converted and others did not. Nor does it address the relative "success" of one mission or denomination as opposed to another, since they offered many of the same material incentives. Furthermore, the material rewards available to Chinese Christians ought not overshadow the additional implications or advantages that conversion might present with regard to Hakka identity. As I will illustrate in the chapters that follow, although the Basel mission became the "Hakka church" largely fortuitously, this label took on special meaning for its members.

Religion adds an important dimension to the study of ethnicity. In the case of such groups as Sikhs, Jews, and Mennonites, religious identity reinforces, is virtually interchangeable with, and may be seen as the basis of ethnic identity. In such cases, religious symbols or practices signal one's ethnic identity. A similar argument has been made in the case of Chinese identity: one view is that certain principles concerning rituals, for example death rituals (J. Watson 1988), are what unify all Chinese.

Alternatively, religious affiliation can conflict with ethnic identity to the extent that religious conversion becomes a means of abandoning or escaping stigmatized ethnic identity, as in the case of Hindu "untouchables" converting to Christianity or Islam (cf. Berreman 1979; Juergensmeyer 1982). Although Hakka might have been considered a stigmatized identity during the nineteenth century, becoming Christian was equally dishonorable, if not more so. Christianity was abhorred by many Chinese as a foreign religion (P. Cohen 1963) that was considered antithetical to being Chinese (cf. Gernet 1985). Especially during nineteenth century, when Hakka were regarded as inferior and Christians were denounced for having abandoned and forsaken their Chinese identity, Hakka Christians were in a sense doubly stigmatized.

While some anthropological studies have demonstrated how religious conversion can serve as a means to escape an identity, others, such as the dramatic examples of revitalization movements, show how the adoption of a new religion can support or increase group cohesion and thereby help maintain group identity (Lanternari 1963, 1974; Worsley 1968). For the Hakka of Shung Him Tong, religion has done both. It has provided a new context in which Hakka identity continues to have relevance, and it has created avenues through which Hakka Christians can attempt to escape the stigma of their ethnic identity by effectively rendering and reinterpreting it in a more positive light.

The especially pious and orthodox beliefs of the early Basel missionaries help account for the specific shape that ethnic and religious identity takes today in Shung Him Tong. As opposed to Chinese adherents to some Christian denominations such as the Roman Catholic church, in which there is at least a superficial incorporation of Chinese forms and symbols into Catholic religious rites, Shung Him Tong Christians, like the early European Basel missionaries, have no tolerance for syncretism in their rituals (see chap. 5). While Catholic rituals create an impression that one can be both Chinese and Catholic, this avenue of expression is not available to the people of Shung Him Tong. The beliefs they have inherited from the Basel mission present them with obstacles and limitations in the expression of their dual Chinese and Christian identity.

To the Hakka Christians of Shung Him Tong, nonetheless, conversion to Christianity has not meant that they must choose between being good Hakka Chinese and good Christians. Their words and actions affirm their belief that they can be both. This has required that they reconstruct their own meaning of Hakka identity within the narrow confines of Christianity in an attempt to reconcile being Hakka, Chinese, and Christian. As I illustrate in the chapters that follow, this has not been a simple, unambiguous, or entirely successful endeavor. It has required that they define Hakka Chinese ethnic identity as located primarily in a common origin and a concept of descent (cf. Keyes 1976, 1981), that is, in Hakka history and genealogy rather than in "traditional" Chinese cultural practices and religious rituals (cf. J. Watson 1988). Yet while some Chinese practices are rejected entirely, others—particularly those related to death and ancestors—are transformed or rationalized in an attempt to reconcile them with what is considered pious Christian belief and practice (see chap. 5).

Hakka ethnic identity, as illustrated by the case of Shung Him Tong Christians, is best looked at not from an exclusively primordialist or instrumentalist perspective but from a perspective that takes into account the way Hakka identity has been historically constructed and influenced by such factors as imperialism and nineteenth-century Christian evangelism. Hakka identity has been molded and influenced by political and economic factors, and by Hakka historians, Hakka Christians, and European missionaries.

My purpose here is not to decide who is "really" Hakka, or to define a static, essential, primordial set of criteria for being true Hakka. Hakka continues to mean different things at different times, in various contexts, and to different people. My objective is to identify what Hakka means to a number of people in Shung Him Tong, and how these views are related to the cultural and historical construction of Hakka identity.[5]

2 History and the Construction of Hakka Identity

Ethnicity, like nationalism, is a relatively new concept. It is of relevance only within the context of the "modern nation state"—although to its adherents it is primordial, rooted in time immemorial (B. Anderson 1983). Ethnicity has not always existed as a category for action or a reason for shared allegiance. The creation of ethnic identities, as with national ones, involves a process in which people become not just the subjects of history but active participants in its making. Thus alliances based on linguistic affiliation, shared local interests, or cultural similarities are transformed into more consciously and widely articulated identities. New ethnic and national identities form what Benedict Anderson has called "imagined communities" (1983). "Invented traditions" (Hobsbawm 1983) are of central importance in the process of forming these communities. An "invented tradition" refers to "a set of practices, normally governed by overtly or tacitly accepted rules and of a ritual or symbolic nature, which seek to inculcate certain values and norms of behavior by repetition, which automatically implies continuity with the past. In fact, where possible, they normally attempt to establish continuity with a suitable historic past" (1983:1). As Hobsbawm writes, " 'Traditions' which appear or claim to be old are often quite recent in origin and sometimes invented" (1983:1); this can be seen in the case of Hakka ethnicity.

Ethnicity is not an indigenous Chinese concept and has not always been easily translated into the Chinese term *minzu* or "nationality," which is a modern loanword from the Japanese. Before the introduction of the modern sociological or intellectual concept of ethnicity, one might argue, there existed several dichotomous Chinese views: of Chinese and non-Chinese, of Han Chinese versus Manchu rulers, of Chinese and non-Chinese barbarians of various types and degrees. But only in the course of nineteenth and early twentieth centuries did difference begin to be conceived of in terms that could be considered "ethnic" rather than linguistic, cultural, geographical, or hereditary.

Hakka ethnicity is said to be rooted in an immemorial past reaching back perhaps as far as the third or the fourth century A.D., but these early so-called "Hakka" were not an "ethnic group" in the sense that we now use the term, with its implications of self-awareness and cognizance of their place in history. At that time, ancestors of today's Hakka were most likely indistinguishable from other Chinese. At some debatable point in time after they came into contact with Min or Yue speakers in southern China, they came to recognize themselves—and became recognized by other Chinese—as culturally and linguistically distinct; they were referred to as immigrants or strangers, as the word "Hakka" suggests.[1] Only later did "Hakka" become a potent ethnic label and the basis for shared identity, action, and belief.

We cannot know precisely when Hakka began to accept "Hakka" as their name rather than thinking of themselves simply as Han Chinese (or people of Tang) or Chinese from the north. Nineteenth-century conflicts and alliances, such as the Hakka-Punti wars (1850–67), corresponded with Hakka and Cantonese linguistic differences (M. Cohen 1968), but this fact does not necessarily determine whether such events are "ethnic." Such social groupings were certainly relevant to the creation of Hakka ethnic identity, but alone they are not sufficient evidence of the existence of "ethnicity" as we now understand it. There are various theories about when the Hakka became an "ethnic group" outlined below, but most of these theories depend on which definition of "ethnicity" is being used. If we consider Benedict Anderson's criteria described above, there is strong evidence that a self-aware and self-proclaimed Hakka ethnicity appeared during the nineteenth century and became increasingly pronounced by the beginning of the twentieth century.

Leong identifies the first consciously "ethnic" statement articulating the origins and "ethos" of the Hakka as appearing around 1808 in a lecture presented by a scholar named Xu Xuzeng (1985: 302–7). Many of Xu's views, and those of other isolated Hakka spokesmen of the nineteenth century identified by Leong, were reiterated by Hakka intellectuals during a period of strong Chinese nationalism after the turn of this century (Leong 1985:307). Certainly by the 1920s, with the emergence of international Hakka associations and the visions and rhetoric they produced, Hakka ethnicity became the basis for action, and Hakka identity alone became sufficient reason for shared allegiance.

As one man from Shung Him Tong explained, it was not until he came to Hong Kong over fifty years ago from an exclusively Hakka region of Meixian that he understood that there were different kinds of Chinese. It was then that he realized that he was Hakka; he joined the Hakka church in Hong

Kong and became a member of the Hong Kong branch of the International Hakka Association. These two institutions helped spell out for him what it meant to be Hakka and helped to create ethnic loyalties that had no previous place in his life.

Historians, both Hakka and western, as well as other scholars and writers, have rewritten Chinese history, infusing it with a new Hakka consciousness, inventing and imagining Hakka identity. For that reason, events and conflicts that were not necessarily conceived of as "ethnic" when they occurred, but which broke down along Hakka/Punti linguistic lines, can in retrospect be interpreted as evidence of an earlier existence of ethnic awareness.

Today it is generally accepted among scholars and Hakka that, despite the likelihood of some intermixing of Hakka ancestors and non-Chinese people, Hakka are of north central Chinese origin and are members of the Chinese nationality. But some of the Hakka I met in Hong Kong, university students as well as rural farmers, are still reluctant to admit that they are Hakka because of the lingering negative implications. Despite the fact that most people of Shung Him Tong village present themselves as proud Hakka, several older villagers expressed a belief that they must defend themselves against the accusations that they are not "real Chinese" and assert the truth about Hakka identity. This they do in part through the telling of Hakka history and in part by infusing Chinese history with Hakka consciousness. The history of Hakka migrations and the Taiping Rebellion are two historical events that help define Hakka identity. If I want to learn about the Hakka, one forty-year-old man in Shung Him Tong told me, I must study these two important episodes of their history. This chapter focuses on the way in which the Hakka are defined by, and written into, Chinese history by Hakka historians, European missionaries, and others.

CONSTRUCTIONS OF HAKKA MIGRATIONS

Interest in the Hakka and their character and customs grew out of, or at least greatly increased, during and after the Taiping Rebellion (1851–64) and the Hakka-Punti wars (1850–67), and reached its height in the 1920s, a period that has been referred to as the peak of Hakka nationalism (Blake 1975). It was during this time that Hakka historians (e.g., T. Hsieh 1929; Luo 1933) began to develop their theories concerning Hakka migrations. Their writings, unlike those of European missionaries who were also interested in the question of Hakka origins, began with the premise that the Hakka were not "tribals" of non-Han Chinese origin or Han Chinese who had mixed with "tribals," but were pure Chinese.

On the basis of genealogical records and linguistic and cultural evidence, late nineteenth- and early twentieth-century Hakka historians and missionaries, like most scholars today, believed that the ancestors of today's Hakka migrated southward from Henan and southern Shanxi provinces in north central China during the early fourth century A.D. and that, by the thirteenth century when they crossed the border into Guangdong province, they were identified as culturally distinct "Hakka" or immigrants (e.g., M. Cohen 1968; Ho 1959; Luo 1933; Nakagawa 1975). Less resolved are the questions of whether the migration in the fourth century A.D. was the earliest migration, what the reasons for the migrations were, and at what point in history Hakka became an ethnic group.

The Hakka migrations, like invented traditions, are crucial because they represent an "attempt to establish continuity with a suitable historic past" (Hobsbawm 1983:1). The specific historic link in this case is between the Hakka present and the Han Chinese past. Hakka genealogies, like those of other Chinese, are traced back as far as possible and are considered "evidence" of pure Chinese as opposed to barbarian status. The Hakka emphasis on a historic genealogy of the group is related to the conception of Chinese identity as tied to the concept of *zu* (genealogical and blood relations; see Blake 1975, 63–95). As one Hakka man in the United States reiterated to me in a recent letter, Hakka have "the purest blood of the Han race because people in Central China intermarried with northern [non-Chinese] people after Hakka moved to [the] South, but Hakka did not intermarry with native people."

Although many Chinese genealogies are considered unreliable or inauthentic by scholars, like many invented traditions, they play a central part in claims to Chinese identity. Histories of Hakka origins and migrations have taken on important symbolic significance, and may also be seen as "myths" or "charters" for Hakka identity (Malinowski 1922; Nagata 1981; Trosper 1981). Hakka migrations can also be interpreted as genealogy "writ large."

The writings of European missionaries are of relevance to the study of the Hakka because missionary views on Hakka identity and origins are still echoed by Hakka writers and by people in Shung Him Tong today. The "historical evidence" of Hakka high-status origins cited by missionaries was used to substantiate the assertions of Hakka historians.

In general, missionaries seem to have held the Hakka in high regard. The Hakka appeared to them to be less xenophobic, more monotheistic, and more receptive to the Christian faith than other Chinese (Bohr 1980:133–34, Eitel 1867).[2] As one missionary wrote, "On the whole the Hakkas are not as bigoted as the Puntis, and the gospel has found easier access to them than the latter" (Lechler 1878:358). To the missionaries, the "great rebellion" which originated with the Hakka, demonstrated that the Hakka were "open to new convictions," and that although the rebellion "turned out a sad failure, yet it might have been attended with better results, had the movement been better directed" (Lechler 1878:358).

Missionaries wrote many articles that focused primarily on the question of Hakka origins. Were the Hakka "a peculiar race or tribe, inhabiting the mountains near Canton and Swatow, who are of a lower social rank than the native Chinese . . . a mongrel race more civilized than the aboriginals, but hardly entitled to rank with the Chinese?" (Campbell 1912:474); or were they "a very distinct and virile strain of the Chinese race" (Campbell 1912:480), "Chinese *de pure sang*" (Piton 1873:225), "genuine Chinese" (Oehler 1922), "not foreigners but true Chinese" (Eitel 1867, 1(6):65) from the north of China (Lechler 1878)?

There are numerous examples of the missionaries siding with the argument of Hakka high status origins. As missionary Oehler wrote:

> The theory of the origin of a tribe from a mountainous corner in
> Fukien has frequently been met with suspicion, whereas among
> authors writing without accurate knowledge of the Hakka history
> the assertion is often found that the Hakka belong to the aborig-
> ines of that province, and are not really Chinese at all—an idea
> which the Punti, who are disinclined towards the Hakka, have al-
> ways been ready to endorse. Against this theory are the facts of
> language, character, and customs, and the impulse to migrate and
> spread out, which in the name "Hakka" finds striking expression.
> This impulse, moreover, is a characteristic of the real Chinese, but
> not of the aborigines. It is safe, therefore, to accept the tradition
> which relates that they migrated about A.D. 900 from the district of
> Kwangshan in South Honan [Henan], where even today the lan-
> guage and customs, especially in connection with marriage and
> funeral rites, are said closely to resemble those of the Hakka . . .
> (1922:351).

According to Lechler, the most reliable sources for tracing the origin of the Hakka were the "family records, which are religiously preserved by the heads of clans" (1878:353). He traced the "pedigree" of "catechist Li" back to the founder of the Tang dynasty in A.D. 620 and cited several other genealogies demonstrating that "the Hakkas descended from the North of China," which explained "the similarity of their dialect with the mandarin" (1878:354).[3]

Missionaries observed that at each stage in Chinese history, when a dynasty was overthrown, those opposed to the new rulers were forced to emigrate. As invaders generally came from the north, the Chinese population expanded southward. In times of relative peace and prosperity, population expansion, or natural calamity, people headed south in hopes of finding new resources and new opportunities. For this reason, Piton argued, "An outline history of the *Hakkas,* is . . . nothing else but an outline history of the *Chinese* in general" (1873:225; emphasis in original). This raised the question of when the Hakka were differentiated from the rest of China's population and when they became known as Hakka.

The origins and migrations of those who later became known as Hakka have been written about by many Hakka scholars. Xu Xuzeng wrote of Hakka culture and northern origins as early as the beginning of the nineteenth century, and several others made similar points (see Leong 1985:302). However, the best known and most famous of the Hakka spokespersons, whose views are still quoted in the publications of Hakka associations worldwide and who is a "household name" among many Hakka, is the historian Luo Xianglin (1933, 1950, 1965, 1974). Luo was also, it is important to note, a leader of the Hong Kong branch of the International Hakka Association and an influential and well-respected member of the church in Shung Him Tong. A significant portion of Luo's evidence of Hakka origins comes from genealogies of Shung Him Tong families, most of whom are descendants of Basel mission converts from China.

As Leong aptly describes it, Luo's work is "a veritable bible for the Hakka" (1980:5), with its unambiguous statements of Hakka beliefs. Luo's main points are as follows:

> (1) Hakkas were originally migrants from the Central Plain, true Han Chinese from the cradle of Chinese civilization, not hill aborigines as their neighbors repeatedly identified them, out of ignorance or malice; (2) Hakkas were historically identified with Han patriotism; they were patriotic loyalists of the Chin in the 4th century, Sung loyalists in the late 13th and 14th centuries against Mongol invaders, and anti-Manchu patriots in modern times, as exemplified by Hung Hsiu-ch'uan and Sun Yat-sen; (3) the Hakka dialect is unmistakably rooted in the prestigious northern, Central Plain speech and in Sui-T'ang phonology; (4) Hakkas justifiably take pride in their women, in academic achievement, and in the possession of all the orthodox Chinese virtues of diligence, frugality, and culturedness in manners and customs (Leong 1980:5–6).

Hakka migrations are written about in several other sources. Here I shall present only enough material to illustrate some areas of disagreement and to illustrate the connection between Hakka and missionary views (see M. Cohen 1968; Hashimoto 1973; Leong 1980, 1985; Luo 1933, 1950, 1965; Moser 1985). Luo classifies Hakka migrations into five successive southward movements. The first period of migration, which lasted from the beginning of the fourth century until the end of the ninth, occurred in conjunction with the southward flight of the Western Jin, originating in Henan, and reached as far as South Hubei, South Henan, and central Jiangxi. The second wave occurred from the end of the ninth century to the beginning of the twelfth. It began as a result of the disorder at the end of the Tang dynasty and the migrations went from Henan to Jiangxi and southern Fujian, and from Jiangxi to Fujian and Guangdong. Northern central Jiangxi was left undisturbed; thus, the earliest immigrants there were unmolested and their dialect today can be readily identified with Hakka (Campbell 1912). The third wave stretched from the beginning of the twelfth century to the beginning of the Ming dynasty in the middle of the seventeenth century. It was initiated by the southward exodus of the Southern Song dynasty and its flight across the Yangtze with the invasion of Mongols, which dislodged people from Jiangxi and southwestern Fujian and forced them into the northern and eastern quarters of Guangdong. By the end of the Yuan dynasty (A.D. 1368), northern and eastern Guangdong were exclusively Hakka. The fourth wave, which lasted from the mid-seventeenth to the mid-nineteenth centuries, began with the Manchu conquest and overthrow of the Ming dynasty. During the Qing dynasty Hakka migration expanded into the central and coastal areas of Guangdong, Sichuan, Guangxi, Hunan, Taiwan, and southern Guizhou. The fifth wave, triggered by population pressure, Hakka-Punti strife in western Guangdong during the middle of the nineteenth century, and the Taiping Rebellion, sent emigrants to the southern part of Guangdong, to Hainan Island, and overseas. This stage continued until the 1940s (M. Cohen 1968; Leong 1980; Luo 1965). The establishment of the People's Republic of China and the announcement that it will reclaim Hong Kong in 1997 has triggered what might be considered a sixth wave of migration out of Hong Kong and overseas primarily to the United States, Canada, Australia, Europe, Taiwan, Singapore, and other regions of Southeast Asia.[4]

Hakka historian Hsieh Ting-yu (1929), who like Luo was a member of the International Hakka Association, followed the theory of Eitel (1867, 1868, 1869), a European missionary who asserted that most Hakka originated in Shandong province, a few in Shanxi province, and fewer still in Anwui. At the end of the third century B.C., they were persecuted and fled southward to Henan, Anwui, and Jiangxi. Beginning in the Han dynasty and up to the fourth century, Hakka rose to positions of power and thus with the fall of the Jin they again had to flee from the Shandong mountains to the south of Henan, Jiangxi, and Fujian.

The period after the tenth century A.D. presents less disagreement among scholars as to the sequence of migrations into Jiangxi, Fujian, and northern Guangdong. By the twelfth century the progenitors of the Hakka were accepted as "being Hakka," that is, as a group with its own language, customs, and way of life showing marked differences from those of other "ethno-stemmas," or ethnic branches (Liu, quoted in Nakagawa 1975:216). According to Luo, this split occurred between the Five Dynasties period (A.D. 907–60) and the Song dynasty (A.D. 960–1127)—that is, before the third wave of migration. Liu is more specific and pinpoints the time when the progenitors of the Hakka formed an independent ethno-stemma as the period of the Five Dynasties and Ten Kingdoms, when, in the mountains where Fujian, Guangdong, and Jiangxi meet, they were independent and isolated from all dynasties (Liu, quoted in Nakagawa 1975:216–17).[5]

Leong (1980) criticizes Luo's scheme of five periods of migration as too simplistic. He also uses Barth's concept of ethnic boundaries in order to argue that ethnic self-awareness does not occur in isolation from other groups as Liu, Luo, and Piton (1873) suggest. On this basis, the conflicts in Fujian province throughout the sixteenth century between the She (a non-Han minority) and the Han who later became known as Hakka provided the setting in which ethnic identity emerged. According to Leong, "These Han Chinese had evolved some distinctive cultural markers, including a separate dialect, and emerged from their non-Han ethnic environment with a heightened sense of Han Chineseness" (1980:14). When in the late sixteenth and seventeenth centuries these people migrated from the area and came into contact with other Han who were culturally different, they first became known as Hakka (1980:14). It was in the seventeenth century that Leong believes the term "Hakka" made its first appearance.

Hsieh Ting-yu believes that the distinction between "settlers" (*kejia*) and "native inhabitants" (*tujia*) has existed since the Tang census of A.D. 780 (1929:217) and was not intended to suggest "racial distinction" but merely implied the literal meaning of *ke* as newcomers. The term "Hakka," he argues, had its origins in the literal meaning of the term and at some later point came to refer to an ethnic group.

Along the same lines as Hsieh Ting-yu, Leong explains that Hakka was merely a way of saying "sojourner households," the same term that was used in local registers to distinguish them from "native households" (1980:19–20). The Hakka preferred this label to the insulting terms used by the native Cantonese. One such term was "Ngai-lou": "'Ngai' is the sound of the first person pronoun 'I' in the Hakka dialect; the Cantonese had fun with the peculiarity (and utter incomprehensibility) of the Hakka speech when they called the Hakkas 'Ngai fellows'. The character 'Ngai' was newly invented with the 'dog' component next to 'righteousness'" (1980:20). Since the Hakka had no one region or "drainage basin to call their own," they had no metropolis to name themselves after, and "the term 'Hakka' was the next best thing" (Skinner 1977:37, in Leong 1980:20).

Anthropologist Myron Cohen (1968) demonstrates how language served to differentiate social groupings. The Hakka became linguistically differentiated from other groups, he argues, at the end of the southern Song (late thirteenth century) during the third period of migration (according to Luo's scheme) from Fujian and Jiangxi into Guangdong:

> When, at the end of the Southern Sung, large numbers of people began to enter Kwangtung [Guangdong] from the north, they were confronted by a population which had come to possess a cultural repertory quite similar to their own. There were differences, chief among them being dialect. . . . [It] was at this juncture that the inhabitants of the mountainous regions of southwestern Fukien entered Kwangtung and became known as the "Guest People" (*K'e-chia*) or, in its Cantonese pronunciation, "Hakka" (1968: 246–47).

According to Cohen, the term "Hakka" took on sociological significance when it was recognized as differentiating the Hakka speakers from the Cantonese speakers with whom they competed for resources.

It is likely that a group of "immigrants" could be distinguished from other Chinese in southern China several hundred years ago, but the process of constructing the Hakka as an ethnic group was most evident during the nineteenth and twentieth centuries. It was only then that a conscious attempt began to "define" the collective identity and allegiance of the Hakka on the basis of their different language, history, and cultural traits. Luo's and Hsieh Ting-yu's writing about Hakka migrations was far more definitive as a Hakka act than were the migrations they described; likewise, later reflections on the Taiping Rebellion were likely to be infused with more Hakka consciousness than was evident among the Taipings themselves.

The questions of the precise point in time of Hakka differentiation from other Han Chinese and the precise place and date of Hakka ancestral origin are not of central significance to this study of Hakka identity beyond lending support to the argument that missionaries and Hakka historians agreed that the Hakka are "true" Chinese of northern origin. More significant is the discourse on Hakka history and identity that was generated by this debate.

The belief in northern origins—which identifies Hakka as at once Chinese and uniquely Hakka—is a central feature of Hakka identity regardless of whether individuals are familiar with Hakka history books or are able to document the northern origin of their own families. Hakka people in Hong Kong today are likely to trace their origin to somewhere in Guangdong province or Meixian or, if pressed further, from Fujian province or "further north," as several young people from Shung Him Tong told me. These details of origin seem to have relevance only to a few individuals and scholars, yet most Hakka consider as unquestionable facts their Chinese origins and the continuous waves of Hakka migrations. On several occasions in Shung Him Tong, I was told that

Hakka "sounds more like Mandarin than Cantonese does" and that this was evidence of their northern origins. Linguists (cf. Norman 1988, Ramsey 1987) now classify Hakka as a southern Chinese language, but linguistic evidence also suggests that the ancestors of the Hakka migrated from the north even earlier than historians such as Luo claim.[6]

THE TAIPING REBELLION

The Taiping Rebellion serves as another important illustration of the construction of Hakka identity through history.[7] The Taiping Rebellion is a "key symbol" (Ortner 1973) of Hakka identity. In Geertz's sense, it serves as a commentary, a "story" Hakka tell themselves about what it means to be Hakka (1973b). It reflects Hakka patriotism and Chinese nationalism, Hakka revolutionary character, Hakka gender roles, Hakka hardships, Hakka determination, and the value of Hakka language, many of the "characteristics" discussed in Chapter 6. To Hakka Christians, it also represents an early example of Hakka "Christianity."

The Taipings and the Society of God Worshipers are also important as an example of how, by the nineteenth century, Hakka-Cantonese dialect difference had become a crucial influence in "the alignment and formation of social groupings" (M. Cohen 1968:286). The Society of God Worshipers, like the Hakka church described in the following chapters, provided an organizational framework through which Hakka interests could be served and Hakka identity expressed (Kuhn 1977:365).

The Taiping Rebellion is also a wonderful example of how history can be shaped and rewritten to serve different interests. Interest in Hakka culture was bolstered by the Taiping Rebellion. European missionaries, who were very optimistic about the Christian elements of the Society of God Worshipers in its early stages, became all the more interested in the Hakka as potential converts. Chinese official sources at that time were, as would be expected, extremely critical of the Taiping rebels whom they depicted as bandits and traitors. According to several Hakka informants from Shung Him Tong, the condemnation and mistrust of the Taipings, fueled by resentment generated during the Hakka-Punti wars, carried over to attitudes and treatment of the Hakka in general.

In the period following the Taiping Rebellion it was portrayed as a despicable incident and many Taiping documents and sources were destroyed or censored. But by the turn of the century, with the decline of the Qing dynasty, Chinese sources began to represent the Taipings in a more positive light and thus the rebellion became a vehicle by which to express certain positive characteristics of the Hakka. Dr. Sun Yat-sen, who some Hakka argue was himself Hakka, and various Hakka writers (e.g., Lou Xianglin and Hsieh Ting-yu) emphasized the heroic role of the Hakka in the rebellion.[8] Sun is said to have admired the rebellion so much that he was nicknamed Hong Xiuquan after the Taiping leader (Moser 1985:247); and according to Teng (1962), Sun's attention to the Taiping Rebellion was an important rallying point in attracting Hakka followers to the cause of the nationalist revolution. Thus, over forty years after the rebellion took place, the reviled bandits and traitors were transformed into patriotic and revolutionary Hakka heroes.

This positive image of the Hakka and their role in the Taiping Rebellion is reflected in the writings of both Hakka historians and European missionaries. Communist writers in the People's Republic of China, however, have placed little emphasis on the significance of ethnicity, and instead depict the Taiping Rebellion as a precursor to the communist revolution, as a "bourgeois-peasant war against the feudalistic Manchu regime" (Teng 1971:4), or as a forceful show of Chinese national consciousness. Regardless of the contradictions such an interpretation could present with regard to communist or nationalist party sympathies, the people of Shung Him Tong, like many Hakka, continue to refer to the Taiping Rebellion with pride.

For readers unfamiliar with the Taiping Rebellion, it is necessary to highlight some of its main features, and the role of the Hakka in it. It followed a prolonged period of dynastic decline, overpopulation, agrarian distress, increased foreign penetration, and growing dissatisfaction with the Manchu rulers. After the defeat of the Chinese by the British in the Opium War (1839–42), foreign invaders imported opium and other commodities to China and as the economy worsened the Manchu government was forced to levy taxes in the form of silver from the people in order to pay for "indemnities." Silver became increasingly scarce as it flooded out of the country (see Kuhn 1978; Teng 1971: chap. 2). With economic disaster, corruption and administrative inefficiency increased. As a result of the war, Shanghai supplanted Canton as China's major port, and more than 100,000 Hakka porters and boatmen were thrown out of work. The economic crunch also forced the closing of Guangxi's silver mines, bringing despair to thousands of Hakka miners. Population pressures pushed as many as 90 percent of Guangxi's farmers into tenancy (Bohr 1980:134). As international conflicts increased, so did local conflicts, and by the time of the first treaty settlement with the British (1842–44), secret societies were actively involved in open rebellion in parts of Guangdong and Guangxi. Guangxi's rivers were overrun with pirates who had been chased from Guangdong by the British navy (Laai 1950). Guangxi's officials became increasingly corrupt, and villagers were forced to protect themselves against bandits, secret societies, and local feuds. Such was the situation when the Society of God Worshipers, under the leadership of Hong Xiuquan, grew into what is known as the Taiping Rebellion.

Hong Xiuquan, the leader of the Taipings, is an oft-cited Hakka hero among the people of Shung Him Tong, although they are highly critical of his unorthodox "misinterpretation" of Christianity. Hong was raised in a Hakka village in Guangdong, and his genealogy, like most Chinese genealogies that claim descent from some famous official or another, traced his descent from a twelfth-century Song dynasty emperor (Hamberg 1854; Newbern 1953:64). As was the case for many Chinese, and especially for the Hakka according to several informants in Shung Him Tong, the hope for raising the prestige and economic status of the family lay in the possibility of a son passing the civil service examinations. Although Hong was considered a promising candidate, he failed the examination several times. After the first two failed attempts, he returned to his village seriously ill and is said to have had a strange dream. Six years later, when Hong read the Christian tract "Good Words to Exhort the Age," he recalled his dream and interpreted it as a calling from God, believing himself to be the younger brother of Christ. Hong and his cousin then baptized each other and began to preach to family, friends, and others who would listen (Kuhn 1978).

Two of Hong's earliest followers included his cousin Hong Rengan, who became the main informant for Basel missionary Theodore Hamberg's 1854 book on the early Taipings, and Feng Yunshan, a distant relative, schoolmate, and friend of Hong's. Among those inspired by Hong's visions was Li Tsin Kau, another Hakka who later became a respected member of the Basel mission. For an account of Li's life and his connection with Hong, the Basel mission, and the Hakka church, see Appendix 1.

A major feature of the Taiping religion was iconoclasm. Like Christian converts, Hong's converts "threw out the ancestor tablets in their homes, gave up Buddhist ceremonies at funerals, and took part in idol-breaking expeditions" (Boardman 1952:13). As a result of local opposition to their iconoclasm, Hong and Feng left to preach to Hong's relatives in Guangxi. In 1845 Hong returned to Guangdong to write and teach while Feng remained in Guangxi and founded the Society of God Worshipers, which within two years attracted several thousand Hakka worshipers (1952:14).[9] In 1847, Hong proceeded to study with the American Baptist missionary Issachar Roberts for several months, but returned to Guangxi without his baptism (Hamberg 1854:31–32).[10]

At first, the God Worshipers were primarily a religious group with Feng as the organizational leader and Hong as the oracle and titular leader; but as the economic situation in Guangxi worsened, the goals of the God Worshipers changed to direct opposition of the Manchu government, local officials, and their Punti allies. The God Worshipers organized themselves to protect their members from the growing violence and banditry in the region, and the security they offered became increasingly attractive to outsiders, especially to persecuted Hakka. As the goal of the God Worshipers came to be defined as the overthrow of the Qing dynasty, it further attracted people who were in opposition to the officials and the Manchus. The religious organization grew into a military community of oppressed Hakka, God Worshipers, and outlaws in opposition to militia, gentry, and government (Teng 1971:62). As Michael describes it,

> what gave this God Worshippers Society its special militant char-
> acter was the fact that it was formed among Hakka by Hakka
> leaders. Once the society was established and its many branches
> were functioning, the Hakka found it an organizational protection
> in their fight against the Punti. Large groups of Hakka, already in
> conflict with their non-Hakka neighbors, joined the rapidly
> growing society. In the villages where they predominated, the
> Hakka congregations took over local control and forced others to
> join. The conflict between Hakka and non-Hakka was thus trans-
> formed into one between the God Worshippers Society and op-
> posing militant organizations (1966:30).

Increasing Hakka-Punti conflicts helped attract new members to the God Worshipers. Hamberg describes one incident involving a wealthy Hakka man who had taken as his concubine a young woman promised in marriage to a Punti man. The Hakka man, who had settled the matter with her parents, re-fused to give her up (1854:48–49). The district magistrate and his officials were overwhelmed with petitions and accusations lodged daily against Hakka, so they advised the Punti to defend their own interests and "enforce their own rights against the Hakkas" (1854:49). Soon after, more violence erupted be-tween Hakka and Punti in the region, involving many villages and leaving large numbers of Hakka homeless, with only the God Worshipers to turn to for help. As Hamberg wrote, these destitute people "willingly submitted to any form of worship in order to escape from their enemies" (ibid.).

Laai speculates that when Hong's goal grew to include the overthrow of the Qing, the leaders of the God Worshipers might have used existing conflicts to further aggravate the relations between Hakka and Punti in order to advance the influence of the society. According to Laai, the members of the society helped to agitate the hostility "so as to bring about the intense feud between the two peoples. Under this situation the Society of God-worshippers served as a reservoir to receive any Hakkas who were dislodged by the Puntis" (1950:176). In turn, the Society of God Worshipers was becoming "not merely a religious organization but also a champion of the Hakka people" (ibid.). Whether the God Worshipers encouraged the hostility is not entirely clear, but eventually it involved them directly.

The first armed conflict between the God Worshipers and outsiders occurred in October 1850. As Hong Rengan described the outbreak to Hamberg, it began when members of a Punti village took the buffalo of a God Worshiper:

> The brethren were highly incensed at such an outrage, and demanded back the buffalo. As this was not instantly complied with, they also seized one or more cows belonging to the other and stronger party. At last an exchange of the animals was agreed to, and the emissaries met and arranged the affairs; but just as they were returning, some of the Puntis, relying on their larger number, fired upon the Hakkas. These, in their turn, attacked the Puntis, and chased them back to their own village (1854:51).

The Taiping "Heavenly Kingdom of Great Peace" was announced as the name of the newly established dynasty in 1851 and Hong was named Heavenly King. Two years later the Taipings captured Nanjing and made it their capital. In 1864, with the aid of British- and French-led troops, the Manchus defeated the Taipings (Boardman 1952; Kuhn 1978; Teng 1971). At its height, the movement had involved two million people (Kuhn 1977:351) and left in its wake thousands of uprooted Hakka, many of whom turned to the Basel mission for shelter and support.

An overwhelming number of the Taipings are identified as Hakka (cf. Bohr 1980:135; Hamberg 1854; Kuhn 1978, 1977:350–51; Laai 1950:167–71; Shih 1967:49–50, 305–6; Teng 1971:54–55). The family members and friends whom Hong first converted were Hakka, and the thousands who initially became God Worshipers in Guangxi were primarily Hakka speakers. As Hakka-Punti feuds in Guangxi increased and Hakka homes and villages were destroyed, thousands more Hakka joined the God Worshipers.

Most of the God Worshipers were poor tenant farmers who rented land from Punti landlords. Many of the bandits, pirates, and members of secret societies who were attracted by the God Worshipers' goal of overthrowing the Manchu dynasty were also Hakka. Unemployed Hakka silver miners, charcoal makers, and dockworkers also joined. Among the members were barbers, blacksmiths, and stonecutters—people whose occupations were disdained by Punti and most likely to be held by Hakka (cf. Bohr 1980; Laai 1950; Skinner 1976:351; Teng 1971:19). The Taiping leaders were mostly Hakka farmers. Most members were poor, but a small minority were wealthy Hakka who Laai speculates joined either for protection or in response to coercion by their relatives (1950:69). There were no high officials or officers, no persons of the intellectual class, and no successful candidates in the public examination. High bureaucrats and literati were the enemies of the Taipings. However, the Taipings were not exclusively Hakka. Included in their ranks were "Chuang, Yao

and Miao tribesmen" (Teng 1971:55) and true to their "Christian universal-
ism" (Bohr 1980:135) they tried to persuade other minorities and Punti to join
their insurrection. This is reflected in a statement Hong made in 1860:
"Whether Hakka or Punti, they are all treated alike" (Michael 1966:40,
1971:18).

People joined the God Worshipers for a variety of reasons. Like many converts to Christianity, the earliest God Worshipers became convinced that their
bad fortune was connected to the worship of idols and false gods: they believed
that by destroying idols and worshiping the one "true God" they would be
saved and their lives would improve. Hong's main appeal was that he
"promised to rescue the Hakka from the disintegration of South China" (Bohr
1980:136; see also Kuhn 1977). As Li Tsin Kau, a Basel mission Hakka convert, explained it, "When we heard Hong's visions, our hearts fell to him and
we thought that our prayers had been answered and that he had been sent by
heaven to bring better times" (Basel Mission Archives 1868a, 1868b, 1885).

The Society of God Worshipers became known as "an organization cham-
pioning the interest of the Hakka people" (Laai 1950:176). As Kuhn argues, the
religious doctrines had not taken on political significance in Hong's village near
Guangzhou but only in the mountainous regions of Guangxi, because in southern Guangdong there existed a "congruence of ethnicity with settlement and
kinship at the basic level of the village," which meant that "no new symbolic
structure was needed to express ethnic conflict" (Kuhn 1977:365). In contrast,
the "fragmented kinship and settlement patterns in Kwangsi [Guangxi] provided ethnicity no firm social base" (ibid.), and the Taiping religion provided
a new organizational framework. In a similar way, Christianity, introduced by
members of the Basel Missionary Society, provided an alternative organizational
framework that attracted numerous Hakka. Among them were friends and families of the Taipings and the Hakka who later founded Shung Him Tong.

The low social and economic status of the Hakka and their oppression by
Punti landlords is a commonly cited reason for why Hakka flocked to the God
Worshipers. The society provided food, clothing, shelter, and weapons for its
members. The same explanation—Hakka material need or deprivation—is
often given for the greater success that Christian missionaries claim to have had
among the Hakka than that which they achieved among other Chinese (Breslin 1980; Bohr 1980).

Other scholars have asserted that the Taiping Rebellion had its roots among
the Hakka people not so much because of their poverty but because the Hakka
"were the social 'out group'," people "without deep social roots" who were
"on the whole more independent, daring, and prone to action than were
the natives" (I. Hsu 1978:282). The oft-cited "revolutionary" or nationalistic

character of the Hakka is also said to explain the part the Hakka played in the Taiping Rebellion and later in the nationalist revolution (Luo 1933:9).[11]

> The Hakka were acknowledged to be revolutionary in character. After the Manchus conquered China most of the guest settlers did not surrender for a long time, and were said to be the last to bow down to the conquerors. Full of nationalistic sentiment, they felt strongly hostile towards the Manchus and desired to restore China to Chinese. With this background *it is no wonder that Hung Hsiu-ch'uan* [Hong Xiuquan] *became the leader of the Taiping Rebellion and that Dr. Sun Yat-sen became the 'father' of the Republic of China; both were Hakkas* (Teng 1971:19; emphasis added).

Some scholars have criticized the Hakka assertion that there is a "causal relationship between the character of the Hakkas and the rebellious or revolutionary activities in which they participated" (Shih 1967:306). But like many Hakka with whom I spoke, Shih considers attention to Hakka culture useful in establishing their contribution to Taiping ideology. Both Bohr (1978, 1980) and Shih ask what influence Hakka beliefs and customs had on Taiping ideology and argue that certain Hakka practices and customs were reflected in those of the Taipings. They share the view expressed by one young woman and an older man in Shung Him Tong, that the Taiping policy of egalitarian treatment of women reflects Hakka values.

Many writers have commented on the "unusual" Taiping treatment of women (e.g., Boardman 1952; Bohr 1978; Eitel 1867, 1868, 1869; Hamberg 1854; Laai 1950; Moser 1985; Piton 1873; Shih 1967; Teng 1971). Women could hold the same civil and military positions as men, foot-binding was prohibited, and marriage was arranged by the bride and groom. Men and women were separated during military training. Boardman suggests that "[t]he higher evaluation of female personality (and also the segregation of the sexes) may have reflected the treatment accorded women worshipers by Roberts and by missionaries" who influenced the Taiping leaders (1952:27). Several Hakka informants with whom I spoke, however, assert that the Taiping treatment of women reflects Hakka customs. Hakka women are known for not having their feet bound and for their ability to work as hard as men: "Hakka men and women worked together in the rice fields and fought together on the battle ground" (Teng 1971:19). As Shih explains, "It was natural for the Taipings to prohibit foot-binding, for the Hakka women did not practice it" (1967:226). As I describe in Chapter 6, this image of Hakka women as hardworking and distinct from other Chinese women persists in Shung Him Tong as a symbol of the differences between Hakka and Punti.

THE CREATION OF HAKKA UNITY

This chapter has described how Hakka historians and European missionaries were both interested in the Taiping Rebellion and shared many of the same views regarding Hakka identity and origins, but for different reasons and with different motives. Missionaries became interested in gaining a better understanding of the Hakka, because it was among these people they sought converts. Hakka historians sought to prove and popularize their own view of their identity through their construction of history. Their position was bolstered by the supporting evidence from missionary historians, while the missionaries—we should not forget—received many of their views from their Hakka contacts.

Nakagawa, a Japanese historian, raises an important issue. He is critical of what he calls the "partnership" between missionaries and Hakka. He argues that following the Taiping Rebellion, missionaries manipulated the "already collapsed" Hakka in order to create disunity among the Chinese, to the advantage of the western powers. Europeans "seduced the Hakka people," praised them "as one of the 'pure and genuine Han peoples' and put the Chinese resistance in disunity" (1975:211). This view is similar to that held by one man in Shung Him Tong who told me "I don't like to talk about Hakka/non-Hakka. This [distinction] disturbed the unification of the Chinese race. This is what the [British] government did, you know, divide and rule."[12]

Colonial governments worked on the principle of "divide and rule," but it is unlikely that nineteenth-century missionaries were entirely aware of the political implications of their work or of the criticism they would face as "handmaidens" of their governments. The explicit and primary motive of the missionaries was to save souls; translating dictionaries and Bibles and studying the culture and history of their subjects were considered first steps in achieving this goal. The words of the missionaries did appeal to the Hakka, but to suggest that they were "seduced" gives them too little credit.

Nakagawa points to the writing of the European missionary George Campbell (1912) as an example of pro-Hakka bias and divisiveness. Interestingly, Nakagawa cites a Chinese translation of Campbell that was published in 1951 by the Perak Public Association of the Hakkas and also in 1923 in *Kaying*, translated by a Hakka of Meixian district. The Chinese translation differs significantly from the original English text.[13] The original does express Campbell's praise of the Hakka, but not at the expense of the "minority races in the mountainous areas," whom he despised, according to Nakagawa (1975:209). The difference between the Hakka translations and the original demonstrate, however, the way in which missionary writing was used to bolster Hakka beliefs and to convey their own superiority.

With their flattering admiration of the Hakka, Nakagawa writes, missionaries' studies appealed to the pride of the Hakka intellectual class and "encouraged Hakka nationalism" at the cost of unified Chinese nationalism. He accuses Luo and other Hakka historians of "avert[ing] their eyes" from the quintessence of the foreign studies of the Hakka, which created colonial subjugation and thus humiliated them by allowing the Chinese people to sustain domination (1975:211). This view was shared by members of the Hakka student association in Japan who criticized the formation of the United Hakka Association in the early 1920s as "retrogressive" and "divisive" (Leong 1985:312). Hakka "nationalists," however, could respond that they already considered themselves in a situation of colonial subjugation—as did many Chinese—by the foreign Manchu rulers of the Qing dynasty. The awakening of Hakka pride may have furthered the disunity between Hakka and Punti, but it could also be defended as a step in the direction of asserting their Han Chinese identity—an essential step in creating Chinese national unity.

Just as the Taiping association enabled the Hakka to rebel against the Manchus, to protect themselves against the Punti, and to assert their claims of being Chinese, so did the Hakka utilize ideas and institutions of the missionaries that they considered beneficial. Hakka writers utilized foreign studies that supported the notion that the Hakka were Chinese of northern origin. On a practical level, Christian missions provided opportunities for escape from post-Taiping oppression, for education and upward mobility, and—as with the Society of God Worshipers—for protection, shelter, food, and medical care for the poor and sick. The fact that the Basel missionaries knew something about the Hakka, including their language and aspects of their culture, and that they welcomed the Hakka and even admired them, must not be underestimated.

After the Taiping Rebellion, joining the Basel mission became a way to remain Hakka and to be with other Hakka. According to one man from Shung Him Tong, he was grateful to the Basel missionaries because they helped create a unified, standardized "beautiful Hakka church dialect" drawing from the Baoan and Meixian dialects, so that all Hakka could communicate with one another. The missionaries also contributed to Hakka's transformation into a written language, another issue of Hakka pride. In different ways, both European missionaries and Taipings provided ideological support of Hakka identity and origins that played an important role in attracting converts.

As I discuss further in Chapter 6, Luo's concern with being Hakka *and* Chinese *and* Christian epitomizes the position of many Hakka of his generation in Shung Him Tong. Hakka such as Luo, Hsieh Ting-yu, and other members of the Hakka association and the Hakka church did not consider themselves passive actors, manipulated and dominated by the Chinese imperial government on one side and the European imperialists and missionaries on the other. Instead they depicted themselves as "true believers," a pragmatic group of people struggling for respect and an improved way of life. Envisioning themselves as Han Chinese rather than tribal or non-Chinese barbarians was a way for the Hakka to assert superiority over non-Han and to view themselves as equal—if not superior—to other Chinese. Christianity was one means by which they reached this goal.

As did the Society of God Worshipers, the Basel mission Hakka church became a vehicle through which Hakka identity could be maintained, imagined, and articulated in positive ways. Joining the church became a strategy for escaping oppression without giving up Hakka identity. The Society of God Worshipers, like the Hakka churches in the nineteenth and early twentieth centuries, went beyond lineage organization in expressing the common interests of the Hakka by providing the organizational structures that helped bring together those who became influential in the invention and articulation of Hakka identity.

3 Shung Him Tong:
The Imagined Community

In the center of the village, down a narrow pathway that leads between the old church building and the new one, stands a row of modest concrete homes, at the end of which is an impressive courtyard. Voices of the choir rehearsing a new hymn drift inside the courtyard walls while children play there, surrounded by bamboo poles of clean laundry left to dry in the sun every day except Sunday. The walls enclose a wide, single-story house divided in two. On one side of the building women chat, rinse the rice, and prepare the evening meal, while a man sits in the family hall reading a newspaper. The other side of the house is quiet and boarded up. Years ago, the Lings and the Pangs, two of the most important families in the village, built the house. Today, members of both families are still represented in the village, but most of the Lings have moved to Hong Kong Island or overseas and only use the house on those special occasions when they visit. The other side, housing members of the Pang's extended family, still teems with life, especially on Sundays when more children and grandchildren abound.

The village holds many other reminders of the members of these two prominent families. In the cemetery there are numerous graves marked with the name Ling, and at the center of the slope is the grave of Ling Kai Lin, the former pastor for the Basel mission, who is given credit for founding the village. Across the hill on another slope is a large, brightly painted red cross that marks the grave of Pang Lok Sam, another important figure in the village history.

Today, life in Shung Him Tong appears peaceful. So little mention is ever made of conflict that it is difficult to imagine the opposition faced by the settlers who first arrived in 1903. The village, however, did not suddenly appear on that date, nor was it called Shung Him Tong at that time; but within thirty years it grew into an active Hakka Christian community. To make sense of the success that Ling and other Hakka Christians had in settling and establishing themselves in Lung Yeuk Tau when other Hakka before them had failed, it is necessary to understand their connection to the Basel mission; the broader historical, social, and political context of the New Territories; and earlier patterns of Hakka and Punti settlement in the area. As I show in this chapter, there were certain advantages to being a member of the Hakka Christian community.

THE EVACUATION AND EARLY HAKKA EXPANSION

The first Han Chinese to settle in the region of Baoan district, which later became the New Territories of Hong Kong, were predominantly Yue (Cantonese) speakers who arrived around the tenth century A.D. When they arrived the indigenous non-Chinese inhabitants were assimilated or pushed out by those who became known as the Punti or "native inhabitants" (Balfour [1940] 1970; Barnett 1964; see also Hayes 1962, 1977, 1984; Siu 1984; J. Watson 1983).[1] The Teng are believed to be the first of what Baker called the five "great clans" or dominant surname groups to have arrived in the area (Baker 1966). The other four surname groups arrived before the beginning of the Qing dynasty in 1644. Some Hakka also arrived then, but it was not until the middle of the seventeenth century at the end of the period referred to as the "evacuation" (1662–69), and later during the nineteenth century (Luo's fourth and fifth waves of migration), that Hakka began to arrive in large numbers.

The overthrow of the Ming dynasty and the Manchu establishment of the Qing was the turning point for Hakka immigration to the area. Concerned that the coastal populations would collaborate with Ming loyalists who had fled to Taiwan, the Manchus issued a proclamation in 1662 announcing an evacuation of the coastal areas inland fifty *li,* or approximately seventeen miles, to be accomplished within three days. The reluctant evacuees were not provided with food or shelter and it was reported in a local gazetteer that as many as a fifth of them died (cf. Lo 1965:92). A second more stringent evacuation followed and the boundary was moved even further inland (Balfour 1970:175–79). Eventually the evacuation was called off because of the disruption and major losses in tax revenues it caused, but during that time, many villagers perished and some Punti villages disappeared completely. This helped open up the way for Hakka immigrants.

As the people of Shung Him Tong proudly tell, the governor of Guangdong knew that Hakka could cultivate the most wretched land while the Punti scorned such hard work, so he initiated measures to fill the void with indigent Hakka, and around 1730 Hakka from the poorest regions of the province began to arrive along the coast (Lo 1965:93–94). At first the Hakka lived as clients interspersed among their Punti patrons who "provided them with land, provisions, implements and probably even housing" (Lo 1965:94). The arrangement was mutually profitable. Hakka provided the Punti with much needed labor and increased the productive power of their land, and the Hakka were afforded sustenance. The Punti were not threatened by the Hakka because they had already claimed the best land, they were the overwhelming majority, and they were backed by a strong kinship and territorial organization (ibid.).

Hakka immigration continued uninterrupted throughout the eighteenth century and the first half of the nineteenth century. Immigration, paired with a high birthrate, resulted in an increase in the Hakka population. Hakka settlements gradually became less dispersed and Hakka reclaimed more of the "wasteland." According to Lo, the Hakka's lower standard of living enabled them to outbid Punti tenants for land leases from Punti landlords (1965:95). As my Hakka informants concurred, the Hakka placed "less stress than did the Puntis on sumptuous marriages, funerals, showy apparel, elaborate festival celebrations, and the like," which enabled them to accumulate savings and buy land whenever it was available (ibid.). New land holdings created new Hakka settlements, and old Punti settlements declined as antagonism and competition between the two groups increased.

The evacuation was also a turning point for Hakka lineages such as the Liao of Sheung Shui who had been in the New Territories before the evacuation. Because they shared the same economic and political interests as Punti, they began to identify themselves with them, rather than with the later Hakka arrivals (Baker 1968:41). In the case of the Liao, Baker argues that the cultural and linguistic process of "becoming Punti" had started several generations before the evacuation, so by 1819 Sheung Shui was sufficiently Punti not to be listed under the Hakka section of the local census (ibid.).

LUNG YEUK TAU

Shung Him Tong is situated in the northeastern region of the New Territories in Lung Yeuk Tau, less commonly known as Lung Shan Heung (Faure 1986:181n. 3, 220n. 46), an area that has been the ancestral home of one branch of Teng for over five hundred years.[2] The Teng, the largest and most powerful higher order lineage in the New Territories, controlled the greatest number of the largest plots of flat, fertile land in the river valleys. In the northwest corner of the New Territories, the Teng settled in the villages of Kam Tin, Ping Shan, and Ha Tsuen and controlled Yuen Long market (see map 1).[3] By the late fourteenth century, Teng settled in Lung Yeuk Tau and Tai Po Tau in the eastern New Territories, and they collected rent from land in Sha Tin (Baker 1966; Faure 1986:28).

Population figures are unavailable for the nineteenth century, but Hong Kong government records from 1911 indicate that, by the beginning of the twentieth century, Hakka in the New Territories outnumbered the Punti (Balfour 1970; Hong Kong Government 1911: table 12). The population of the northern New Territories, whose "usual language spoken at home" was listed as Hakka, outnumbered those who spoke "Punti": their numbers were 37,053 and 31,595 respectively.[4] Although these figures indicate that the Hakka were greater in number, they were also poorer, they were generally later arrivals in the area, and they settled and farmed the less productive lands of the higher elevations, often as the tenants of the Punti.

The Hakka population was not scattered evenly throughout the New Territories. According to the 1911 report, Hakka speakers in the Sai Kung region, for example, outnumbered Punti almost three to one, and in Sha Tau Kok there were almost twenty-five Hakka for every Punti. Yet in Sheung Shui, the region that included Lung Yeuk Tau, Punti still outnumbered Hakka, who comprised only slightly more than one fifth of the population (Hong Kong Government 1911).

As was noted in Chapter 1, Lung Yeuk Tau comprises five walled villages and six unwalled villages scattered over an area of roughly two square miles (see map 2). Today opinions vary about whether Shung Him Tong should be considered part of Lung Yeuk Tau. In the past, Lung Yeuk Tau referred unambiguously to the geographical area dominated by the Teng and to the social group composed primarily of members of the Teng lineage who held settlement rights in the area (Faure 1986:2). Outsiders who worked for the Teng as servants or tenant farmers, some of whom might have been Hakka, were not members of the lineage and were not considered members of the community.

While the majority of the population of Lung Yeuk Tau in the nineteenth century was Teng, throughout the early part of the twentieth century the Hakka population continued to increase. Today most Teng have either retreated to one of two main villages in Lung Yeuk Tau or have left the area. The other Lung Yeuk Tau villages house a mixture of Hakka, Cantonese, and other non-Christian newcomers. When the first Hakka Christians began to arrive in Shung Him Tong at the turn of this century, few if any of the residents of Lung Yeuk Tau were Hakka or Christian. Today in Lung Yeuk Tau, outside of Shung Him Tong, less than 10 percent of the Hakka population and even less of the Punti population is Christian.

In 1897 the population of what was then called Chong Hom Tong (lit., Pine Cliff Pond; Hong Kong Government 1905), now Shung Him Tong, was fifty-five, of whom most if not all were Teng. By the time of the 1911 census, Shung Him Tong's population was thirty-eight, of whom most if not all were Hakka surrounded by 632 Punti in the other areas of Lung Yeuk Tau.[5] Although the census data may not be entirely accurate, they suffice to show that when a few Hakka immigrants came to Lung Yeuk Tau in 1898, they were clearly in the minority (see table 1).

Table 1. Population of Shung Him Tong

Year	Population
1897	55[a]
1911	38[b]
1930	100+[c]
1950	236[d]
1972	400[e]
1987	1300[f]

[a]Hong Kong Government, Crown Block Lease (1905)
[b]Hong Kong Government Census (1911)
[c]Pang (1934)
[d]Ingrams (1952)
[e]Sagart (1982)
[f]Fanling District Office (1987)

BRITISH RULE AND THE TENG DECLINE

The decline of the power and property of some Punti lineages in the New Territories may have begun as long ago as the period of immigration after the evacuation, but the appropriation of the New Territories by the British also contributed to their decline. Before the British, there existed a system of land tenure in which dominant lineages claimed ownership rights to much of the land in the New Territories (see R. Watson 1985, 55–59; J. Watson 1983). Members of the dominant lineages pocketed "taxes" from those who farmed land that was not registered with the Chinese government. When the British began to register land, "taxlords" claimed it was their land and that they had collected "rent," not "taxes." Some land was leased in perpetuity to tenants who owned the right to farm the land and who could in turn lease their rights to other tenants. In a variant of the distinction between surface rights and subsoil rights common in southern and central China, the landlord owned the "bottom soil" of the land, which gave him the right to collect rent. Other arrangements included short-term leasing of land (see R. Watson 1985). By 1905, the Hong Kong government had registered all land that had proper ownership deeds. In cases in which no deed could be produced, "the cultivator was usually proclaimed the owner" (R. Watson 1985:59). The Teng of Ping Shan claim they owned more land in pre-British times, but at the time of the British land survey their tenants fraudulently claimed ownership (Potter 1968:100).

According to Faure, with the arrival of the British, the Lung Yeuk Tau Teng lost their control of bottom-soil rights, which "changed the fundamental political situation of the New Territories" (1986:164).

This revised system of land ownership greatly benefited the Hakka at the expense of the Punti landlords. As explained in a speech by the district commissioner of the New Territories in 1955:

> In 1899 we found that although the Chinese documents of title
> were in the name of the Hakka clans, the adjoining Punti clans
> had the right of paying the land tax and charging the Hakkas a
> much higher land tax. We [the colonial government] broke that
> system by issuing Crown leases direct to the Hakkas and compen-
> sated the Punti "tax-lords" by grants of vacant land, free of
> Crown rent for the first five years. Everybody ought to have been
> happy, but today it is only the older Hakkas who remember
> clearly how the British enfranchised them, while the Punti clans
> preserve the tradition of how we robbed them. . . .
> Basically therefore, the Hakka are our friends and the Puntis are
> our enemies. But I naturally have to treat them all alike (Hong Kong
> Government 1955:4).[6]

The British land policies served not only to undermine the economic power of the Punti but also to ally the British with the Hakka.

Many volumes of land records were destroyed during the Japanese occupation of Hong Kong, but enough exist to make some general statements regarding land ownership in the Shung Him Tong area. Beginning in 1903, Hakka Christians, mostly from Baoan district (later called Xinan, now Shen Zhen) and the areas closest to Hong Kong, arrived in Shung Him Tong (see map 3; see also app. 2). Later, Hakka families also came from Hakka regions further inland; from regions of Meixian (then called Jiaying, or Kaying in Hakka), the town and district of Wuhua (then called Changle, or Tschonglok), and the towns and villages of Zhankeng (Tsim Hang), and Meilin (Moilim), where the main Basel mission churches were located. By the 1930s there were people of eight surnames (Ling, Pang, Tsui, Cheung, Chan, Yao, Tsang, Cheuk) living in Shung Him Tong. Little by little, land that once belonged to the Teng was sold to Hakka immigrants, and the Tengs receded to the northeastern most regions of Lung Yeuk Tau.

The Crown Block Lease shows that by 1905 Pastor Ling, recognized as the founder of the village, and his family owned small plots of land that totaled 20 percent of the land in and around Shung Him Tong (approximately ten and a half acres). That land was presumably bought from the Teng. Teng individuals, families, and corporate groups owned approximately 30 percent or fifteen acres of the land in that area, and the rest was listed as Crown Land. Within

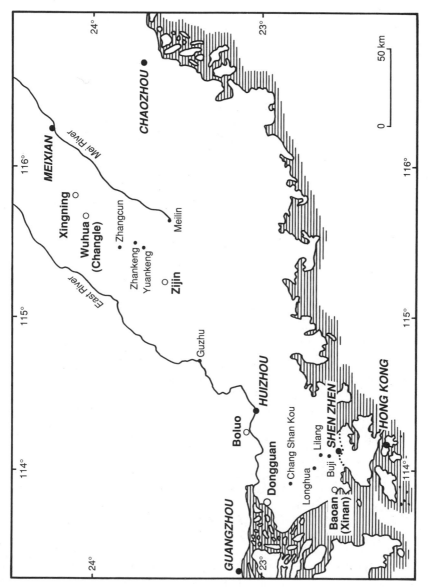

Map 3.   North and South Central Guangdong Province. Adapted from Hashimoto (1973) and Loercher (1879).

the next twenty years, the Teng had sold all their land in Shung Him Tong, and church families owned all the land that did not remain Crown Land. Between 1913 and 1918, another important member of the Shung Him Tong community, Pang Lok Sam, had acquired a total of approximately three acres in Shung Him Tong, mostly at public auction.

Although the specific reasons for the decline in power of the Lung Yeuk Tau Teng would only be revealed by a detailed study, the general description of the process of decline of powerful lineages described by Baker is in accord with the explanations I heard from the people of Shung Him Tong:

> The weakening of a lineage by virtue of failing manpower or misspent wealth must have been marked by the gradual collapse inwards of its land-holdings, more distant ones being sold first . . . There must have been lineages which descended from power to weakness and perhaps extinction. The Teng lineage of Lung Yeuk Tau seems to be a case in point. At one time powerful enough to produce major scholars . . . and to play the main role in establishing a market town, it has declined during the last century until now its village is no longer sacrosanct. The borders of the territory of such a lineage must gradually have shrunk, retreating little by little to geographic frontiers closer to the village (1968:173).

The people of Shung Him Tong agree, but place the emphasis on what they consider the "moral decline" of the Punti, which they contrast with the moral strength of the Hakka Christians. In the words of one elderly village man:

> The Teng had lived in the area for a long time and they didn't like newcomers. We were threatened and treated as aliens, outsiders. We had a hard time. . . . The Teng were very rich people, but in Chinese we say that a family can never be rich for more than three generations. Perhaps this is because by the third generation the sons have forgotten how to make money and are lazy. . . . Well the Teng were lazy. Perhaps they smoked too much opium and played mahjong all the time and gambled and lost their money. . . . Pang Lok Sam and the Lings, they got the land from the Teng through their mortgage company. The Hakka have the reputation of going through China and usurping the land from the wealthy landlords by working very hard.

Another man, a descendant of the village founders, explained that in order to get money for gambling, opium, and concubines, the Teng mortgaged their land to the company that had been started jointly by Pang and Ling. When these Teng could not pay back the mortgages, Pang and others had the opportunity to buy the property. A young woman teacher said that, among other things, the decline of the Teng was tied to the fact that there were not enough Teng men to work the fields since many had left to work in the city or overseas.

Geomantic features or *feng-shui* (lit, "wind" and "water") are often cited in the legends and history of the New Territories as factors that help explain the rise and fall of lineages (Faure 1986; Sung 1973, 1974). Even though the people of Shung Him Tong know of *feng-shui,* they do not tell *feng-shui* legends as though they believe them to be literal truth. The tales they tell about the past are divided into two types, "history"—assumed by those telling it to be true and correct—and "stories" about outsiders who believe in *feng-shui* or about the power of Christianity over *feng-shui. Feng-shui* is discussed in further detail in Chapter 5; here I will limit my discussion to a legend of the founding of the village told to me on separate occasions by two different members of the church, one an older missionary and the other a middle-aged schoolteacher from Shung Him Tong:

> The village is set at the foot of dragon mountain and is bordered by Phoenix river. Before the Christians arrived, the Punti farmed some of this land, but no one dared to live here because of the powerful *feng-shui.* So when the Christians asked to settle here they said "why not let them try?" Shung Him Tong people came and built their houses here and no harm came to them.

The schoolteacher ended the legend by saying, "That [experience] tested the Christians' belief in the strength of Christianity." The missionary said, "The Punti then understood that the power of Christianity was stronger than that of *feng-shui.*" With such a conclusion, we would expect to find Punti flocking to the church and converting to Christianity, but they did not. Instead they seem to have revised their view of the *feng-shui* and now consider that the land is ideal for burial sites; several wealthy Cantonese families have attempted to build large auspicious family graves in the area.

CONSTRUCTION OF THE "IDEAL VILLAGE"

A young woman from Shung Him Tong told me that she praises God for the miracle of the village. Like many other young people whose parents and grand-parents helped establish the village, she is aware of the hardships they faced founding the village in the heart of Punti ancestral lands.[7] Awareness of local history is due in part to stories recounted in casual conversations, sermons, church bulletins, and commemorative publications of the church and the Basel mission (cf. Cheung 1984; Luo 1974), which draw freely from a handwritten history of the village compiled by one of the earliest settlers, Pang Lok Sam. Much of the material from Pang's book is also reproduced in Luo Xianglin's famous history of the Hakka in support of his theories of Hakka migrations

(1965).[8] Pang's history, like Luo's, has not been read by most members of the community, but both are well known and have informed many people's views about the identity of the community and the Hakka in general.

Pang's manuscript includes a section on "public history," or the history of the village institutions. In it Pang describes the establishment of the church, cemetery, school, roads, and bridges and tells of how the settlers overcame the hardships they encountered along the way. The second section comprises eleven family histories, each written by the male head of household (see app. 2).

The authors of the family histories stress the importance of keeping genealogies and express their belief that it is one's duty to know one's family history. The manuscript was written, according to Pang, with the main purposes of preserving the history of the village for future generations and encouraging them in their duty to their families and the community. In his introduction he writes of his concerns: "Whether or not a society can flourish depends not only on the pioneers who prepare the way but also on the successors who carry forth and develop the endeavor. If no one pioneers, even a good place will not be discovered. If no one keeps it going, a flourishing community will decline. To start a business is difficult, but to keep it going is never easy either" (1934:1). Below, I draw freely from Pang's book, church histories, and material gathered in conversations with villagers, church members, and relatives of people who lived in Shung Him Tong. All of the written and oral versions of Shung Him Tong history attest to the reasons for Hakka migration to Lung Yeuk Tau during the nineteenth and twentieth centuries. They left Guangdong because of poverty, population pressure, increased Hakka-Punti conflicts, and dissatisfaction with life in their native villages as well as the promise of a better life in the "peaceful" British-governed New Territories.

All of the first immigrants to Shung Him Tong were Hakka, mostly from the Baoan district in Guangdong (see table 2), and most were either already Christian or became Christian soon after moving to Shung Him Tong. Several were retired missionaries who had worked for the Basel mission in Guangdong or Hong Kong, and almost all claim to have been the victims of persecution, violence, or robbery in their native villages. Some violence was a result of Hakka-Punti feuds, but, as many of the life histories of early Chinese Christians in the Basel Mission Archives describe, converts were often blamed for local misfortunes. They were beaten, their houses were burned, and they were evicted from their villages (see app. 1).

A striking number of the household heads and their sons were missionaries who had attended Basel mission schools. As an older man from Shung Him Tong wrote to me in a recent letter, "Tens of thousands of students of my grandfather's generation and downwards received their good and proper education from the Basel mission secondary school in Nyenhang [Yuankeng]."

Table 2. Household Heads in Shung Him Tong in 1932

Name	Arrived in SHT	Native Place
Chan Yuk Choi	1900	Lilang, Baoan
Chan Kwai Choi	190?	Lilang, Baoan
Ling Kai Lin	1903	Buji, Baoan
Ling Ban Chung	1903	Lilang, Baoan
Pang Lok Sam	1905	Longhua, Baoan
Cheung Wo Ban	1913	Mahum?, Baoan
Cheuk Hing Ko	1917	Longhua, Baoan
Tsui Yan Sau	1925	Zhankeng, Wuhua
Tsui Yan Wai	1926	Zhankeng, Wuhua
Tsang Wing Fai	1927	Huiyang
Yao Dou On	1927	Huiyang
Tsui Kwong Chung	1931	Zhankeng, Wuhua
Tsui Kwong Wing	1931	Zhankeng, Wuhua

Source: Pang (1934).

This included many of the Lings, Pang Lok Sam, and others from the village. Many older settlers chose to retire in Shung Him Tong rather than in their native villages. Religious networks—school and church acquaintances—seem to have been the main system through which people learned of and came to settle in Shung Him Tong, but kinship and native place ties were also factors.

In 1897, the year before the New Territories were leased by the British, a few Hakka immigrants surnamed Kong arrived at Dragon Mountain from Lilang. They remained only a few years, however, because it was difficult to make a living among the hostile local inhabitants. Most people of Shung Him Tong today are not aware of the Kongs and begin their history with Pastor Ling Kai Lin, who is known as the "official" founder of the village; but the Kongs in a sense paved the way for others to come later.[9]

Ling Ban Chung, a distant relative of Pastor Ling, whose native place was also Lilang, heard about Lung Yeuk Tau from the Kongs, and with his nephew he moved to another Lung Yeuk Tau village named Ma Wat, where they rented a house and some farmland from a Teng family. Pastor Chan Lok Chun, also originally from Lilang, had been working in Hong Kong for the Basel mission when he too decided to buy some land and move to Tsz Tong village at the suggestion of the Kongs. Pastor Chan had trouble with his workers and neighbors and within a year lost most of his investments, so he returned to Sham Shui Po to continue his mission work. When he left, two Christian kinsmen named Chan and a man named Hong rented, farmed, and later acquired his land. In 1899, opposition to British rule caused local disturbances so Ling Ban Chung temporarily returned to Lilang and only later returned to settle permanently in Shung Him Tong.

Pastor Ling Kai Lin, born in 1844, was the son of Ling Chun Ko, who had been converted to Christianity by Theodore Hamberg of the Basel mission. Ling Kai Lin's father had moved to Lilang with Hamberg when they were expelled from the nearby village of Buji. Kai Lin's father then helped to establish a chapel, a boarding school for boys, and a theological seminary in Lilang, where he taught the Bible and Kai Lin studied.

Ling Kai Lin dedicated most of his life to the Basel mission and, after thirty-six years of service, decided to retire. As he explained in his letter of resignation, his health was not good; his older relatives were too weak to go to the sermons, and the younger ones too lazy, so he needed to spend more time with them (Basel Mission Archives 1899, 1900). His retirement was granted, and in 1903 he bought land in Shung Him Tong and settled there with his eldest son, Ling Sin Yuen, who was also a preacher. Then the Lings invited friends and relatives to come and work for them as tenant rice farmers. In 1903 there were people of the surnames Chan and Ling in Shung Him Tong, most of whom worked for Pastor Ling.[10] There are three explanations given for the way Pastor Ling learned of Lung Yeuk Tau. The best-known version is that he was in contact with his distant relative Ling Ban Chung (their great-great-grandfathers were brothers; see app. 2, fig. 2), who recommended and then arranged for him to buy land there. As Pastor Ling told his son Sin Yuen, their native place was not a peaceful place to retire, since robbers and bandits were all about, but he had heard of Lung Yeuk Tau in the New Territories, where even chickens and dogs were not disturbed, the population was low, and the land was vast and suitable for cultivation.

Pastor Ling might also have heard of Lung Yeuk Tau from Pastor Chan, who was also from Lilang and worked for the Basel mission. An article written by Pastor Ling's grandson (Sin Yuen's son) Ling Dou Yeung adds more background to the story (Lin[g] 1974). According to him, Pastor Ling's youngest son, Sin Fong, was an engineer involved with the initial surveying of land for the Kowloon Canton Railway. When he finished his work on the section of the railway that reached Shen Zhen, he crossed over the Shen Zhen River to the New Territories in order to confirm Ling Ban Chung's claims and to find a place where people of his native village might come and settle. According to Ling Dou Yeung, Sin Fong picked a very suitable site, one that even modern *feng-shui* experts would agree is probably the best in the region.

The usual story in the village today is that the first tenant farmers became Christian *after* they moved to the village, but according to Ling Dou Yeung, those who decided to migrate to Shung Him Tong were already "believers" from the church in Buji. They at once began farming the hillside plots under the supervision of Ling Sin Yuen, who each week traveled back and forth between Buji and Shung Him Tong by horse. They created a small place of worship, which the villagers called Cheung Hing Tong (lit., the Hall of Long-lasting Prosperity; Lin[g] 1974; Sagart 1982), and the village also came to be known by that name.[11] Later, Pastor Ling changed the name again because "it seemed to refer too much to our family" (Lin[g] 1974), and when the church was founded it was called Shung Him Tong.

Pastor Ling's sons had all been educated at Basel mission schools in Guangdong, and all are reputed to have attained an unusually high level of education—continuing their education well beyond secondary school. None worked as farmers, and villagers today speculate that they were each able to contribute money to purchase more land in and around the village. Sin Fong's work for the Kowloon Canton Railway, one older villager thinks, allowed the Lings to prosper by investing in land they knew would increase in value because of its proximity to the railroad.

The arrival of the Hakka newcomers to Lung Yeuk Tau was not without incident. The local Punti were opposed to outsiders, particularly Christian ones.[12] When Ling Ban Chung proposed to build his family two small houses in Shung Him Tong, the Teng claimed that it would destroy the *feng-shui* of their ancestral graves. Pastor Ling took the case to British authorities on Ban Chung's behalf, and the government intervened to allow the houses to be built. For the sake of keeping the peace, Pastor Ling agreed to the local Punti leaders' request for twenty-five Hong Kong dollars with which to pay for a banquet to appease their ancestors. This conflict was the first of several in the history of the village. In each case, rather than let the local Teng elders settle the conflict, the Hakka took the matter directly to the British authorities.

The immigrants envisioned Shung Him Tong as a home that could provide them with all that their previous home had lacked materially, socially, and spiritually. In the preface to Pang Lok Sam's history, Reverend Ho Syu Dak, a leader of the Basel mission in Hong Kong that later became the independent Tsung Tsin mission, wrote the following description of the imagined community of Shung Him Tong:

> An ideal village should have the following: public roads for transportation and communication, a church for spiritual activities, a school for educating the young, a hospital for healing the sick, and a cemetery. In this model village everyone would be satisfied with

their home and happy with their work. Everyone would live by the old lessons: love their neighbors, look after their friends, and help each other. . . . In the mid autumn of 192[?] . . . I found such a model village in Lung Yeuk Tau, New Territories, Hong Kong. . . . I often visited this village and was so impressed that I was reluctant to leave. On close examination I found it complete in every way except that it lacked a hospital, but this was not a problem because there was a public Red Cross clinic nearby. All villagers, of a total of over 100, were Christian. They loved their neighbors as much as they loved their families, so the village was called "Christian Gospel village." I awoke to find that this was the model village I imagined. My dream of the past years came true; and anyone who wants to build an ideal village should try to learn from this one (Pang 1934, preface).

The church, school, and cemetery are still key features of the village today, with the church as the focal point of the Christian community. The church stands in a prominent location at the front of the village and is the first thing seen on approach. Behind it are nestled several rows of single-story stone houses that were built in the early years of the village.

The Church and the Cemetery

From 1903 to 1905 Pastor Ling and his eldest son, Sin Yuen, had been spreading the gospel among their tenants and other Hakka in the area. By the winter of 1905 there were ten converts, so Pastor Ling requested that the Basel mission send an evangelist to the village to help set up a church. In response, they sent Pang Lok Sam, who was to become an important figure in the village, in the Hakka community, and in the New Territories.

Pang had previously spent two years working as a missionary in the Wuhua district of Guangdong. His home there had been plundered and his family robbed, so he decided to move away. When his younger brother died in 1901, he applied to the mission for a transfer to Baoan so he could be closer to his grieving mother. He then heard of Shung Him Tong, which was within the British leased area where "law and order were maintained and life was peaceful" (Pang 1934). After being transferred to Tai Po and Sham Shui Po in the British Territory and discussing his plans with his family, he used what he had saved over the years to buy some land in Shung Him Tong.

Pang helped Pastor Ling with church work, dividing his time between Shung Him Tong, Tai Po, and Sham Shui Po until 1909, when he was assigned to work primarily in Shung Him Tong. The following year he and Pastor Ling built the large double house that the two families continue to share today. Pang served as head evangelist in Shung Him Tong until 1913, when "he chose to devote himself to the growth of the New Territories" because his "other business" became too demanding (Cheung 1984:1; see also app. 2). He nevertheless continued to play a major role in the growth of the village and the church.

By 1922 the small cottage that had served as a sermon hall was too small, and Pang was instrumental in arranging for the construction of a new church that was completed in 1927. After providing a place for Christians to live and worship, Pang wrote that it was important to find them a place to rest when they died, a place where relatives could come to show respect. In 1931 Pang applied to the government for land for the cemetery (see Hong Kong Government 1931). The request was approved, and the cemetery was established on a hillside in back of the village. The villagers pride themselves on this achievement and claim that Shung Him Tong is the only church in the New Territories with its own cemetery.

Pang also played an important role in facilitating the independent status of the Tsung Tsin mission, the successor to the Basel mission in Hong Kong.[13] In 1934 the Tsung Tsin mission urged Shung Him Tong to become self-supporting. The three veteran pastors Ling, Pang, and Cheung Wo Ban took turns delivering the Sunday sermon and Cheung conducted the family visitations. The church continued to run normally and saved five hundred Hong Kong dollars annually. In 1937, because of the Japanese occupation of China, there was a large influx of refugees into Hong Kong, and the church grew, with Hakka Basel mission converts from areas around Baoan and others from as far as Meixian. On January 1, 1940, the church was officially declared self-supporting and representatives from the other Tsung Tsin mission churches participated in the celebration.

Beginning one of the worst periods in the memory of the people of Hong Kong, the Japanese occupied Hong Kong from December 1941 to August 1945. Shung Him Tong remained open, served by Pastor Man Ji San throughout the occupation. Many residents returned to their native villages in China, however, and as a result, church attendance was cut by as much as two thirds. The Tsung Tsin mission organized a group of two hundred people who walked for up to six days back to their old homes in Baoan, Huizhou, and Wuhua, while some went as far as Meixian (see map 3).

Those who remained in the village were forced to grow their own food and collect shrubs and grass from the hills for fuel, so that by the end of the war the hills were completely denuded of vegetation. The village school was closed down and used as a prison and detention center by the Japanese. Today stories about the ghosts of tortured prisoners wandering the Chung Him School grounds still circulate among the students. After the Japanese surrendered, church members returned en masse from China.

With the establishment of the People's Republic of China in 1949, church membership continued to grow at a rapid pace. Landlords, Christians, and Chinese nationalists fled to Hong Kong, some deciding to settle in Shung Him Tong, in the new adjacent village of On Lok, or in nearby Luen Wo market. In 1951, with gifts, donations, and a grant of five thousand Hong Kong dollars for charitable institutions from the Royal Hong Kong Jockey Club, construction began for a new two-story church that would seat three hundred followers. Meanwhile Pastor Man was transferred and was replaced by Man Fuk San, who later retired to the Hakka Christian community in North Borneo. He was replaced by Reverend Chow Tin Wo, who later left to pursue further study in Switzerland and Scotland. The most recent pastor, Tong Siu Ling, was born in Meixian. Two of his brothers are also pastors for the Tsung Tsin mission.

The School

The high value that Chinese traditionally place on education is shared by the people of Shung Him Tong and the Hakka in general, who regard education as the one most important route for upward mobility. As Pang wrote, "Education can improve a man's life, contribute to society and promote greater civilization in the world" (1934:7). According to many Hakka Christians, education was one of the main incentives for their ancestors to convert to Christianity. Even though the Hakka were represented in the Qing government examination quotas, Hakka often felt they were discriminated against or did not have the same advantages in preparing for the examinations.[14]

According to the northern New Territories district officer I spoke to, by 1949 the population of Shung Him Tong was per capita the most educated in all of urban or rural Hong Kong. The sons and daughters of Ling Sin Yuen all had university degrees, mostly from American universities. In Shung Him Tong education continues to be a priority. Church-affiliated schools, as I was told by the church evangelist, are considered an important means of teaching children to be good Christians and of attracting non-Christians to the church.

In theory, education has been readily available to children in the New Territories since the 1920s. But one New Territories temple inscription suggests otherwise, reading, "The descendants of those whose names do not appear on this tablet are not allowed to study in this temple" (Lun Ng 1984:251n. 5). Faure has written that by the "early twentieth century, no male child in the land communities of the eastern New Territories was totally deprived of a chance to attend school" (1986:147). The people of Shung Him Tong, however, felt otherwise. They believed that there were no schools in the area where they could send their children. The courses taught in the nearby Teng ancestral hall were taught in Cantonese, which excluded many monolingual

Hakka children. Moreover, classes were taught in the hall where ancestors were worshiped, which also made the school unappealing to Christians.

Shung Him Tong church and village leaders decided that they had to establish their own school for Christian and non-Christian Hakka children. In 1913 Pastor Cheung taught classes in a one-room building that served as a temporary school. A new primary school was built in 1925, founded by Pang Lok Sam and his brother-in-law Tsui Yan Sau, who was also the founder of the famous Wah Yan College in Hong Kong. A year later the primary school was expanded into an upper and lower primary school and dormitories were built to house students who lived a long distance away; the school was again expanded in the 1970s.

In 1923, Pang Lok Sam applied to the government for land to be used for the school.[15] After the government established that the school would be a philanthropic venture rather than a commercial one, they agreed that the land could be used for the sole purpose of a Hakka school (Hong Kong Government 1923). Until at least the 1950s the students were all Hakka with the exception of a few Mandarin speakers. This clause of the agreement was later amended, and today the school is no longer restricted to Hakka students. Today, however, the wealthier youths of Shung Him Tong often attend more prestigious schools in Hong Kong or Kowloon.

Roads and Bridges

Just as the church and school serve as monuments to the growth of the village, roads, bridges, walls, and fences also elicit stories about the history of the community. As Pang wrote, "There was once a dispute concerning the blockage of the road. It is worth recording so as to reveal the malicious ways of the world and how cruel people can be" (1934:13).

The people of Shung Him Tong were actively involved in improving their community. Besides the church and school there were other projects—such as building an embankment along the edge of the river to protect the area from floods during the typhoon season—which were geared toward improving their lives. Roads and bridges were constructed to facilitate the journey to and from market, to bring students to the school, and to bring more worshipers to the church. But such projects were also the grounds for dispute, especially with non-Christian, non-Hakka neighbors in the surrounding communities.[16]

The road connecting Shung Him Tong to the outside world presented several challenges to Hakka Christian leaders. After Chung Him School was established, Pang Lok Sam went to the Tai Po district board to ask that the narrow wooden bridge crossing Phoenix River into Shung Him Tong be replaced. He received no response until a young Teng boy drowned in the river during the typhoon season at the dragon boat festival. The government then approved the request and contributed 900 Hong Kong dollars to the project.

The main route connecting Shung Him Tong with the larger market town of Sheung Shui had always passed through land that later became On Lok village. In the 1920s, across the river from Shung Him Tong, On Lok was developed into a posh residential community of "country homes" for wealthy Chinese businessmen and professionals, most of them Cantonese. By the late 1920s, the conflict between residents of Shung Him Tong and the Cantonese developers of On Lok came to a climax.

Throughout the 1920s there had been trouble all over the New Territories with bandits and thieves, so Pang and the heads of about twenty wealthy families from Shung Him Tong, On Lok, and other nearby villages organized Luen On Tong (United Peace Association) for mutual aid and protection. The organization included both Hakka Christians and non-Christians, some of them relatively recent Cantonese immigrants to Hong Kong, and possibly one or two older Punti families. The members kept gongs in their homes to sound in case of trouble and arranged for guards around their homes and fields. The association also arranged that the villagers be allowed to keep firearms to protect their property. Luen On Tong held four banquets a year for its members. At one banquet in 1928, Fung, a landlord from On Lok village, asked Pang if Shung Him Tong villagers could take a different route to the Fanling train station rather than through On Lok. Pang answered no and sensed that there would be trouble over this issue in the future.

Shortly after, Fung declared that Shung Him Tong villagers should find an alternate route and that the people of On Lok would not allow them to cross their property. They erected a barrier around their village and placed guards at the gates. These entrances were closed at 9:00 P.M. and only reopened again at 9:00 A.M. When Pang first learned of this, he assumed it concerned the safety of the On Lok villagers and made no objection. But the next year on January 1, the path from On Lok to Shung Him Tong was blocked, and Pang reported it to the Tai Po District Office. The district officer assigned a police inspector to investigate. It turned out that the On Lok villagers had bought the land along which the path ran from the government a year earlier. The district office recommended that the Shung Him Tong and On Lok village leaders negotiate. Ling Sin Yuen, Cheung Wo Ban, Pang Lok Sam, and Tsui Yan Sau invited the On Lok village leaders to hold a meeting, but two meetings later, still no agreement had been reached. A few months later a lawyer from On Lok arranged a meeting in the Tai Po District Office and offered the following conditions:

1.   Only students and villagers can use the path;
2.   An annual one-dollar fee should be paid by each user;

3. Passage is allowed in both directions;
4. The path is open during daylight hours only;
5. People must pass on foot;
6. No cows are allowed;
7. No funeral processions are allowed;
8. The route must be agreed on in a contract.

Shung Him Tong representatives objected to the conditions. A month later Fung decided to block the path. The next evening On Lok guards fired several shots and claimed that Shung Him Tong villagers had tried to clear the obstructed path at night; they discovered them, fired a warning shot, and Shung Him Tong people allegedly returned fire. The following day the police inspector sent someone to bring Pang Lok Sam with his two rifles and pistol to the police station to be examined.

A European Basel missionary from Switzerland who was studying Hakka language in Shung Him Tong at the time of the incident wrote a letter to attest to the fact that Pang Lok Sam did not fire the shots.[17] A week later Pang and Ling again met with the On Lok lawyer but they reached no settlement. The district commissioner recommended that Shung Him Tong hire a lawyer. Pang, concerned that this would mean a great financial burden for the village, decided to take a different tack.

The next day, Pang arranged for a meeting of Shung Him Tong leaders and advocates at Chung Him School. Reverend Ho and Pastor Tsang of the Sai Ying Pun Basel mission church also joined the meeting and helped the Shung Him Tong representatives plan how to lodge their appeal. The following day they went to discuss the case with three members of the Heung Yee Kuk (Rural Consultative Committee), the organization of rural representatives that had been set up to serve the interests of the people of the New Territories. They finally agreed that Pang, who had been influential in founding the Kuk and was then the chairman, would send a letter to the Tai Po District Office and request that it be forwarded to the governor (Pang 1934).

Pang Lok Sam is thought to have been very effective in his way of approaching the government. In the letter to the Tai Po District Office dated April 1930, Pang Lok Sam and Ling Sin Yuen wrote:

> For several decades our villagers have gone to Fanling, Sheung
> Shui, Shen Zhen, etc., by way of the bridge to On Lok that leads
> to the main road. All along there was no problem. . . . In 1913,
> seeing that there were many school-aged children in the area,
> Pang Lok Sam contributed money to build a temporary school. In
> 1914, with a grant of HK$2,000 from the government, we built
> Chung Him lower and higher primary schools. . . . The total ex-

penditure was HK$10,000. . . . Later, since the wooden bridge
had decayed, the government gave us a grant of HK$990 to repair
it. . . . HK$1,976 were spent in the construction of the bridge,
with HK$280 contributed by five wealthy families of On Lok vil-
lage. Clearly, the construction of the bridge was considered important by the government; and the bridge was considered necessary by both the government and the villagers of On Lok. For the
past twenty-five years worshipers have taken this path to church.
Once people live in a place, they need roads. Where there are
roads, there are also bridges. This is why the government has the
good policy of providing financial support for people who need to
build bridges. . . . In fact the government provided funds to build
the bridge because it is along the route that children take to go to
school. So the bridge is for the school, which contributes to education. If the bridge is abandoned, the school is also, indirectly,
abandoned. (From letter from Heung Yee Kuk to the governor,
in Pang 1934).

Quickly and unexpectedly, the matter was resolved. No doubt Pang's political clout and his relationship with the Kuk was a major factor. By order of
the government, the police inspector sent a detective sergeant to On Lok the
next day. Fung was instructed to make the path accessible, and Pang Lok Sam
was informed that the dispute would be settled by the government in due
course. By the end of the year, the government decided to buy back four acres
of land in On Lok for public access. The land was bought from the On Lok
Investment Company for eighty-seven Hong Kong dollars. As Pang wrote,
"With the blessing of God we could finally come to a satisfactory conclusion
after a series of twists and turns" (1934:16; see also Hong Kong Government
1930). The construction of the road and the bridge is still a matter of pride for
the villagers of Shung Him Tong. The list of donations and the plaque com-
memorating the new road and the bridge still stand. Since then three additional
bridges have been built connecting Shung Him Tong to the main road, the
most recent completed in 1987.

POLITICS AND THE PEOPLE OF SHUNG HIM TONG

From the beginning of their arrival in the New Territories, the people of
Shung Him Tong showed an exceptional ability to protect their interests and
establish themselves in their community. The successful establishment of the
church, school, and cemetery and the resolution of the conflict over the path
through On Lok village are testaments, in the minds of the people of Shung
Him Tong, to "God's power." But these same events also demonstrate their

ability to deal with the political situation in the New Territories and the material benefits of belonging to the Hakka Christian community.

Luen Wo Tong was another voluntary organization started by Pang Lok Sam. It was less elite in its orientation than Luen On Tong, described above, and had many more members. It served the interests of Hakka Christians from Shung Him Tong and helped to link them with Hakka outside of the village. Membership, restricted to Hakka only, was attracted from throughout the Fanling region, including On Lok and Lung Yeuk Tau. Luen Wo Tong was established in the late 1920s and was, as one of Pang's sons described it, "a Hakka organization to protect them when they were bullied by the Punti." In the words of a retired government official who lived in Shung Him Tong for a few years as a child, it was "designed to resist pressure from the Puntis."

Luen Wo Tong also established certain rules and standards for its members. At weddings, birthdays, anniversaries, and other occasions, the same man explained,

> instead of giving gifts of an unlimited amount, it was limited to thirty cents. . . . They tried to standardize this practice so it wouldn't be a strain. Otherwise you'd be embarrassed because to your friends you'd feel obligated to give something. . . . If you overspend then you hurt your purse. So one of the things they decided was when a man dies and they need someone to carry the coffin you pay him eighty cents and no more. If you are invited to peoples' wedding, you need only contribute your share of thirty to forty cents, but no more. It's a sort of code of practice among Hakka, you see. Although the real intention, the unwritten one, was so one wouldn't be pressured by the Punti, see. It was a survival thing.

Another man described how the organization owned a building and bowls, cups, chairs, and other things "so that members could use these things for big banquets rather than have to rent them from big expensive restaurants." In those days, he said, "When you were invited to weddings you were obligated to give sixty cents, which was a hardship for some people. Pang Lok Sam made a stipulation that excused poor people from this obligation." After the war, by the late 1940s, he went on, "This association was not so necessary." As he explained, a government official who was originally from Shung Him Tong "discouraged the association because he said it helped to reinforce the distinction between Hakka and Punti. He said not to make there be differences. By then, anyway, there was little trouble."

Luen Wo Tong was one way for the people of Shung Him Tong to protect their interests. Their mission school education, knowledge of foreigners, wider church contacts, and ability to deal with the British government enabled such prominent community leaders as Ling, Pang, and others to successfully resolve the problems they encountered. By relying on their own leadership or allying themselves with the district office, Hakka Christians were able to circumvent the traditional political authority of the Punti. While in the nineteenth century the Teng might have resisted the establishment and expansion of Shung Him Tong, their power in the twentieth century was seriously undermined by the arrival of the British administration, who, in many respects, considered the Hakka their allies. As illustrated by the incident of the new path through On Lok, Hakka Christians were even able to successfully achieve their goals in competition with wealthy Cantonese developers.

Like several other Hakka Christians, Pang Lok Sam had considerable influence outside the boundaries of Shung Him Tong. He was a leader in the New Territories as a representative and founder of the Heung Yee Kuk and was involved in founding the International Hakka Association. He also organized Luen Wo Tong for the mutual benefit and protection of all Hakka, both Christians and non-Christians, and Luen On Tong, which allied him with wealthy Hakka and non-Hakka families. When the ever-increasing Hakka population of Lung Yeuk Tau and the wider region encountered problems with landlords or even in family matters, Pang was often invited—by both Hakka Christians and non-Christians—to mediate. Pang also served as an important link to the British government and was known to be a close personal friend of the governor, Sir Cecil Clementi. As Smith (1985) has aptly demonstrated, religion was instrumental in the upward mobility of Chinese Christians. Mission-educated Chinese Christians in Hong Kong often attained positions as middlemen in business and politics. Members of the generation after Pang Lok Sam, Ling Sin Yuen, Cheung Wo Ban, and Tsui Yan Sau were just as successful. One of Tsui's sons, Paul Tsui, became a high-ranking official in the Hong Kong government. Cheung's son worked for the Hong Kong Government Lands Office, and one of Ling's sons became the first president of the Chinese University of Hong Kong.

In the first three decades of Shung Him Tong, the founders managed to establish a church for communal worship, a school to provide high-quality education for their children, and a cemetery where their ancestors could rest. Homes were built; roads were constructed and expanded. The people of Shung Him Tong became renowned in the New Territories, and the church attracted an increasing number of Hakka followers who shared the vision of this imagined Hakka Christian community.

4 The Hakka Church Community and Daily Life

On the surface, day-to-day life in Shung Him Tong does not appear to differ greatly from that of the neighboring non-Christian Chinese villages. Every morning before dawn people from Shung Him Tong set off to catch buses, trains, and taxis to work or school, while others set out to work in the vegetable gardens and still others head to the market to buy or sell fresh vegetables, meat, and fish. Younger women, particularly those who work outside their homes, do not go to the market every morning but stop there on their way back from work, and they are criticized by older women who are extremely particular about fresh food. Some women head off to the market after taking children to school or to the bus stop, then afterward meet their friends at the teahouse or the food stall for rice porridge. For older, retired men and women, such activities as searching for the freshest vegetables or fish at the market, meeting friends, and reading the newspaper at the teahouse or the park are regular parts of the day. After the market, women return home in plenty of time to clean the house and wash the clothes before preparing lunch. Washing machines are becoming more common, but many women still do laundry by hand.

It is when the marketing, chores, baby-sitting, and washing are finished that the activities of Shung Him Tong Christians and others differ. Older men from Shung Him Tong can be seen chatting while they sit on park benches in Luen Wo market, or setting off to attend special meetings at the church, but they are rarely, if ever, seen participating in card or board games. Elsewhere in Lung Yeuk Tau, one commonly hears the clatter of mahjong tiles, or catches scenes of women playing cards through the doorways of their homes. But in Shung Him Tong, if these activities go on at all, it is behind closed doors. The only exception is the local shop in Shung Him Tong, where the sound of mahjong is often heard. This, I was told, is because "outsiders" come there to play.

The Hakka church is the focal point of Shung Him Tong, not only in a physical and symbolic sense but also in terms of the social organization of the community. Villagers commonly work and go to school outside of the village, and they have non-Hakka and non-Christian friends, coworkers, acquaintances, and sometimes spouses, but in many ways the community is set apart, labeled by outsiders and experienced by members as different. Shung Him Tong has inherited this historically constituted separation as a legacy that continues to mark it off from its neighbors and to identify it as a Hakka Christian community. As will become more apparent in the chapters that follow, some members, particularly younger ones, feel a degree of ambivalence about the Hakka nature of their community, but it is not something they can easily change. Despite their various ties to the outside world, their identity, social life, entertainment, and many weekly activities center around the Hakka church.

Over 90 percent of the residents of Shung Him Tong are considered to "belong" to the community, and, as was mentioned earlier, the vast majority of these people are Hakka. People belong by virtue of their ties to the church, whether through the fictive kinship relationships of church "brotherhood" and "sisterhood" or through actual kinship ties to the original founders of the church and village. People who rent houses or farm land in Shung Him Tong and do not belong to the church are generally not considered members of the community or "church family." Membership in the church through baptism and confirmation serves not only to integrate new members into the community but also to reassert the social, political, and moral status of its members. Daily activities, family life, gender roles, and the political and economic organization of Shung Him Tong are all tied to the church and help to define the identity of this Hakka Christian community.

CHURCH ACTIVITIES AND THE RHYTHM OF THE WEEK

Sunday Service

Each Sunday at ten in the morning the church bells sound, announcing to Shung Him Tong and the surrounding villages that Sunday school classes and the women's prayer group are about to begin. At eleven, the bells chime again and groups of Hakka Christians of all ages approach the church; in the summer months, they wield umbrellas to protect themselves from the scorching midday heat. Older women, dressed in loose black pants and blouses, arrive holding the hands of squirming grandchildren. Hakka worshipers come from as far away as Hong Kong Island by car, or they arrive by taxi or minibus from the Fanling train station, the housing estate, or the nearby market town of Luen Wo. One minibus delivers several elderly people to church each Sunday from the home for the aged in Sha Tin, which is administered by the Tsung Tsin mission. Most church members, however, arrive on foot from Shung Him Tong, or from across the On Lok bridge, and a few families come from other villages in Lung Yeuk Tau.

The church elders are very proud of the new church, designed by an architect with kinship ties to Shung Him Tong and membership in one of the other Tsung Tsin churches. The building is considered very "modern." Its square lines, narrow vertical windows, and pinkish beige and blue concrete walls contrast with the old, stucco, mission-style church just a few yards down the road. When the new church was completed in 1983, the cross was removed from its bell tower and the old church building was unceremoniously rented out as a storage unit. The new church has a small parking lot in front, a playground in back, and on the ground floor a small library and office, along with four large classrooms used for Sunday school and kindergarten classes. Upstairs are the main hall and two small apartments—one for the church evangelist and the other for official guests or seminary interns who sometimes stay for a few weeks during the summer. Directly above the two apartments is a larger one that houses the pastor and his family.

The main hall is two stories high. Forty pews, with a capacity to seat over three hundred people, fill the room. A deep red carpet divides the pews down the center aisle leading to the platform at the far end of the hall. The eye is automatically directed to a large, plain wooden cross suspended at the center of the far wall. Beneath the cross is a table with a vase of fresh flowers arranged each week by a member of the women's youth group. On the left side of the platform are some seats, the podium for the main speaker, and a lower podium for the translator, who renders the sermon into Hakka or Cantonese. To the right are the organ and the choir pews. The podiums, the organ, and the choir frame the cross at center stage. Empty of people, with little that suggests that it is "Chinese," Shung Him Church could easily pass as a suburban North American Lutheran church.

Before the service begins, a small crowd always congregates in the shaded entrance and the foyer, while the children remain in the playground until the last minute when the church bells sound. One often hears the cheerful sounds of reunions spoken in Hakka as old church members return for visits from overseas. Later, these members are formally welcomed by the pastor or chairman during the service. People are careful not to make too much noise since the women's prayer group, led by the pastor's wife, can be seen through the window of the classroom reciting prayers. Children are quickly ushered in to join those who arrived for the early Sunday school class, while ushers pass out programs at the door of the church hall and help the elderly to their seats. As soon as the women's prayer group adjourns, the young adults who are in the choir hurry into the room to don their robes and collect their musical scores.

By quarter past eleven, everyone who will attend the service has taken a seat upstairs. During the hot season the overhead fans churn the humid air and the sun pours in the windows; members of the congregation fan themselves with programs or paper fans while waiting for the service to begin. On ordinary Sundays around 150 people comfortably fill the hall. On special occasions such as Christmas or the Chinese New Year, as many as four or five hundred people line the aisles and crowd outside the main entrance. Some make the yearly trip to Shung Him Tong from as far away as Holland, the United Kingdom, Canada, or the United States, and others, who attend only occasionally, are sure to come on such special occasions.

Old and young men alike wear western-style trousers and button-down shirts, but women dress in a variety of styles, largely indistinguishable from other people in Hong Kong. Toward the front of the hall is a cluster of older women in more traditional garb—dark trousers and blouses, gold and jade earrings and bracelets, their smiles sometimes displaying gold-capped teeth. Their hair is neatly tied back and sometimes hidden under the traditional black rectangular scarf with embroidered band.[1] A middle-aged group of women wear polyester pantsuits in dull or dark prints—some with mandarin collars—and have their short, curly hair brushed back from their faces. Younger women and girls wear anything from brightly colored "hightop" sneakers, leggings, and designer T-shirts to more conservative stylish dresses. At first glance it is clear that women in the audience outnumber men and that families do not generally sit together. Men and women frequently sit in gender-segregated groups with their friends rather than their spouses, with the exception of young married couples.

The service follows the same formal, reliable pattern each Sunday. The organist begins, the congregation rises, and the minister, the chairperson of the assembly, the chairman of the board of directors of the church (who is also the director of the choir), the translator, and the eighteen or so members of the choir enter in a slow procession. The ushers leave the extra programs at the door for latecomers and stand in front of their seats. When the last members of the choir reach their places, the congregation sings a hymn. Then everyone is seated and recites a silent prayer. The chairperson stands at the lower podium, greets the congregation, and leads a hymn and another prayer. Then the congregation is seated and the chairperson reads a scriptural passage from the Bible. The congregation stands again and in unison they recite a passage from the hymnbook such as the Lord's Prayer or the Ten Commandments, followed by the doxology. The congregation is again seated while the choir sings a hymn. This is followed by the sermon.

The sermon is the longest part of the service. Usually it is delivered in Hakka in a very somber tone by the regular minister of the church. The "female evangelist," a student from the theological school, other ministers from the Tsung Tsin mission, honored visitors from the Basel mission in Switzerland, or other Hakka ministers from "sister" Chinese churches overseas sometimes deliver guest sermons. If the speaker can speak Hakka, the translator renders the sermon one line at a time into Cantonese. Less often, if the sermon is delivered in Cantonese, it is translated into Hakka. The translator is usually the pastor's wife or one of the young women in the choir or on the board of directors.

Following the sermon, the congregation again stands with heads bowed while the speaker delivers a prayer. Another hymn is sung and then the congregation and the speaker take their seats while the chairman of the board makes his announcements. These, like the introductory remarks of the chairperson of the assembly, are often in Hakka and are generally not translated into Cantonese. The news items are also written on the back of the program so people who do not follow the spoken Hakka can read along. Announcements include topics such as who will usher, collect donations, and teach Sunday school the following week; the amount collected in donations the previous week; the homes that will be visited for family worship; and other meetings and special activities.

After the announcements the chairperson passes out the collection bags to the four people assigned to collect donations. Occasionally there is a "double" collection, part of which goes toward evangelical missions or the new Lutheran seminary. In what appears to be a conscious attempt at balance, the four collectors are without exception two men and two women, and generally one of each gender is younger and the other older. Every individual usually contributes something: children are taught at an early age to put a coin in the collection bag, and even the youngest children's youth group has its own miniature collection bag. After the donations, all stand and sing another hymn, the minister delivers the benediction with his arms spread wide and his eyes closed, and all are once again seated to recite a silent prayer. After a few moments the organist begins and the minister, officials, and choir slowly file out of the room, followed by the rest of the congregation.

The tone of the service is always somber and unemotional, as is the brand of Christianity practiced by this community. The service follows the same general pattern week after week with a few minor variations on the weeks of baptisms, confirmations, and communion. Hymns are usually selected according to the liturgical calendar; the first and last hymns of the service are the same each week, and there is little variation in the recited prayers. Only once during the year I attended Shung Him Tong Sunday services was there an unusual outburst. A woman who had never been baptized was asked not to receive communion. She began to shout abusively and was quickly ushered out of the hall. People sitting near me apologetically referred to her as "mentally imbalanced," and the service continued as usual as though nothing had happened. While to the outsider the service may appear dull, to the members the dependable weekly repetition of this community ritual provides as much comfort and reassurance as the message of the sermon. Each week Hakka Christians enter their sacred place of worship, and then they return once again to the mundane, less predictable existence of their everyday lives.

Church Groups

There are a variety of church groups in Shung Him Tong, each of which suggests a different social category. There are groups for children, youth, young adults, professional young adults, women, and bible study, as well as two weekly family worship services and the church board. Many of the categories overlap. For example, some of the older married women who attend the prayer group belong to the board of directors. A few members of the older youth groups are also represented on the board; young professional adults may also belong to the regular youth group. None of the church groups is directed specifically toward men or boys in particular, and young men are less well represented in the older youth groups.

Several men in the community explained that the church, as a Hakka church, is conscious of treating women as "equals." Although the Sunday ritual might seem to superficially support such an impression, this is in fact not the case. There are roughly equal numbers of men and women who officiate at the Sunday service, but men in the church tend to hold the positions of greater prestige and authority. Two men and two women—one older and one younger—always collect the offerings each week, and two men and two women always serve as ushers. Most often the sermon is delivered by a male pastor, but the female evangelist also occasionally has her turn. Men and women from the board of directors are both offered the position of chairperson of the weekly assembly, but the chairman of the board of directors who reads the weekly announcements is always a man. Women may be visible, but they play a far more active role in the "service" or "support" roles of the church, as translators, Sunday school teachers, secretaries, and evangelists in the surrounding communities, while men fill most of the more prominent and powerful roles of pastor, treasurer, school principal, chairman of the board of directors, and so on. The importance of maintaining the idea of "liberated" Hakka women is examined in more detail in Chapter 6.

Sunday is the main day for church activity, but meetings and study groups structure the entire week. After the service there is usually a meeting of the church board of directors. The board of directors includes the minister (a man) and the evangelist (a woman), who are regular employees of the church, and twenty-three board members. Board members are elected every two years, but in fact are usually only replaced if someone retires from his or her position or moves away. Four of the positions on the board—two for men and two for women—are reserved for church elders and are positions that are held for life. These elders are not necessarily active in church affairs. During the year I was there, two elders—including Pastor Ling's grandson and his wife—resided overseas and a third, also related to Pastor Ling, lived in a home for the elderly. In such cases, the importance of having Lings represented on the board outweighed their being physically absent.

The chairman of the board of directors is selected from among the members of the board. In theory anyone is eligible, but in fact the one resident male elder had been the chairman for several terms by the time I began my research. By virtue of his role as chairman, his status as a descendant of one of the early village pastors, and his particularly authoritarian personality, the chairman was considered the single most influential person in the church. The role of chairman is potentially the most powerful and influential position in the church, but, as with the role of the pastor, the amount of authority he exerts depends largely on the ambition and personality of the person who holds the office. The chairman, by virtue of his role, has the power to make and veto decisions concerning the administration and everyday affairs of the church.

At the time I conducted my research, the chairman was considered very conservative, he was not known for initiating major changes, and he had the power to override the suggestions of other board members. For example, although several board members were in favor of having air conditioning installed in the sermon hall, the chairman did not support the plan so it had to be shelved until the time when he retired, or as one person said, "Until he goes away on holiday." As it happened, a year after I left Shung Him Tong, this chairman, who was by then in his eighties, resigned his position and was replaced by his eldest son-in-law. As I was informed in a letter, one of the first things the new chairman did was to have air conditioning installed.

Members of the board of directors may hold offices or belong to church planning committees such as the kindergarten planning and supervising committee, the cemetery management committee, the church publications editorial board, and the playground and church premises planning committees. Special offices include treasurer, secretary, accountant, director of the youth groups, director of the women's league, and principal of the kindergarten. Most of the special roles and offices are held by men, and men also serve as the Shung Him Tong representatives at the Tsung Tsin mission synod meetings. Among the board members are roughly an equal number of men and women, mostly married couples, covering a range of ages, but it is well known that the men play a more visible and influential role in making church policy. One young woman whose parents were both board members said that her mother, like other women board members, speaks up at meetings far less than her father and tends to just go along with his point of view.

The board of directors forms a very special and elite group and is said to comprise the pillars of the community. Indeed, becoming a member of the board or having a family member represented on the board reflects highly on the entire family. When I first arrived in Shung Him Tong I was advised by one older board member that I must interview those who are the most important and influential in the community. All of the names he listed were male board members. Another man in his early forties recommended that I be sure and talk to members of what he called the "old and the new set." When I asked him who he recommended, he also listed male members of the board of directors, and as in the first man's list, each person was a well-educated professional who could trace agnatic or affinal kinship ties to the early pastors or founding families of the village.

The distinction he made between the "old set" and the "new set" was an interesting one. Although these labels were meant mainly as a way to distinguish the older from the younger members, age was not the only difference, and the labels were used to refer to others besides board members. Members of the old set were more directly related to the founders of the community and were from families who had been Christian for several generations. The younger set were either unrelated or less closely related to the founding families or had recently "married in." Their families were generally "recent" converts who had been Christians for two generations or less.

Board members considered part of the old set traced a direct kinship tie to the founding families and tended to be more conservative in their views regarding the church. One board member was the son, another the grandson, another the nephew of one of the three founding males. With one older board member the tie was less direct, but he traced his kinship tie to the founding families by going back over five generations to their common native village in China. These men agreed with many of the younger board members that an important goal was to attract more members, but, as is discussed in more detail later in the chapter, they were generally opposed to changes away from being a "Hakka church."

The board members considered representative of the new set were three brothers in their thirties and early forties. They were younger than most of the other male board members, and they did not have blood ties to the founding families. They did, however, have ties to the old set through marriage, and each of their wives also served on the board at one time or another. The three brothers held a somewhat less conservative view regarding the direction of the church and its Hakka identity. Despite the fact that they were not born into the village, and that they had not been born into a Christian family, they were widely considered "model" church members who set a good example for others by virtue of their university education, their commitment to the church, and their upward mobility and success.

In a letter I received in 1991, a friend from Shung Him Tong wrote that "the aged members are gradually releasing their duties to the younger ones." Since I left Shung Him Tong, members of the community who represent the new set—those who have not emigrated to Canada or elsewhere—have effectively replaced the old in many of the church leadership positions. As of 1991, the new chairman and vice-chairman were still both related by blood or marriage to the founding families.

In 1986, I was told categorically that all of the board members were Hakka, but later it became clear that there were several exceptions. One woman board member had been adopted by a prominent Hakka church family, and although most people thought of her as Hakka, one person speculated that perhaps her biological parents were not Hakka. One man was of Chaozhou origin, but he had been a teacher at Chung Him School for several decades, was a well respected and dedicated member of the community, and spoke Hakka fluently. Two other women were "not born Hakka," but like the other non-Hakka on the board they spoke Hakka fluently and were jokingly referred to on a number of occasions as "honorary Hakka." One of these women was the wife of one of Pang Lok Sam's sons, and the other was the wife of the staunchly Hakka pastor who often served as the translator during the church service. These exceptions do not seem to interfere with the ideological construction of the community as Hakka.

There are several different youth groups. The "senior" youth group meets on Saturday evenings and is open to anyone who has finished fifth form or who is out of school and working. The middle youth group is for people in middle school between first and fifth forms, and members range in age from fourteen to nineteen years. The third group meets early Saturday afternoon and is for those between sixth primary and fifth form, who are between ten and fifteen years old. Youth groups are run by the evangelist, a young woman in her early thirties who is a regular church employee, and teenage and young adult women volunteers. One young woman explained that since the new evangelist arrived several years ago, the structure of the youth groups changed and has become more serious: "There used to be just one youth group [for all ages] and I would come to play. Now children come to pray not play." At one middle youth group meeting I attended, the young people sat in silence for almost fifteen minutes at a stretch as they were asked by the evangelist to contemplate the questions of whether they were filial to their parents and whether or not they had been active enough in "spreading the Word."

The new evangelist considers it her first duty to proselytize and has worked hard to get the youth involved in more Bible study, prayer, and evangelism efforts. I once casually commented to a senior youth group member that there were many kinship links between members of the church. The young woman I mentioned this to, a secretary in a Kowloon firm, responded defensively and said, "Our youth group is working hard to change that." Most of the young people, especially the older youth group members, believe it their duty and obligation to introduce more people to Christianity, regardless of whether they are Hakka or to whom they are related—although, as discussed below, they have had limited success. They are critical of those who do not join in organized evangelical efforts or invite outside friends and coworkers to the church.

The younger children's meetings consist largely of supervised play, singing of hymns, and Bible stories, while the older children and adults conduct a more formal Bible study. For adults there is more prayer, sharing of ideas and experiences, and discussion of Bible passages. Song, prayer, study, and "giving witness" play a large part in the "senior" youth group meetings.

At one Saturday evening meeting for senior youth there was a "circular" prayer that lasted almost half an hour. Twenty people, including the evangelist, sat in a circle and prayed in complete silence. Another activity included a formal written examination on the scripture they were to have prepared for that week. Later, the evangelist corrected the exams and recorded weekly scores. Hymns were sung at intervals throughout the evening. Some tunes were more popular than those sung during the Sunday service, and hymns were sometimes sung in a lively and casual spirit with one person shouting out the language to sing in after each verse: "Hakka!" "Cantonese!" "Mandarin!" "English!"

The topic of the evening was "time" and the young people were to discuss the meaning of time as it related to the Bible and to their lives. The highlight of the discussion was when a young woman received nods and whispers of approval for "giving witness" and sharing her ideas about how she once divided up her time into work time, study time, family time, and fun time and never felt there was enough until she was "born again," after which all her time became more fulfilling as Christian time.

Every fourth Sunday of the month there is a lunch meeting of members of the group for young professionals. With the help of the evangelist and the use of her kitchen, several of the women members heat up cans of Campbell's soup or Ramen noodles, make sandwiches of white bread and Spam, and serve Jell-O salads. This group of young unmarried adults ranging in age from early twenties to thirties contrasts with the regular young adult youth group. Although membership of the two groups overlaps somewhat, the young professionals are slightly older and more affluent than members of the regular "senior" youth group. Some are pursuing college or university educations, while those who have finished school work as teachers, administrative assistants, nurses, and doctors. One reason given for the formation of this group is that the members "don't have enough time to attend the weekly Saturday evening youth group meetings." The professional youth group tends to exclude the young people who work in factories or who are unemployed. Its members correspond in a general way with those young people who are the descendants of the old set. The professional youth group meets less frequently than the other youth groups because it is presumed that its members must devote more time to their careers. As one young woman put it, it is "less serious" than the regular youth group. Some members are known to occasionally go to discos with their outside friends, and they do not have the same degree of involvement with the church projects and outings as is expected of other youth group members. Consequently, the members of this group seem more likely eventually to leave the community and the church. Because of their ties to the older set and the village founders, however, their "less pious" behavior is not openly criticized, but they do evoke some criticism from older villagers and resentment from other young people. The newer, less well-connected, and less affluent or occupationally successful youth group members feel they are required and expected to demonstrate a higher standard of Christian spirit and commitment, and in many instances they do.

In addition to the regular weekly meetings, members of the older youth groups organize bicycle rides, picnics, games, competitions, music classes, talent shows, and field trips into town for the younger children. Choir rehearsals, occasional joint meetings with one of the twelve other Tsung Tsin mission youth groups, and planning committee meetings also fill the week. Informal soccer, tennis, badminton, and volleyball games often take place on Sunday afternoons. Festival events such as Christmas, the Chinese New Year, and Easter are celebrated at the church each year, as are life-passage rituals of birth, baptism, confirmation, marriage, and death. Churchwide outings for people of all ages are also arranged, such as a trip to the Chinese University gardens and restaurant. During the summer there is a day camp for the younger children and, for the older youth group members, a joint outing with the youth group members from other Tsung Tsin mission churches to an outlying island or mountain camp for several days. At Christmastime, a caroling group pays a visit to nearby hospitals and the Tsung Tsin mission home for the elderly. In 1987, the 140th anniversary of the year the European missionaries from the Basel mission arrived in China, a year-long calendar of celebrations was planned. A special Tsung Tsin missionwide choir was formed and a variety of celebrations, banquets, programs, workshops, and special services took place at different Tsung Tsin mission churches.

JOINING THE CHURCH, JOINING THE COMMUNITY

Speaking Hakka

Hakka language is one of the most important symbols of Hakka identity, at least among the older people of Shung Him Tong. To the younger church members it is far less important, and a declining number of youth make an effort to speak it. But as yet, it remains an important feature of Shung Him Tong identity. While I was in Shung Him Tong, one older man began to teach a Hakka language class one evening a week. Enrollment was not overwhelming; it included five young women and one of their mothers, all of whom hoped to improve their Hakka reading and writing skills. The teacher taught the Hakka "church dialect," which was different from his own native Meixian dialect, and he used the Hakka Bible as his text. As he explained, the church language is more like Baoan Hakka, because that is where the Basel missionaries went first. It "is a beautiful language" that is more easily understood by Hakka from many regions. The teacher was very proud when one of his young students soon gained enough confidence from the class to volunteer to translate the Sunday sermons.

Shung Him Church, many members say, is the only place they can go to speak Hakka. Many who live several miles away say this is why they continue to commute to Shung Him Tong on Sundays. Some, especially the older church members, lament the shift to include a Cantonese translation of the sermon, which they consider regrettable but necessary for the growth of the congregation. When I asked one elder why he had read the announcements from the Sunday service in Hakka, he answered in an exasperated tone of voice, "There must always be *some* Hakka!" Explaining the reason for the translation of the sermon, he continued, "Only the oldest women do not understand Cantonese; more of the young people don't understand Hakka. They learn Cantonese at school, they speak it with their friends, they want it in Cantonese." Another older man explained to me that he had resigned himself to the idea that there must be more Cantonese: "If it is in Cantonese, the young people can bring their friends along."

"The young people *no longer speak* Hakka." "The young people *don't want to speak* Hakka." "The young people *don't understand* Hakka." "They speak Cantonese at school, they *don't want to* speak Hakka." I commonly heard these sentiments expressed with various degrees of remorse. Some church members, and especially the chairman of the board at the time, stood firm and insisted on keeping at least part of every service in Hakka. "This is a *Hakka* church!" one board member said emphatically when I asked him if he thought the service should be in Hakka or Cantonese. Another board member, representing the more popular view among the younger set, said, "Hakka is a thing of the past. We've got to be practical about these things." His emphasis was more on attracting new members than on preserving the Hakka character of the church, an example of the growing tension between Hakka and Christian identity in the church community.

Today in all Hong Kong schools the language medium is Cantonese with the exception of some English-language schools. From primary school on, students are required to learn English. In the past few years there has been more discussion of requiring students to learn Mandarin, the official language of the People's Republic of China, rather than English. Considering the number of years that most students study English, the standard is remarkably poor. Hakka was once the main language of instruction at Chung Him School but today all classes there are taught in Cantonese.

Certain occupations are stereotypically Hakka. As one man put it, "One place you can be almost certain to hear people speaking Hakka is at construction sites." In most work places, however, there is no question but that people speak Cantonese, with a few using some English. It is not uncommon, as one young factory worker said, to have worked with someone for years before realizing that they also speak Hakka. In the home and among family members, many Shung Him Tong people still speak Hakka, including many with one Cantonese parent. The pastor's family and many of the Pangs, Cheungs, and Lings speak Hakka at home and among themselves. At the teahouse or at the market the older Shung Him Tong women often speak in Hakka, and a few of them speak only Hakka. As mentioned above, many non-Hakka who learn to speak Hakka are referred to as "honorary Hakka."

Weekly family worship visitations are conducted in Hakka unless, as is rarely the case, there is someone present who does not speak it. The pastor, originally from Meixian, is far more comfortable speaking Hakka than Cantonese. Although he has lived in Hong Kong for over twenty years, his attempts to speak Cantonese are clumsy and difficult to understand, and often elicit giggles from the young people. Even though people speak Hakka at home and hear it at church on Sundays, the general impression among most people in Shung Him Tong is that Hakka language is slowly fading away because the young people are increasingly reluctant to speak it. Most of the young people I met in Shung Him Tong can understand and speak Hakka, but they may be reluctant to speak it. A lack of interest in the language, however, does not necessarily correlate to a weakening of Hakka identity.

I was on a hike with several young women, members of the older and middle youth groups, on a hot summer afternoon. As we meandered across the spine of Dragon Mountain, past shelters that some said were built to hide from the Japanese, I asked my companions why they did not speak to one another in Hakka. They pointed to two young women, "Ming Lee," who worked in a factory and had only belonged to the church for a few years, and "May," a nurse from an older church family, and said accusingly, "Because of them." Ming Lee adamantly defended herself and explained that although she does not know how to speak Hakka she can understand it. She insisted that her mother was Hakka and her father half Hakka, much to the surprise and doubt of her friends. May was not so defensive but merely explained to me that she does not like to speak Hakka, although her parents and her sisters often do, and that she still considers herself Hakka. As a well-established member of the church, she did not feel the same need as Ming Lee to defend her Hakka identity.

In general, the younger its members, the less likely a church group is to conduct its meetings in Hakka. Hakka-speaking seminary students are also becoming increasingly difficult to find for summer internships. While I conducted my research, three theology student evangelists worked for the church. One was a summer visitor who spoke no Hakka; the second was the woman evangelist mentioned above, who had been there several years and who spoke some Hakka. Her parents, she thought, may have been part Hakka, though the language was never spoken in her home when she was growing up in urban Hong Kong. She was surprised to find that people in Shung Him Tong all spoke Hakka. When she went to Canada to continue her studies, another young Hakka woman replaced her. This third intern had come to Hong Kong to study, and her family in Malaysia still spoke Hakka at home. "We are lucky to have her," one older board member told me. "She is Hakka." He explained that the board, when hiring, tries to find a Hakka speaker first, and then opens the candidacy to qualified nonspeakers. Qualified Hakka speakers are getting harder to find and are consequently in great demand.[2] Hakka ministers from other Tsung Tsin churches and elsewhere often say that they enjoy visiting Shung Him Tong because there they have the opportunity to speak Hakka.

In the wider Hong Kong context, Hakka language is far less prevalent than Cantonese. At school, at work, and on television and radio, people hear mostly Cantonese, though some also listen to English and Mandarin programs. Hong Kong has experienced nothing like the 1989 Hakka demonstration in Taiwan to demand Hakka-language television programming that marked the beginning of a Hakka movement (Martin 1992). Hong Kong Hakka have not actively demanded Hakka programs or equal time for Hakka language. The church and home are two of the few remaining contexts in which Hakka is spoken.

Recruiting Converts

Translating the sermon into Cantonese, improving the playground and church facilities, opening a nursery school, and offering extra evening classes and social activities are all efforts to attract new members to the church. Two evenings a week I taught English conversation classes. Fifteen children attended, many of them encouraged by their parents to bring their English homework assignments, and one evening a week four to eight adults attended. The church board hoped that these classes, like the new larger playground constructed in back of the church, would attract new churchgoers. Judging from the English classes, however, a vast majority of the students were already church members, and those who were not were Hakka from Lung Yeuk Tau or Luen Wo market who showed no intention of joining. Some non-church members attended the class just until their English examinations were finished or until they had succeeded in their English-language job interviews.

Twice a week the pastor, the evangelist, and usually two or three other church members go on family visitations. In the evening, as they approach the house that is being visited, they can be heard singing hymns while the pastor plays his accordion. Each family who belongs to the church is visited at least once a year. These families are urged to invite extended family members, friends, and neighbors to attend the visitation—especially those who do not already belong to the church. During the visit, everyone prays, sings hymns, and listens to a short sermon before sharing refreshments and informal conversation.

In terms of broader evangelical efforts, many members of Shung Him Tong are actively involved or at least contribute money to overseas missionary work geared specifically toward attracting Hakka converts. In 1987 several young people from Shung Him Tong, including the evangelist, attended a conference of the Chinese Christian Organization for World Evangelism, which was held in Taiwan. One session that was organized by members of the World Hakka Evangelical Association focused on the question of attracting more Hakka converts worldwide.

Evangelism is encouraged among the youth groups more now than it was a decade ago. Members of the youth group go out in groups large and small and sometimes join members of other Fanling churches to pass out religious leaflets at nearby housing estates and in shopping malls. They are not reluctant to make a Christian spectacle of themselves in public. Once, I was invited for a hike and picnic with several youth group members. When we reached our destination, the young women picked a scenic but crowded spot in the park that was surrounded by clusters of other people who were out to enjoy the fresh air and, I presumed, the peace and quiet. As soon as we unloaded our packs, my seven companions unselfconsciously pulled out their songbooks and began to sing hymns and read out loud from the Bible, pleased to draw attention to themselves and their cause. On other, more formal occasions, leaflets are brought along and people are individually approached.

Non-Christian Hakka in the neighboring villages sometimes invite the pastor to say a prayer and lead a hymn at the funeral of a Hakka non-Christian. I have never heard of one of the Punti families making such a request. The pastor and a small entourage from the church say they are pleased to attend these funerals because they present a good opportunity to attract new members to the church, although they suspect these Hakka non-Christians just "want all the blessings they can get." In some regards these Hakka non-Christian neighbors are in a good situation. As fellow Hakka, they can easily activate their connections with the Hakka church, but as non-Christians they have better relations with Punti than the Hakka Christians.

Baptism and confirmation records from Shung Him Tong indicate that the number of new members has dropped considerably since 1981. Between 1947 and 1970 the number of baptisms averaged over fifty per year, while between 1981 and 1986 the average dropped to twenty-five (see fig. 1). Board members, youth group members, and a few ordinary church members are concerned about this downward trend. They consider it their duty to bring in new church members, but for a number of reasons they have had limited success.

One reason is that between 1980 and 1986 the number of churches within a two-mile radius of Shung Him Tong has increased from four to six (G. Law Ward 1982:63). These include another Lutheran church, a Baptist church, an Assemblies of God church, a Catholic church, and a new Chinese Evangelical church run by a friend and classmate of the Shung Him Tong evangelist. Cantonese is exclusively spoken in these churches. People from Shung Him Tong who have visited other churches have gone to either the currently popular Assemblies of God church or the new Chinese Evangelical church.

Although some people who move from the village no longer attend church, or choose to join a different church, many continue to return to Shung Him Tong, at least on occasion. Shung Him Tong has not lost a significant number of its members to the other nearby churches, but the church leaders are concerned that potential new members—especially young ones—prefer other churches over Shung Him Tong. Young people consider Shung Him Tong a "village church" and some think it is "too old-fashioned" in contrast to the other churches, which have larger youth groups, many more social activities, and "rock and roll hymns," and which are generally considered "more modern, more lively and more fun for young people." Indeed, Shung Him Tong— as it is imagined by the older members—in some ways maintains the older Basel mission tradition of South German Pietism.

Unlike many of the nineteenth-century Anglo-Saxon Protestant missions, which emphasized a liberal view of "progress and democratization" in their vision of "modernization," the South German Pietists were concerned with the maintenance of "traditional village patterns and village life and the idealization of the village community" (Jenkins 1982:88). The same might be said of the traditional core of values of Shung Him Tong.[3] As one woman in her mid-thirties explained, during her youth many of her friends' parents would

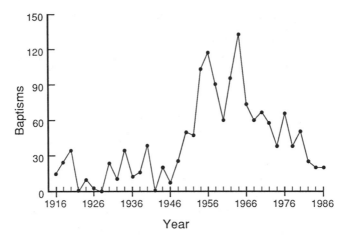

Figure 1. Baptisms at Shung Him Tong, 1916–86.

not allow their children to go to the cinema; even Christian films were pro-hibited, as were dances. Today, it is still hard to imagine a Shung Him Tong youth group organizing a dance or singing rock and roll hymns as is done at the nearby Assemblies of God church, run by American missionaries.

Another factor that serves to alienate rather than draw potential converts is an air of superiority among the Hakka Christians that may also stem in part from the Pietist tradition. As Jenkins has written, the Pietists believed that they were living a higher life than their neighbors, and they often seemed to be "looking down" on their neighbors (1989:3). In Shung Him Tong there is lit-tle tolerance of other religious practices and ways of life. Many non-Christians feel no desire to join the church because such a move would mean a change of life-style and would alienate them from friends and relatives who might go to bars or discos, gamble, play mahjong or card games, or attend horse races—all activities openly condemned by Shung Him Tong Christians.

The issue of attracting new converts also points to the growing tension be-tween Hakka and Christian identities. Many younger church members believe Shung Him Tong will never appeal to young people as long as it remains a "Hakka church." There are few if any young people who think of themselves as Hakka in such a way that they would consciously join the church *because* it is Hakka, as in earlier times. Many who already belong to Shung Him Tong, however, feel more at home there than at other churches, and the fact that it is Hakka—a place where their mother tongue is spoken—may be more im-portant in contributing to this feeling than they consciously realize. Non-Hakka, especially Punti, are likely to steer clear of the church because of its strong Hakka reputation. Some church members are optimistic that, as the youth group grows and becomes more active under the leadership of the energetic new youth group director and evangelist, new young people will be attracted to the church regardless of its Hakka character. Others believe it is the character of the church that must change.

While some people will not join Shung Him Tong because they consider it too old-fashioned, others merely lose interest and stop attending. This is more often the case for people who move out of the village; for those who remain in the village, social pressure is brought to bear. One young woman who grew up as a member of the church moved away many years ago and now attends only on occasion, for the sake of her father. Acquaintances in the village speculate that the church no longer suits her life-style and her career in the police force. Certainly, her diverse circle of friends and her interests are far removed from those of many of the church's young people.

Other explanations I was given for the decreasing membership were the lower birthrate and continuing emigration from the area. When On Lok village was torn down to make way for a new industrial estate during the mid-1980s, many of On Lok's residents, including a growing number of Hakka Christians who had lived there since the 1940s, were relocated into nearby high-rise housing estates. They sent their children to the more convenient estate schools and day-care centers, and enrollment at Shung Him Kindergarten and Chung Him School dropped. Most church members from On Lok continue to come to church, but there is no longer a growing neighboring community from which to attract new members.

Unlike On Lok, the Lung Yeuk Tau villages to the east of Shung Him Tong are composed of a much greater proportion of Punti villagers who reject Christianity. They are considered "more resistant" because they are already integrated into communities with their own ancestral halls, temples, and shrines. Hakka non-Christians in those areas are often influenced by a desire to remain neutral or to maintain good relations with their Punti and non-Christian neighbors—something that might be more difficult if they were Christian. As the people of Shung Him Tong are quick to point out, most of the church members are relative newcomers to the area. Many of the more recent members immigrated to the area from China in the 1940s, 1950s, and 1960s; they are overwhelmingly Hakka, and many were already Basel mission converts when they arrived in Hong Kong.

Today there are few ethnic tensions between Hakka and Punti in Lung Yeuk Tau and the surrounding areas, especially as compared with the first three or four decades of this century. For this reason, by the late 1940s Luen Wo Tong faded out of existence and church members no longer felt the need to play as much of a role in local leadership as did Pang Lok Sam and other early residents. Non-Christian Hakka from surrounding communities have less urgent reasons to join the church or to ally themselves with Hakka Christians. The benefits they might receive from closer interpersonal relations with more affluent or powerful church members do not provide enough incentive to join the church. Yet as potential Hakka converts they are welcomed and feel free to attend church functions and to enroll their children in the church school. My Hakka landlady's teenage daughter, for example, attended church on Christmas for the "treats" (a little bag of edible sweets) that are handed out and for the merriment, but shrugged off the invitation to join the church or any regular youth group activities, which she considered boring. Her extended family also felt free to invite the pastor to bless funerals and marriages as a peripheral part of the ceremonies, but they had no intention of converting and claimed to have "no religion."

There are different ideas among the people of Shung Him Tong regarding the reasons why people convert to Christianity. Many of them were raised as Christians and have never questioned their faith. Several church members voice the opinion that people must be "down and out" before they will consider becoming Christian. In the words of one man: "The time to convert someone to Christianity is when they've just lost the shirt off their back at the horse races. If you approach a man who's just won, he'll say 'why?' But when people are unhappy or poor they will accept Christ. . . . A rich man won't become a Christian like a poor man will. That's the time to approach them."

Serious misfortune is the most frequently cited reason for the "questioning" of one's faith, both in the biographies and testimonials of the early Basel mission converts and at present. For example, one nineteenth-century convert, Wong En Kau, whose biography is recorded in the Basel Mission Archives, had a younger brother who was killed by a tiger. This incident made him question the power of the traditional deities. As he recounted to a Swiss Basel missionary, "After two years of doubt about the deities, two Christian preachers arrived at . . . my uncle's village." He heard them preach about salvation and eternal life: "I told them of my doubts concerning the traditional deities and of the bad fortune my family had suffered—the death of my brother, economic misery because of my father's gambling. At home I told my mother about Christianity. She was happy to be given fresh hope" (Basel Mission Archives 1874). He and his mother decided to

> ban all heathen ritual objects from the house and to destroy them. The relatives were very angry with us and didn't understand why we should oppose the traditional religion. Even my wife opposed me. But the holy ghost helped me to ignore the hostility around me. On March 22, 1868, my mother, my uncle, and I were baptized by Missionary Lechler. Soon after she was baptized, my mother died and my relatives' hatred reemerged. They treated me

as though I was a leper. The Christians . . . helped me to bury my
mother. To my surprise, my wife finally made her way back to
me and her ears were open to the gospel. . . . The relationship
with my relatives and the rest of the village worsened and my wife
and I had to leave (Basel Mission Archives 1874).

Wong also benefited in material ways from his association with the missionaries:

Two months later Missionary Lechler employed me as a teacher
for the primary school. . . . During the day I taught, and in the
evening I worked as a translator of the Bible. In 1870 my wife
was baptized and since that moment my household has been a
member of the Christian community. At the age of thirty-two, I
was allowed to enter the school in Lilang to become an evangelist,
and after two years at the school I became one. I am aware that I
am incapable of the task, but with the help of the Lord, I shall
succeed (Basel Mission Archives 1874).

In a letter to the home mission in Basel in 1868, missionary Charles Piton
wrote from Nyenhang of three new converts whom he believed would make
good Christians. One had asked to be baptized previously, but Piton suspected
"only economic motives"—that is, a desire to be employed as a teacher—so
he delayed his baptism. The second convert was a blind man with a tragic story:
once wealthy, his family had been plagued with opium use, gambling, prostitution, and three cases of fratricide. The convert had a bad reputation, but his
illness, which resulted in blindness, "changed his life," and he converted to
Christianity. The third was hired by Piton to do construction work on the new
chapel. He learned about the gospel, and after two years, when Piton was "sure
of his intentions," he was baptized (Basel Mission Archives 1868b).

In Shung Him Tong today, it is still said that some old people join the
church to "receive blessings" or to gain the benefit of burial in the church
cemetery, where their graves will be tended and they will not be forgotten.
Young people in particular are critical of men and women who are baptized
just before marrying a Christian so the ceremony can be held in the church but
who then do not become regular members.

As one younger board member explained, there are many people who
come to the church for material help: "They are less educated and less literate
and they want to improve their lives." Reflecting on the past, many third or
fourth generation Christians unabashedly imagine the scenarios leading up to
their own families' conversions: "People were poor and they needed help. So
they approached the missionaries for help and they received education and
jobs." Such economic motives for converting gave rise to the common perception of Chinese Christians as "rice Christians." One difference between

Chinese Christians and other Christians, according to Francis Hsu, is not that the Chinese alone have practical motives for converting but that only the Chinese are frank in admitting their pragmatism about religion (1981:273). Still, the people of Shung Him Tong find such pragmatism far more acceptable in their own forebears than in their contemporaries.

As one Shung Him Tong man, a retired accountant, explained, "The more prosperous the church, the more people it will attract." As the Basel mission opened more schools and hospitals, he said, the numbers of converts increased:

> A hundred and forty years ago the Basel mission came and they built a school in China. They educated a lot of good people. The other counties in Guangdong were not as educated as Meixian. Because of Christianity there were better schools and better work. The schools were first for Christian children and then second for those who were not yet Christian—but our children came first. The Christians made better profit and made progress faster than non-Christian Hakka. There was already an idea of the importance of hard work and education, but the church provided the means for this education. At first not many people went to the church. The missionaries were rich though, and from a powerful foreign country, so when they started paying people to go to school and then later hiring them in their schools and hospitals and churches, people got more interested. People were sometimes sent overseas for more education and bit by bit the church became prosperous and the church members brought more prosperity to the church. . . . When they got this education from the mission schools, the Hakka people could start to go anywhere they wanted in the world and get jobs there. They were often hired by the government so they worked hard and they struggled for power. At first it was not easy to get the Hakka people to be Christian. They aren't easy to convert. But as the missionaries realized how important schools and hospitals are to the people, they were more and more successful. As the church becomes more prosperous, more people will come to become Christian. It's a better way to find a better life and a better job.

One younger European Basel missionary criticized the Chinese churches in Hong Kong for often "using social welfare to buy members." In the 1960s, for example, when foreign churches donated food for the poor, Chinese churches—including the Tsung Tsin mission—often insisted that people be baptized before they receive food. To many Chinese Christians, this must have been the logical order of events: if churches provided food to non-Christians, what would be the incentive for people to join the church?

Among young people recently converted or born into Christian families, I heard no explicitly expressed practical or material explanations for being "born again." Instead of focusing on the benefits that come from joining the church, they emphasize the conversion experience and the personal crises that precipitate it. Certainly no younger member would admit to material motives for joining.

Ming Lee is a recent convert. She became Christian several years ago after she was seriously injured at the factory where she worked. Several schoolmates from the youth group came to visit her in the hospital. They prayed for her and urged her to do the same. When she recovered she joined the church. She was living near Luen Wo market at the time; her brother was "wild" and her family was not happy or well off. Later, by chance, her family moved to the edge of Shung Him Tong. Her father, a construction worker, had agreed to build a house for a Catholic man who lived on the outskirts of the village in exchange for the use of some land where he could also build himself a small house. After they lived there for a few years, Ming Lee convinced her mother to attend the church. Now she is quite eager for people from the church to know that her mother is Hakka and her father, despite the fact that he rarely comes to church, is half Hakka, making her three-quarters Hakka. Before she became a member, this young woman had never thought of herself as Hakka. To her, this is an important factor in "fitting in" with other church members. Another young woman joined when she was unhappy and lonely; and several others explained that when they were away from home for the first time, although they were already Christian, their faith was strengthened and renewed.

Today, the church does not offer the same material incentives for members that it once did. People do not need the physical protection of the church community; nor do they need the church leaders to back them up in claims to build houses or send their children to school. Wealthy church members no longer serve as patrons to young non-Christians, providing tuition and moral guidance in hopes of their eventual conversion. Although many young converts like Ming Lee are from fairly poor families, they receive no immediate economic benefits by joining. Young people are occasionally employed as teachers or secretaries at the church, which better qualifies them to later find jobs outside, but these positions are rare and are normally filled by qualified people from outside (in the case of teachers), or young people whose families have long been members of the community (in the case of church assistants). Ming Lee did attend the English class in the hopes of eventually improving her job prospects, but so did the non-Christians who attended.

Today, education is readily available in Hong Kong and is not limited to mission schools. Though the church runs a nursery school, most toddlers of church members attend other schools. Today many church members send their children to the most prestigious schools they can afford—English-speaking nursery schools and private schools whose graduates are accepted at the best primary schools. The church nursery school is cheaper than many; it is smaller and does not have a reputation for attracting teachers as good as those found at wealthier urban schools, and the students are mainly from nearby villages. Many of its pupils come from non-Christian families who consider the church nursery school convenient and inexpensive although not of the highest quality. Education, medical care, and social welfare are provided by the government, and although the Tsung Tsin mission and other churches contribute to such programs, it is not necessary to be Christian to receive benefits. Thus, most church members today refer to the benefits of being Christian in terms of the spiritual and emotional enrichment of their lives rather than the material benefits that they say prompted previous generations to convert. This is not to say that recent Christian converts do not expect their lives to "improve" in a variety of ways once they have made the decision to be a "better" person.

One Sunday a visiting seminary student delivered a sermon in which he read a section from "The Parable of the Great Banquet" (Luke 14:16–23). Comparing the church with the banquet, he urged the congregation to invite more people, pointing emphatically at empty spaces in the pews. The sermon evoked a strong response from "Tin," a church member and schoolteacher in his forties, who told me that the speaker was "right in theory but not in practice." When I asked him to explain, he said, "In theory everyone wants to bring in new members, but in their hearts they do not." There are many new member drives, special programs, and gospel meetings, but new people come two or three times, he said, and then "they stop coming because they feel excluded—like outsiders" because they are not "members of the big families who control the church."

At the root of the problem in attracting new members is the very fact that first attracted and now binds together the older members: it is a Hakka church. The members of the church are torn between wanting to attract new members and keeping Shung Him Tong a Hakka church. As one older male board member said, "It goes against the teachings of Jesus Christ to conduct the services in Hakka and thereby exclude other people who might want to join our church." But the same man, on a different occasion, revealed his ambivalence by stating with pride, "Ours is not like other churches; ours is a Hakka church." Many church members, especially among those of age forty or over, say that they attend the church in Shung Him Tong village because their friends are there and because it is Hakka, even though some of them live far away. The very distinction of the church as Hakka is what makes it attractive to many present members, but it is also what people like Tin think makes it unattractive to potential new members.[4]

Focusing their efforts on recruiting non-Christian Hakka into the church would appear to be one solution. But church members seem reluctant to define their conversion goals so narrowly and "therefore exclude non-Hakka." Furthermore, few non-Christian Hakka in the region are as interested in joining the church as they were in earlier decades. Some seem to identify more with their non-Christian neighbors—regardless of whether or not they are Hakka—than with Shung Him Tong Hakka Christians. Others identify with the people of Shung Him Tong as fellow Hakka, but not with their Christianity. One Hakka neighbor who was forever exhorting me to "speak Hakka, not Cantonese!" told me that, despite his habit of decorating his house with lights at Christmastime, he had absolutely no interest in becoming Christian— though if he did, the church he joined would be Shung Him Tong. Decreasing material incentives and a decreasing interest in Hakka identity throughout the Lung Yeuk Tau and Fanling regions are both factors that help explain why greater numbers of local Hakka do not join the church, and why some members leave both village and church.

Many people of Shung Him Tong are somewhat resigned toward the direction the church must take away from its Hakka origins. Although the older church members insist that parts of the service remain in Hakka language, they sense that the Hakka character of the church will inevitably diminish. Of the thirteen Tsung Tsin mission churches, Shung Him Tong is one of only two in which the sermon is still delivered primarily in Hakka. The other eleven churches are urban and conduct services in Cantonese, although two of the larger churches conduct two services each Sunday, one in Hakka and one in Cantonese.

Village Residence and Church Membership

During the first month of my research, as I met people at the church or walking through the village, I was repeatedly told that "everyone in the village is Christian" or "everyone in Shung Him Tong village belongs to the church." Before long, it became obvious to me that these statements were overgeneralizations, harmless exaggerations, or even wishful thinking. It was not until I was several months into my fieldwork that I learned that such overgeneralizations represented a particular view of the social reality of Shung Him Tong.

As we were walking through the village, on our way to the teahouse in Luen Wo market, my companion a young schoolteacher, mentioned an upcoming wedding to which "the whole village is invited—*everyone* will be there."

I pointed to the nearby house of some recent arrivals to the village and said, "Will they be there?"

"No, no, not them," she answered.

As we continued to walk through the village, I pointed to another small house and said, "What about the people who rent that house?" Again she answered no. Frustrated, I then pressed my companion to explain exactly who would be at the wedding—who comprised this "everyone"? She said that all the members of the "old" established Christian families in the village were invited. To Yee Ling, herself a descendant of one of the first families, "everyone" signified those in her own social category: relatives of the Lings, Tsuis, Cheungs, Pangs, and others who were active members of the church.

Recent arrivals and tenants in Shung Him Tong do not automatically become members of the community, but through a variety of avenues they can eventually be numbered among those who are respected members of the church, if not descendants of the founders. Such avenues include marriage to a respected church member, service in a church office, and exemplary behavior, all of which were factors in the acceptance of the three brothers mentioned earlier. Thus, for the most part, "everyone who is anyone" in Shung Him Tong is Christian and belongs to the church.

Not all who attend church are considered full-fledged members of the community, but members of the community are almost always members of the church. Community members need not live in Shung Him Tong, but as discussed above they must have a legitimate claim through kinship ties to a founding family or by model behavior—which usually means success and moral uprightness as well as contributions of time and money to the church. There is one interesting exception to the church membership requirement, however, with regard to the Catholic families in the village.

Catholics, to the people of Shung Him Tong, are not considered "Christians" at all but rather, as one young woman explained, little better than "idol worshipers."[5] Yet, in certain social situations like weddings, there are two Catholic families who are considered to be members of the community. Both are Hakka, originally from Meixian; both are descended from old Shung Him Tong families; and both have members considered eminent in wider Hong Kong circles. The Tsuis were related to the first Basel mission convert in Wuhua and belonged to a Basel mission church. They were also related by marriage to Pang Lok Sam; Pang's wife was named Tsui, and her famous brother was the founder of Wah Yan College in Hong Kong (see Tsui Dou Leung in Appendix 2). Another prominent member of the Tsui family, Paul Tsui, was a district officer and also the first Chinese person in Hong Kong to hold the post of secretary for Chinese affairs. One branch of the Tsui family still belongs to Shung Him Church; the Catholic branch retains honorary membership in the community for certain occasions, and its members are cited as examples of educated and successful Hakka.

The people most frequently held up as model members of church and community, although they are not related by blood to the old families, are the three brothers on the board of directors. In contrast to members of the old set, these brothers had to work their way up to respected positions in the church. Indeed, the story is told like a fairy tale, complete with the eldest son's marriage to a woman who was both the granddaughter of one of the first village pastors and the daughter of a most respected church elder. Informants told of the parents of the three brothers, Hakka refugees from China who were forced to borrow money from their neighbors to plant the sweet potatoes they hawked in the market. They discovered Christianity, joined the Shung Him Church, and continued to work hard to put their children through school. All attained a college education—one daughter became a minister, one son attained a high position in Hong Kong's department of social services, and the other sons are in equally successful professions. All three men married women from old Shung Him Tong families, and they are looked up to as the future leaders of the church. Education, economic success, and model Christian behavior are considered the key elements of their high status in the community.

Another factor should not be neglected in the acceptance of these men as worthy members of the community. They are Hakka. Church members readily identify them as Hakka and even say that they display important Hakka traits of determination and hard work. Unlike Ming Lee, they do not need to announce or defend their Hakka identity in order to fit in; it is understood.

ECONOMICS, EDUCATION, AND POLITICS

Economic status and political views are two of the most difficult topics to learn about in Shung Him Tong and in Hong Kong in general. I was warned by Yee Ling and other friends not to make hasty judgments about a person's economic situation, since a person's wealth is difficult to discern. As Yee Ling explained, someone who lives in a small run-down shack and is always working in the fields may have wealth stashed away for his children's education, for a new house, to spend for a New Year's Day banquet, or to emigrate. A woman who works as a farmer or a construction worker might have her teeth filled with gold and wear expensive jade bracelets, but they may be her only savings. Some people choose to appear wealthy and successful and flaunt their wealth by building new houses and buying new cars, while others choose to appear poorer than they are for fear that they are tempting bad fortune, or arousing the envy of their neighbors. Christians of Shung Him Tong claim they are not afraid of bad fortune, and yet they do not flaunt their wealth.

Of course, one way in which Shung Him Tong people are encouraged to demonstrate their wealth, or at least their generosity, is to contribute to the church. Weekly church contributions are anonymous, but annual contributions are carefully listed and published in commemorative bulletins, as are one-time donations to special fund-raising drives such as those for the new church building, or for the celebration of the 140th anniversary of the Basel mission-aries' arrival in Hong Kong. Reminiscent of the carefully recorded and dis-played lists of contributions made for festivals, new temples, and ancestral halls in other parts of Hong Kong, these lists of contributors serve to memorialize one's name and status in the community. The logic from *The Protestant Ethic and the Spirit of Capitalism* (Weber [1930] 1958) would suggest that perhaps these contributions—as markers of wealth—are merely indications of "grace." To the people of Shung Him Tong, however, the donations are considered purely altruistic acts of generosity, and any suggestion that the Chinese con-cept of "buying" blessings from deities is in operation is of course condemned as erroneous (cf. C. K. Yang 1961:321). Nonetheless, as is discussed further in Chapter 6, some Shung Him Tong people believe that those who are "good Christians" are more likely to be "blessed" with success and happiness, though they admit that, in keeping with both Christian and traditional Confucian views, it is wrong to attempt to "calculate" reciprocity in such a way.

Larger contributions are expected from prominent members of the church, and board members are usually more generous than others. Contributing to church fund-raising campaigns serves at least to exhibit and reinforce, if not to raise, one's status in the eyes of the community. I was told of several "model church members" and their "generous contributions" of land and money to the church. People were impressed by contributions that were larger than they expected, and they still remember names of people who contributed money to build the On Lok bridge or land on which to build the church or cemetery.

A Shung Him Tong church member who works for the department of so-cial welfare explained that, although there are some elderly people in Shung Him Tong who are "poor" in that they would qualify for public assistance, they all have sufficient food, shelter, and clothing. Some people who qualify for public assistance may not accept it, he said, "because they are proud and they prefer to work." Another man told me that the Hakka, even more than other Chinese, are too proud to accept charity. A distinction begins to emerge between the charity handed out by the government and the assistance given by missionaries in the past. Help from missionaries was acceptable because it provided education or employment, means through which to improve the fu-ture of one's family. Charity as an end in itself is unacceptable.

Many of the descendants of the four older families of Shung Him Tong con-tinue to do well economically and are consistently those who make the largest monetary contributions during church collection drives. Their houses are gen-erally larger and have been remodeled to include more modern amenities than others in the village, though most houses in Shung Him Tong have telephones, televisions, and indoor plumbing. Descendants of the older families also send their children to expensive private schools and universities, often overseas. Most have professional occupations and own land in the New Territories. Descendants of the four original families have also moved to Hong Kong Island, Kowloon, and farther abroad. The overall opinion of these community leaders is that they have been blessed with economic success because they are good Christians. If they were to partake in un-Christian behavior such as gambling, drugs, or illegal activity, they would take the chance of forfeiting their success.

In 1950 D. Y. Ling (Lin[g] 1951) conducted a study of the economic situation of sixty farming families in the Fanling region. Twenty-eight of the families surveyed were from Shung Him Tong, where he found an extremely high tenancy rate of over 95 percent (1951:32, 19), higher even than those of coastal parts of China in 1945, which never reached 90 percent. Shung Him Tong residents told Ling in 1950 that tenant farming had greatly increased since 1920, when 50 percent of the farmland was cultivated by its owners (1951:19). The main reason for this shift was the source of labor. The "big" landowning families such as Tsui, Pang, and Ling never farmed their own land. At first poorer relatives farmed the land of their wealthier kin and eventually were able to buy small plots to farm themselves. By 1949, the large influx of refugees who fled to Hong Kong from China provided a cheaper source of labor. Land that had been used for rice cultivation shifted to vegetable crops that were in higher demand because of the rapidly expanding population and increasingly efficient transportation.

In 1950, the number of absentee landlords in Shung Him Tong was extremely low. According to Ling, in places such as Shung Him Tong, where the landlord typically lived on the farm with his tenants, "the effect [of tenancy] on the economy of the place, is not as bad" (1951:32). In Shung Him Tong, tenants and landlords seemed "to live [together] in a rather happy partnership or relationship; and this happy partnership has resulted in the development of some local cooperative effort quite useful to the life of the community" (ibid.). What appeared to Ling to be a happy partnership between his landlord relatives and their tenants might appear to other, more critical observers as exploitation facilitated by kinship ties (see R. Watson 1985), as well as religious ones.

Today, farming around Shung Him Tong is done almost exclusively by Cantonese emigrants from Guangdong who do not belong to the church (see Strauch 1984:192; Topley 1964). Some of the older church members once farmed for Shung Him Tong landlords, but today most of them have retired. The great majority of people from Shung Him Tong work outside of the community in a wide variety of occupations, including shopkeeping, factory work, construction work, architecture, business, banking, real estate, teaching, law enforcement, civil service, medicine, and so on. Some commute to work in Kowloon or on Hong Kong Island, while others work in nearby market towns or industrial estates.

Unlike emigrants from nearby villages who return to Hong Kong to live when they retire, it is said that former residents of Shung Him Tong seldom build new houses there. Many come back to visit, but few to live. There are several reasons for this. Shung Him Tong people believe that, because the church provides them with greater exposure to western ideas and education, they are better adapted to life in western communities. Many Shung Him Tong people already speak English and have attended North American or European universities, and thus they assimilate more easily in America and Europe. In contrast, people of Shung Him Tong believe that villagers from elsewhere in Lung Yeuk Tau never learn English, stick more closely to Chinese relatives and acquaintances, and never feel at home in overseas communities—so they return to retire in their native villages.

Shung Him Tong people also believe that they fit in better overseas because they can activate an extensive network of church connections, which helps them to integrate into the community. Indeed, several households, motivated largely by the shift in government in 1997, have recently emigrated to Vancouver and Toronto, where they already have kin and friends from Shung Him Tong, and where they have joined Hakka churches established by people affiliated with the Tsung Tsin mission. Their social networks have a broader foundation than those of non-Christian Chinese, which are based more exclusively on kinship.

Another important factor is that emigrants from Shung Him Tong are not usually "working class" and do not settle in urban "Chinatown ghettos," but instead are more likely to live in middle- and upper middle-class suburban neighborhoods. A number of emigrants from Shung Him Tong work overseas in the restaurant business (a common phenomenon in the New Territories; see J. Watson 1975), but a large number are very well educated and work as ministers and missionaries in overseas Hakka churches, or in other professions.

One indication of overseas returnees to the New Territories are the three-story Spanish-style "villas" that have sprung up in many areas. In Shung Him Tong there are relatively few new houses of this kind. In addition to the reasons already given, Shung Him Tong people are discouraged from building houses because they do not share the rights and privileges of the Punti or "indigenous" villagers. Villagers with indigenous status have the legal right to build houses in their village for all male descendants. Unlike indigenous villagers, Shung Him Tong people today must petition for the right to build houses, the dimensions of their houses are strictly regulated, and they must pay fees from which native people are exempt.

Although many people consider themselves well rooted in Shung Him Tong, to others it is not the Hakka Christian promised land. Despite efforts to build the ideal community, they are still marginalized by government restrictions and regulations that prevent them from having the same rights as the Punti. When people return to Shung Him Tong, it is to visit the church and their friends, not because of material incentives to build a home there. This fact has important implications for the future of the community and its growth.

As one person contemplating a move to Canada explained, the Hakka are emigrants and are always looking for better places to settle; they still remember the discrimination their families faced in China and are making plans to emigrate before reunification in 1997. Since the failed Democracy Movement in the People's Republic of China in 1989, even members of prominent village families who claimed they would never leave Hong Kong have recently attained visas and are applying for foreign citizenship. Mr. P., a board member in his sixties, explained that he plans to get foreign citizenship as an "insurance policy"; later he will make the decision of whether to continue to reside in Hong Kong.

Just as attaining scholarly status and positions in the government bureaucracy by passing imperial examinations reflected well on the entire Chinese lineage in the past, so are university degrees and high government posts generally thought to reflect well on the people of Shung Him Tong today. Shung Him Tong is well known in Hong Kong for the large number of "scholars" it has produced. Among its most renowned are Paul Tsui, the first Chinese person to serve as secretary for Chinese affairs of the Hong Kong government, D. Y. Ling, the first president of Chung Chi College at the Chinese University of Hong Kong; and a number of other government officials. Even before the 1950s, the Ling family alone is said to have produced over twenty graduates of American universities. Many members of the educated elite of Shung Him Tong have died or emigrated, but they are still considered members of the community and go far in reinforcing the image of the "successful Hakka Christian."

The Rural Committee, composed of village representatives, was formed by the British government in Hong Kong in order to provide representation to indigenous (pre-1898) New Territories villages. Village representatives were selected from Punti and old Hakka families and only the heads of household of indigenous families were entitled to vote. In 1982 the law was changed and people who had been village residents for more than seven years were given representation (Strauch 1984).

Unlike residents of other regions of the New Territories, however, the people of Shung Him Tong have shown little interest in village-level politics in recent years, for a variety of reasons. One is the drastic decline, mentioned earlier, of ethnic conflicts and competition in the region. Although several well-respected members of the church board would seem to make likely candidates for the office of village representative, they explain that it would not be worth their while. Mr. P., a descendant of one of the founders and a respected member of the church community, would be an obvious candidate, but as several people said to me, "Why would he want to? It's too much trouble and not really any power." One church member said that Shung Him Tong people do not consider the village representative system a way of gaining power and prestige. Representatives have to bother with settling minor disputes that take up a lot of time.

As Shung Him Tong villagers pointed out, the Rural Committee is more important to indigenous Punti villagers, while they themselves "have the church to depend on." Several board members are long-term friends and acquaintances of higher-level government officials and still have ready access to other networks of communication with the government, although there has been little need to activate these networks in recent years. When I asked for examples of how these networks are useful, informants could only provide cases from the early decades of village history. As Tin explained, "for example, when Shung Him Tong wanted the bridge built across from On Lok, Pang Lok Sam went right to the government and the bridge was built."

In the church community there are numerous people who have attained high government positions by virtue of their education; village representatives are usually less well educated. The process of becoming a village representative is also thought to require certain "immoral" activities of which the people of Shung Him Tong disapprove: one must, as one man explained, "pay people for their support which is not agreeable to church people."

Shung Him Tong has a village representative and a vice-village representative. These are elected positions, but so few people are interested in them that the same representatives have been reelected for as many terms as they are willing to serve. Many people feel that the man currently serving as the village representative "is not very interested in the position." He is the descendant of the Catholic Tsuis, is not a member of the church, and is rarely seen in the village. The vice-representative is more active in the community and is considered partially responsible for initiating such projects as the widening of the road and erecting new streetlights in the village. Because no one else wants the job, he is considered satisfactory, but not a model member of the community. He is a distant relative of the Lings and a nominal church member, but not a member of the church board. His reputation suffers because his family does not regularly attend church, and they run the corner shop, "which attracts bad characters" and where people from outside the church go to play mahjong.

To established members of the community today, in contrast to Pang Lok Sam's time, involvement in the village level of local government is not considered worthwhile. New residents of Shung Him Tong village who hope to become integrated into the community as full-fledged members must place greater value on church affairs. They cannot risk charges of corruption if they want to be considered good Christians. It is only to more marginal members of the church community, or to those who do not belong to the church at all, that local government seems worthwhile.

MARRIAGE AND THE "CHURCH FAMILY"

In church the pastor refers to the congregation as "brothers and sisters," and young people often refer to each other as "my brother" or "sister in Christ." The congregation, however, particularly members of the old families and those who know each other well, follow the old rural Chinese pattern of referring to each other by kin terms such as "father's younger brother," "mother's younger sister," "mother's older sister," and so on. This is not unusual for a village community where there is continuing and frequent interaction among members (see R. Watson 1986), but in the case of Shung Him Tong these informal terms of address are often used with church members who have moved away, and can be used to distinguish between those who are accepted as members of the community and those who are not.

In contrast to the traditional Chinese pattern of village exogamy, marriage between residents of Shung Him Tong is fairly common. When asked, most people say that the ideal marriage is with a member of a different Tsung Tsin mission church—church exogamy. Shung Him Tong villagers, unlike the people of other parts of Lung Yeuk Tau, consider conversion to Christianity the primary requirement for a spouse. The ideal prospective spouse belongs to one of the churches affiliated with Tsung Tsin mission; otherwise, membership in another Protestant church is acceptable. If the prospective spouse is not Christian, he or she is usually baptized before the wedding. During the nineteenth century the Basel mission arranged marriages between Christian boys and girls from their schools. The present-day mechanism for introducing Christian young people is the Tsung Tsin missionwide youth group, youth group summer camp, and associated missionwide activities.

Many parents say they would be pleased if their sons or daughters married someone who is Hakka, but they consider this factor secondary to the requirement that he or she be a Chinese Christian. Young unmarried people say that Hakka background is not important, but in fact many marriages are between Hakka. The majority of married couples over forty in Shung Him Tong are Hakka, but there are numerous cases of Hakka men marrying Cantonese or non-Hakka women, including the church pastor and one of the board members. One older man told me "it doesn't matter" whether one's wife is Hakka or non-Hakka; yet his father, Pang Lok Sam, was seriously disappointed by his choice of a non-Hakka, non-Christian marriage partner. His father told him, "There are plenty of good girls in Wuhua who are Hakka and Christian. Why not pick one of them?" His wife converted to Christianity before marrying him; if she had not, he said, "my father certainly would not have permitted" the marriage. In many ways his wife, described by her daughter as strong and extremely hardworking, is archetypally Hakka.

While I was in Shung Him Tong, a number of young unmarried women complained to me that there were not enough eligible young men at the church and felt it unlikely that they would marry within the community. In the several years since, this has not proven to be the case. Despite the traditional Chinese attitude that villagers should not intermarry because they "grow up together and do everything together like brother and sister," many Shung Him Tong married couples—including several very recent ones—grew up together in Shung Him Tong.

The pattern of marriage in Shung Him Tong varies according to generation. The first arrivals and their children, who were married adults by the 1940s and 1950s, grew up together in a relatively small community and usually married people from outside the village, often from other Tsung Tsin mission churches. Today, young people grow up as neighbors but often attend different secondary schools and see each other only at church. The community has also grown to include recent immigrants from other parts of the New Territories. Today, marriages between members of the church community are more common than they were in the past and are no longer considered distasteful.

In the past five years, there have been at least four marriages between members of Shung Him Tong, all of whom are expected to become pillars of the community. As a friend wrote in a recent letter, "We are glad that these youngsters are getting married within the same Church group, so that they will not get scattered." Although I did not collect statistical information regarding marriage patterns, it is clear that village endogamy is unusual in the New Territories and more prevalent in Shung Him Tong because of its Hakka, Christian, and multisurname nature. This pattern has important long-range implications for the community because, as the man quoted above suggests, men and women who grew up in Shung Him Tong are more likely to perpetuate its traditions. On the other hand, this pattern means that fewer people are being brought into the community by marriage, which again demonstrates how the church is caught between its need to expand and its mandate for insularity.

The postmarital residence pattern in Shung Him Tong is also unlike the traditional Chinese pattern. Shung Him Tong has never been strictly patrilocal and the ideal of the extended family (cf. M. Wolf 1968) is rarely realized. Many sons and daughters of the village founders have moved away, but some have remained. There is no single overarching pattern of residence. The present households include men and women who were raised in the village and others who settled there after marriage. In still other cases, neither spouse grew up in the village. As in all of Hong Kong today, residence is often influenced by such practical considerations as space, expense, and access to work, family, and friends. Shung Him Tong has advantages in these regards. Although it is far from Kowloon and Hong Kong Island, public transportation is such that one rarely hears of a commute of over an hour. Some young couples, however, prefer the convenience of living in a modern high-rise to remaining in the village.

As in other parts of Hong Kong, women marry at a later age than they did in the past and are often expected to work outside the home and contribute to the family income. Women are still primarily responsible for household chores and child rearing, but today these duties are more likely to fall on older mothers and mothers-in-law, while young women are more likely to be wage earners.

A few marriages in Shung Him Tong are arranged. This is more likely to occur with daughters from poorer or less-educated families. Several young women from the village had marriages arranged with young men who worked overseas and "did not have the time to look for their own wives." In most cases, the couple met a few times before the marriage took place, and soon after the young woman went overseas with her husband. Often older women at the church attempt to "introduce" people. In general, young people of Shung Him Tong resist the idea of arranged marriage as old-fashioned.

While I was there, a young man from Shung Him Tong who had moved to New Jersey with his parents and brothers several years earlier to work in a restaurant returned to marry a young woman from Luen Wo market. In this case the woman was not Christian so the wedding was not permitted to take place in the church. Before the tea ceremony, the minister was asked to come to the groom's house and bless the wedding. The minister asked the young woman if she spoke Hakka, which she did not, so he proceeded to bless the couple in halting Cantonese, which evoked several giggles from the onlookers. Hymnals were passed out, and the crowd of people who had gathered at the doorway after the Sunday service joined in and sang.

The church officially disapproves of divorce and polygyny, but as one older church member, Mr. C., explained at length, church policies are less strict today than they were when he was young:

> In those days the church controlled much power. The [polygy-nous] person would be expelled from church and the whole family would probably leave as well. Now the church is not so strict . . . and so powerful and they have the attitude that they will leave it to God to judge people. The soul is more important than ordinary rules. Today less people have more than one wife—very few—but if they do they will probably leave the church willingly, and later if they repent they will come back.

As he suggested, though polygyny is disapproved of by the church, everyone wants to have children—preferably a son—and to many polygyny is preferable to being childless. I asked him to give me an example:

> There was one church member whose wife had no children. He divorced her because he thought 'she is no good to my family, I will send her away' so the man married another wife and had children and later came back and repented. All he wanted was to have children! He had them, so he came back to the church and no one would prevent him. You see, to the Chinese people there are three important rules of Confucius and the most important is to have children—at least a boy to carry on the line.

"Did anyone at the church mind?" I asked. He answered:

> In the Bible there are many people with more than one wife, and to the Chinese it is most important to have children so how can the church possibly tell them that it is wrong? They must decide for themselves. The church would not expel someone from the church for divorcing, they would say it is for the person to look into themselves and to decide what is wrong and what is right. If a person wanted to have another wife just for pleasure then that is not right. Certainly that is not right. In the past people wanted more than one wife mainly to have children and especially if the first wife had none, and second because they could afford it. If it was a big family, more wives could do more work.

As reflected in the words of Mr. C., both Christian and non-Christian Chinese place great importance in maintaining the line of descent. Although Christians often say they do not mind whether the child is a boy or a girl, sons are still considered especially important and the celebration after the birth of a boy is often more elaborate. Some members of two very large and prominent families still follow the naming pattern for their sons that was established by a poem written by a Christian ancestor several generations earlier. That way, they explained, many generations from now, all patrilineal descendants of the same generation will be easily identified because they will have one of the several given names in addition to the same surname. This practice is also considered a display of respect for the ancestor who wrote the poem.

Because of the importance of maintaining the line of descent, several Shung Him Tong families who would otherwise have been childless are known to have adopted the son of a relative. In several instances, offspring of maternal kin were adopted. Adoption of a male relative also occurred for a Christian man who died without an heir about thirty-five years ago. In that case, a nephew of the deceased became his "son" for purposes of continuing his line of descent and visiting his grave at Easter. The natural father—brother of the deceased—continued to play the role of pater, but it was understood that the adopted son's own sons would contribute to his uncle's (i.e., his adoptive father's) line of descent.

Christian and non-Christian Chinese both believe that they have obligations to their ancestors, and one of these is to maintain the line of descent. The main difference, as discussed in the following chapter, is not so much in the practices and behavior surrounding the care of the ancestors—although these do differ—but in the Christian need to justify their actions as secular. Despite this constructed difference, there exist important continuities between Christian and non-Christian Chinese beliefs and practices concerning filial piety and familial duties and obligations. For Shung Him Tong Christians, furthermore, the obligation to continue the line of descent applies not only to their biological families but to the church family as well.

Plate 1.   Early Christian Converts. Reprinted by permission of the Basel Mission Archives.

Plate 2. Mission Station in Lilang. Reprinted by permission of the Basel Mission Archives.

Plate 3.   A Hakka Woman. Reprinted by permission of the Basel
Mission Archives.

Plate 4. A Christian Family. Note the woman's bound feet, which suggest that she is not Hakka. Reprinted by permission of the Basel Mission Archives.

Plate 5.   Old and New Churches, Shung Him Tong, 1987.

Plate 6.   Shung Him Tong Village.

Plate 7.　The Cemetery.

Plate 8.   At the Grave of Pang Lok Sam.

5   Christian Souls and Chinese Spirits

Unlike many of their non-Christian neighbors in Lung Yeuk Tau, Shung Him Tong Christians are never seen visiting ancestral halls or Buddhist, Taoist, or other temples. They have no village shrine dedicated to the earth god, and at the Chinese New Year and other festival occasions they do not set out tables in front of their homes displaying generous offerings of food and incense. They do not decorate their doorways with lucky red paper couplets or images of door gods, and they have no household altar at which to worship the kitchen god. In the location where one would expect to find incense burning at an ancestral altar, instead there might be a photograph of a family gathering or a picture of an Anglo-Saxon Christ tending his flock. Shung Him Tong Christians do not consult astrologers or almanacs for auspicious dates for marriages or burials, nor do they hire *feng-shui* experts to advise them on the placement of new houses or the orientation of graves for their ancestors. They do not recognize or celebrate such festivals as the Hungry Ghost Festival (Yu Laan Jit) or the birthdays of various gods and goddesses, and they frown on or belittle those who do. One woman in her thirties told me that even as a child she was amazed that some people worshiped their ancestors. She and her sisters would hide in the bushes behind the millionaire's large horseshoe-shaped grave on the hill, and when his relatives bowed and made offerings "we would pretend that they were worshiping us!"

As was described in the previous chapter, Shung Him Tong Christians are extremely conservative and orthodox with regard to their Christian church service. The church building itself, and certain church ceremonies, are virtually identical to those of any number of other conservative Protestant churches in Europe and North America. They believe exclusively in one Christian God and are alternately hopeful, frustrated, intolerant, and pitying of those who refuse to give up the worship of ancestors or "false" gods and idols. These orthodox beliefs and practices are a source of pride to Shung Him Tong Christians, and they are critical of people who do not share their faith, including Catholics. One Catholic woman married to a devoted member of Shung Him Church complained that its members repeatedly try to convert her although they know that she faithfully attends a Roman Catholic church each Sunday. One week, when her husband could not attend church, Shung Him Tong elders pointedly asked him whether he was letting his Catholic wife lead him astray.

Although many obvious religious practices distinguish the people of Shung Him Tong from Chinese non-Christians, other beliefs and practices suggest a certain degree of affinity with their non-Christian neighbors. Church services are strictly Christian, but certain festival occasions are traditionally Chinese, as are certain aspects of life-cycle rituals. The first day of Chinese New Year, for example, rivals Christmas as the day with the largest church attendance of the year. Ching Ming, a spring festival in remembrance of the dead, occurs at about the same time of year as Easter, and the people of Shung Him Tong consider Ching Ming and Easter "equivalent" in certain respects.

Like their non-Christian neighbors in Lung Yeuk Tau, the people of Shung Him Tong also wear new clothes and haircuts to celebrate the Chinese New Year, and at the midautumn festival they eat special cakes and climb to a place where they can watch the moon at night. Like their neighbors, they are concerned with the proper burial and care of their ancestors; and despite the fact that they do not hire *feng-shui* experts, the physical construction of their village, like that of their neighbors, adheres to basic geomantic prescriptions.

One might easily dismiss the coexistence of such traditional Chinese and Christian religious practices as an illustration of the generalization that Chinese people are "pragmatic" about religious belief and practice, and that "when Chinese assume a monotheistic faith they tend to treat it in a polytheistic spirit," incorporating elements that are currently relevant to their lives and letting go of irrelevant elements (F. Hsu 1981:274).[1] However, these behaviors are not so readily explained. There is in fact very little in Shung Him Tong that fits the strict definition of religious syncretism, in the sense of an integration of elements of one religion into another. Nor can the Christians of Shung Him Tong be said to treat their religion with a "polytheistic spirit."

The concept of religious syncretism does not adequately describe the belief system of Shung Him Tong Christians because they have created a distinction between Christian religious beliefs and practices and Chinese religious beliefs and practices, which they have reinterpreted as "secular." Their construction is more accurately described as a dual system of beliefs (Nash 1981:7) than a syncretic blending of two systems into one. In other words, Christian practices are maintained as strictly orthodox, and Chinese practices and festivals that have not been reinterpreted as secular are criticized, avoided, or deemed of little concern.

Why, one might ask, do Shung Him Tong Christians maintain this dual, segregated system of beliefs, and why do they feel the need to justify the continuity of their Chinese beliefs? One reason for these attempts at justification is the conservative manner in which early Basel missionaries presented Christianity. One very open-minded Basel missionary lamented to me, "The early missionaries forced Christianity on them in their own narrow terms . . . and they created a dislike by the converts for their own roots." Unlike some Protestant and Catholic churches in Hong Kong with doctrines more tolerant of the integration of Chinese features into Christian practice—allowing, for example, kowtowing and incense burning at the graves of relatives—Shung Him Tong prohibits such "indigenization."

It may be, too, that my questions prompted the people of Shung Him Tong to justify their actions more than would otherwise have been the case. One can imagine them needing to rationalize their behavior to an anthropologist or foreign missionary in discussions that would never come up with each other. However, this factor is not likely to have been greatly significant because it was usually my informants who brought up the continuities between their actions and beliefs and those of non-Christians.

Shung Him Tong Christians agree that their behavior resembles that of non-Christians on the surface, but their underlying motives, they insist, are always different. Although the motives they articulate seem very different from those of non-Christians, are they really? Do the practices described below, such as burning the possessions of a dead man, simply reflect a convenient means of disposal and a desire to "disinfect" the premises? Another interpretation is that Hakka Christians maintain certain Chinese practices as "insurance." In other words, they may not be so different from the non-Christians who they criticize as wanting to "have their cake and eat it too" when they invite the Christian pastor to say a blessing at funerals. In this Malinowskian sense, certain practices could be said to serve a psychological function by reducing the tension surrounding such stressful situations as illness and death. By burning the dead man's possessions they are indeed disposing of them, but they are also following the proper traditional Chinese procedure for ridding themselves of any possible lingering evil spirits.

One can easily argue that the continuity of Chinese non-Christian practices serves such psychological functions for individuals. More relevant, and more important to this study, is the question of what such practices say about dual Chinese and Christian identity. The maintenance of traditional Chinese practices by the people of Shung Him Tong is a way to assert—to themselves and others—that they are Chinese. The rationalizations that Shung Him Tong people are quick to offer, contrary to their apparent logic, do not indicate that the two systems have been easily reconciled. The constant need to segregate, define, and redefine boundaries and to rationalize the two belief systems reflects, instead, the tension that exists between them. The contradictions between their Chinese and Christian religious beliefs can be resolved only temporarily through such actions. A similar problem exists in attempts to reconcile the Christian and Chinese facets of their identity. People of Shung Him Tong would like to be "good" Chinese and "good" Christians, but in practice these two identities, like the belief systems they represent, give rise to certain logical contradictions.

There are three main objectives to this chapter: first, to describe certain Chinese and Christian beliefs and practices and to illustrate the way in which they coexist but are consciously constructed and articulated as discrete; second, to consider the extent to which this dichotomy successfully reconciles Chinese and Christian beliefs; and finally, to analyze the creation of this dual system for what it says about Hakka Christian identity.

RITUALS FOR THE DEAD

James Watson has suggested that in late imperial China the standardization of ritual was of central importance in the "creation and maintenance of a unified Chinese culture" (1988:3). He asserts that "to be Chinese is to understand, and accept the view, that there is a correct way to perform rites associated with the life-cycle" (ibid.). In imperial China, according to Watson, there existed a variety of *beliefs* concerning death and the afterlife, but there existed a uniform *structure* of funerary rites, and "the proper performance of the rites, in the accepted sequence, was of paramount importance in determining who was and who was not deemed to be fully 'Chinese'" (1988:4).

While it is beyond the scope of this book to determine to what extent Chinese Christians follow the proper structure of funerary rites (1988:12–15), it is clear that Shung Him Tong Christians fail to follow at least two important requirements: they do not burn offerings for the dead, and they do not set up ancestral tablets.[2] Such behavior may well prompt the accusation that Chinese Christians are not fully Chinese. But Hakka Christians—through their actions and beliefs—provide a powerful critique of such a "cultural" and ascribed definition of Chinese identity. Like many Chinese in the People's Republic of China who did not or could not strictly adhere to orthopraxy in their death rituals over the past two decades, they still assert that they are Chinese (Whyte 1988).[3]

Although their non-Christian neighbors may consider them no longer Chinese since they have accepted a heterodox foreign religion (see P. Cohen 1963), people of Shung Him Tong say that adherence to Chinese religious belief and practice is not a necessary criterion for determining Chinese identity.[4] Instead, they argue that there are certain *secular* Chinese beliefs, values, and practices that make one Chinese. They refer in particular to beliefs and practices that involve ancestors and that relate to history and descent. As one woman from Shung Him Tong explained, she and her fellow villagers share with all Chinese "certain basic Confucian values"—a need to care for and demonstrate respect for their elders, and a desire to maintain the line of descent. She implicitly argues, like Eberhard and many others, that "Confucianism is rather a system of ethical rules and moral behavior than a religion" (Eberhard 1952:6–7).

C. K. Yang (1961) and Liu have described Confucianism as a system of "moral orthodoxy" that has coexisted with "religious pluralism" (1990:2). Buddhism, Taoism, and Chinese "popular religion" all "flourished peaceably alongside Confucianism" (ibid.). As Liu explains, "This religious diversity coexisted with moral orthodoxy—moral because its precepts were primarily socioethical, and orthodox because such precepts were themselves linked to religious and cosmological notions" (1990:2–3). Although Christianity is obviously unorthodox in this regard, there are ways in which certain socioethical morals can be viewed as compatible. Focusing on Neo-Confucianism, de Bary has suggested that "the orthodox tradition, even more than a set moral code or philosophical system, was a life-style, an attitude of mind, a type of character formation, and a spiritual ideal that eluded precise definition" (1975:24). In light of such a statement, we can see why Chinese Christians might claim—despite their blatantly unorthodox practices—that they are orthodox with respect to Chinese rules of the "right and correct view."

Like non-Christian Chinese, Shung Him Tong Christians are especially concerned with filial piety, maintaining the line of descent, and the proper care and remembrance of the dead. Although Shung Him Tong people do not treat their ancestors in all the traditional ways, they commemorate them, show respect for them, and care for them in ways that they believe do not conflict with their Christian beliefs.[5]

The Shung Him Tong Cemetery

In Hong Kong, where land is at a premium, some traditional burial practices have had to be altered, yet the burial and care of the dead is of no less importance now than it ever was. Unlike their Teng neighbors, the people of Shung Him Tong do not meet the legal requirements—documented residence prior to 1898—that entitle them to burial in the hills. Yet like the Punti, they have a strong sense of identification with their village and feel the importance of being buried just outside the residential section of the village, in the vicinity of their home, church, and kin.

The people of Shung Him Tong cannot take for granted that the village is theirs. Government restrictions remind them that they do not share the same privileges as the Punti, and they will not forget that in the past they were unwelcome outsiders whose residence in the New Territories might well have proven temporary like many immigrants before them. When the village was first established, people commonly returned to their native places in Guangdong to die, or had their remains transported back at a later time. With the establishment of a cemetery for the community, this practice became uncommon. By burying the dead in their own cemetery, the people of Shung Him Tong were better able to show respect to their ancestors, and they also demonstrated—to themselves and the Punti—their intention of remaining there permanently. In effect, they became symbolically rooted to the place. They might still engrave "Baoan," "Wuhua," or "Huiyang" on their headstones, but the native place in Guangdong is of secondary importance to Shung Him Tong, the place where the ancestors' bones lie permanently at rest.

"When a man's parents die, . . . [i]t is his duty with all his heart and strength" to locate a "propitious spot" for their burial (Freedman 1966:134). In *Under the Ancestors' Shadow,* Francis Hsu wrote that "a 'good' graveyard is the concern of every family, rich or poor" and that "a family which has to entomb its dead in a public graveyard is an object of pity" (1948:43). Although Hsu wrote of the people of Yunnan in the 1940s and Freedman quoted a nineteenth-century source, the same can still be said with regard to the people of the New Territories in the 1980s. The Shung Him Tong cemetery is a source of pride and security to the church members. As described in Chapter 3, the cemetery was established through the persistent efforts of early church and village leaders:

> In 1931, recognizing the importance of a cemetery, Pang Lok
> Sam applied to the government for the use of Chung Shan [Pine
> Hill] to the south of the village. The government approved his
> proposal and gave two months notice for the graves of non-Chris-
> tians to be cleared from the hill. Wood from the pine trees grow-
> ing on the lot were donated to the church and sold to pay for the
> supplies and labor needed to build a road to the cemetery, and a
> gate (Pang 1934).

The people of Shung Him Tong are opposed to burial in public cemeteries because of the cost, because the distance from their homes might discourage visitation, and because they would not be buried among other Christians. In the huge public cemeteries, graves are automatically assigned the next available spot and are disinterred every seven years. People of Shung Him Tong are afraid that ancestors might be spread out in different cemeteries and lost in anonymity. In addition, for some elderly villagers, the negative connotations

of low social and economic status are associated with burial in a public cemetery. Public cemeteries in Hong Kong carry the negative implications of
"graveyards for the poor" described by Freedman (1958:77–78), whereas the
Shung Him Tong cemetery resembles the "family sites" that house the rich
(ibid.).[6]

The advantages of the Shung Him Tong cemetery are its exclusivity, its af-
fordability, and the fact that the entire family can be buried in one place. The
elderly of Shung Him Tong are reassured to know they will be buried in a familiar place on the periphery of the village, surrounded by other Hakka Christians. They know that their descendants will always know where they are
buried; graves at the Shung Him cemetery are permanent and therefore less
likely to be neglected. Permanent graves are also important to the living as a
concrete reminder of the connection between the past and the present.

The Shung Him Tong graveyard rules are different from those of other
Chinese cemeteries. A sign posted outside the gate reminds visitors that Chinese traditions should not be followed, including graveside offerings of food
and the burning of paper money, incense, and the like. Only flowers may be
offered and flowerpots must have holes in the bottom to prevent mosquitoes
from breeding in the stagnant water. The cost of an assigned grave site is four
hundred Hong Kong dollars; the cost of selecting a particular site, twenty-four
hundred. Burial of ashes costs three hundred Hong Kong dollars, with an extra charge of two thousand Hong Kong dollars to choose a specific location.

Longtime residence in Shung Him Tong or kinship ties to the early families does not entitle one to burial in the cemetery. The Shung Him cemetery
rules permit only church members and Tsung Tsin pastors who have served at
Shung Him Tong (and their spouses, but not their children) to be buried in
the cemetery. "Members" are those who were baptized or confirmed at the
church. People who move away from Shung Him Tong, including those who
move abroad yet wish to remain members, may attend another church but they
must maintain "contact" with the Shung Him Tong by occasional visits or annual contributions. Burial in Shung Him Tong cemetery can be seen as the final and most reliable statement of community membership.

People were not disturbed or surprised that I spent time recording information from grave markers in the cemetery. I was told by Mr. C., an old friend
of Luo Xianglin, that Luo also spent much time "connecting the past with the
present," gleaning material for his research from the Shung Him Tong cemetery. To Luo it was not only a Christian cemetery but also an important source
of Hakka history and a representation of collective memory. On each grave
marker is written the name of the deceased, his or her years of birth and death,
his or her place of birth if other than Shung Him Tong, and sometimes the
date of burial. Names of spouses and children are also engraved on most mark-

ers. Black-and-white photographs of the deceased, four inches by six in size, are set into all but the oldest grave markers.

Like any written history, the Shung Him Tong cemetery reflects a particular view of history with its own bias toward those who are most powerful or influential within the community. In death as in life, some receive more benefit than others and status is not only recorded but also vied for (see also Freedman 1966:118, 142; Freedman 1958:77–78; Nelson 1974:274; R. Watson 1988:203–27). Unequal status is reflected in the location of the grave, the materials used to construct the grave and marker, and in the upkeep of the grave site (see also de Groot [1897] 1964:832–33). Preferred spots are those located at the center of the cemetery toward the top, but not too high and not too far to the sides, as these areas are easily overgrown by weeds. According to one villager, the preferred spot is high but not too high, visible and with an open view. Traditionally, she told me, Chinese people prefer to be buried on hills for fear that coffins at lower elevations will be damaged by water. Most of the founders of the village are buried in the center of the slope in the area that was once the top of the cemetery, surrounded by bushes. As descendants of these people are generally distinguished from newer members by their economic status, they are somewhat more likely to be buried in the higher and more central locations of the cemetery. As new space is cleared at the upper parts and sides of the slope, these spots become preferred in contrast to the assigned graves and the lower parts of the hill.

What Francis Hsu wrote of family graveyards in Yunnan also holds true for the Shung Him Tong cemetery if we substitute for the idea of a "family graveyard" a "community" one: "In principle, entombment should follow a certain order with respect to generation, age, and sex. Seniority in generation and age entails entombment on the upper terraces; if on the same terrace, a senior should be entombed at the left of a junior. A man and his wife should be entombed side by side; the man on the left of the woman. The left-hand side is regarded as the side of higher honor" (F. Hsu 1948:43–46; see also de Groot [1897] 1964:832).

However, in Shung Him Tong as in Yunnan, these principles are rarely observed in practice: "not only are tombs miscellaneously arranged but also husbands and wives are often placed at a distance from each other" (F. Hsu 1948:46). The ideal principles are not strictly followed because "individual achievements have become the all-important factor and may supersede all other principles of rank in the arrangement of tombs" (1948:47), as well as the problem of space.

In Hsu's study, important members of the lineage took precedence over those who ranked higher in order of generation, age, and sex. In Shung Him Tong the same principle applies: the founders of the community still occupy central locations in the cemetery, with the exception of Pang Lok Sam, who was buried in a Chinese-style horseshoe-shaped grave that he selected for himself on a private hillside across a small valley from the cemetery.[7] Villagers of less wealth or renown are now buried in overgrown corners, and more recent members of the community who find site selection unaffordable appear to be buried in low spots and around the edges.

Overcrowding in the cemetery has recently become a cause for concern. Approximately ten people are buried in the Shung Him Tong cemetery each year, at which rate the forty or so remaining plots will soon be filled. People can no longer reserve grave sites so family graves can be together; the size of each new grave has also been restricted. Early graves in the cemetery were often larger than is currently allowed and a few were in the horseshoe shape common to the New Territories.

As there are relatively few spaces left in the cemetery, decisions must be made concerning its future. Some points are certain: unless families choose otherwise, none of the existing graves will be moved. People are encouraged to select cremation or burial in smaller plots of bones only; such options cost less. A shelter in which to house urns containing cremated remains might also be constructed. The problem, as two members of the cemetery planning committee explained, is that "Chinese people don't like to be cremated" (see also Whyte 1988). One possibility is to build up the sloping edges of the hill to increase the surface that can be used for graves. Another possibility that has been discussed is to stack coffins within one grave "Hong Kong high-rise style," or to disinter graves after a certain number years.

Funerals

Superficially, Shung Him Tong funerals may be either more "western" or more "traditional" in appearance. Yet no matter how western, they still reflect concern with the proper, respectful, and safe disposal of the dead, as well as concern with the social ties that once existed between the dead and the living. These concerns are themselves not particular to the Chinese, but the extent to which they are articulated and the attention they are given may be considered characteristically Chinese.

Most families hold Christian-style memorial services at Shung Him Church or in one of the larger city churches. These memorial services may be seen as the equivalent of "conventionalized weeping speeches" in traditional Chinese funerals in which mourners express their relationship to the deceased, their own sentiments, and the glory of the deceased person's past deeds (C. K. Yang 1961:35–36; see also E. Johnson 1988:139). The deceased is remembered for his or her role in the family and in the church community. At one funeral, before the coffin was taken to the cemetery, a large framed photographic portrait of the deceased was carried around and displayed for all to see. A smaller copy of this photograph was later set on the headstone.[8] As de Groot ([1892] 1964:113–14) described in his nineteenth-century study, among the well-to-do a portrait of the deceased was often commissioned and later placed in a temple or ancestral hall. Its function similar to that of a wooden soul tablet, the portrait served as a place to house the spirit of the dead. Another perhaps less formal portrait might be hung in the hall of the house. This portrait was not believed to house the soul but was "intended to enable the deceased to live on among his descendants" (de Groot [1892] 1964:113). As one might expect, the people of Shung Him Tong do not believe that the portrait houses the soul, but many do hang portraits of the deceased in their family halls for the purpose of remembering them.

As in some funerals in Taiwan (cf. A. Wolf 1970), mourners might wear traditional mourning garb: white clothes, and hemp or burlap cloth draped over the head and shoulders of the sons, daughters, and daughters-in-law of the deceased (see also Freedman 1958:41–45; Ahern 1973:207–8, 211). This is often the case for church members of lower social classes. At other Shung Him Tong funerals, especially those of people with many urban, educated, or overseas Chinese kin, mourners are more likely to wear black suits and ties or black skirts and dresses. Yet even the more western appearance reflects some of the traditional mourning grades.

One man said that, when he was a boy in a Christian village in Wuhua over fifty years ago, one could tell how closely related people were to the deceased by the way they dressed, regardless of whether they were Christian. The first generation of descendants wore burlap clothes, the second wore all white with a burlap belt, the third wore just white, the fourth some white, and the (usually hypothetical) fifth, not considered related at all, would neither dress in mourning clothes nor be expected to attend the funeral. In those days, he said, "There was none of this yarn flower business," referring to the way of dressing at funerals in contemporary Hong Kong. Today, in western-style funerals, the sons and grandsons of the deceased wear black patches of material pinned to their clothes for several days, and daughters and granddaughters wear yarn flowers. Women wear white flowers for the death of their parents or their in-laws, green for the death of a maternal grandparent, and blue for a paternal grandparent, each color marking the proximity of the genealogical connection.[9]

Friends and relatives of the deceased attend the funeral, as do some church elders and board members as an expression of respect for the deceased and out of concern for the survivors. The funeral procession starts at the church and proceeds, after the service, slowly to the cemetery—the coffin driven in a decorated van, and the people walking in a procession behind it. At the grave site, the minister speaks and leads a prayer and a hymn. The guests gradually leave while close kin remain at the grave, each throwing a handful or a shovelful of earth into the grave. In one case, in contrast to the traditional view of red as a joyful color appropriately worn only by those removed from the deceased by four generations (cf. A. Wolf 1970), the family members threw red carnations into the grave. At some funerals, the burlap mourning clothes are also placed over the coffin. Traditionally this was done in fear of the evil spirits that might pollute the garments, but Chinese Christians say they no longer believe such nonsense; the tradition, as one young woman said, merely marks closure.

At both Christian and non-Christian funerals, the family of the deceased distributes small white envelopes, each containing a sweet, a coin, and sometimes a needle. These, following Chinese tradition, are given to help take the bitterness out of the occasion (cf. C. K. Yang 1961:34) and, as Christians say, to mark the change, and to thank the guests for attending.[10] Special envelopes of money are passed out to the workers who have been hired to dig the grave. Christians often use white envelopes made especially for this purpose with a biblical quote and a cross printed on the outside, rather than the usual term *gat yi* (lit., "lucky ritual").

Coffins are ordered from shops in town, and may be of either western or Chinese style. Chinese-style coffins are carved from one piece of wood and cost three or four times the amount of a "western" coffin. The younger generation finds western-style coffins more practical, but the older generation prefers Chinese-style coffins. Two older men recited the following popular rhyme when asked about coffins:

> To be born in Suzhou (where there are beautiful girls);
> To eat in Guangzhou (where there is the best food);
> To live (wear) in Hangzhou (where the best silk is made);
> To die in Liuzhou (which is famous for making coffins).

A necessary part of the funeral includes a simple banquet, to which all who attended the funeral ceremony are invited. While at birthdays, weddings, and other happy events eight to ten courses are served, funeral banquets in Shung Him Tong usually consist of five or seven "simple" dishes. Even numbers—except the number four, which is bad luck because it sounds like the Cantonese word for "death" (*sei*)—are associated with happy events, and odd numbers with sad ones. The number nine (*gau*) is also an exception because it sounds similar to the word for "plenty" or "enough." As Eugene Anderson notes, memorial feasts for the dead are similar to those for other life-cycle occasions, only "smaller" (1988:248). Funeral banquets in Shung Him Tong are not only smaller but involve "plain and simple" food. The abstinence from luxury foods is, according to de Groot, likely to be a vestige of an earlier time when mourners were expected to fast as an expression of sacrifice and grief ([1897]

1964:647, 656). As Thompson explains, "The logic seems to be that the more the mourners fast, the more the dead can feast" (1988:74).

Several people from Shung Him Tong—including men, women, youth, and elders—pointed out to me that some practices surrounding the funerals of Chinese Christians resemble those of non-Christians. As noted earlier, however, Christians felt the need to justify their actions to me as "scientific and logical" as opposed to those of non-Christians, which they claim are motivated by superstition. This was particularly the case with practices involving death pollution. Holding a banquet immediately after the burial ensures that people do not return home and bring bad fortune into the house. A family from Shung Him Tong with whom I discussed this issue agreed that as Christians they "don't have to worry about that kind of thing." However, they have nonetheless taken the traditional precautions against the possible bad luck, and they are aware of the irony of the situation.

Among non-Christians the belongings of the deceased are usually destroyed, with the exception of objects of great value or objects that people have asked to have buried with them. Following non-Christian tradition, several Shung Him Tong people described to me how relatives were buried in a special suit of clothing, or with other favorite possessions (see C. K. Yang 1961:31–32; de Groot [1892] 1964:46–69). For Christians these objects might include a favorite piece of jewelry, or a Bible. Other items of clothing and personal belongings are often thrown away or burned. Burning, the traditional means of sending the possessions of the dead with them to the afterworld, is considered by Shung Him Tong Christians—as I was told by Yee Ling and another young woman—to be merely a good way to dispose of things, or, as a middle-aged woman explained, a means of "disinfecting."

When one member of Shung Him Tong died of cancer a few years ago, all of his belongings including his clothes and bed, were burned or thrown away, although his Christian relatives claimed they knew that cancer is not contagious. The village dumpster was just a few yards away from the house where the man died, but his relatives opted to burn most of his possessions. Several other people I spoke to remembered having been made as children, twenty or thirty years ago, to walk over a pot of burning herbs after attending a funeral. Non-Christians explain this as a way of keeping the spirits away from the house, while Shung Him Tong Christians, again in an attempt to secularize what appear to be religiously motivated actions, say it is merely a way to "disinfect" and prevent the spread of disease.

Ching Ming

Tin, a Christian schoolteacher, offered the following legend of the origin of the Ching Ming festival: "In ancient China, a young man was told by a sage to take his family and go to the top of a mountain. He did so. Upon return-ing home, he found that all those who had stayed below were drowned. From then on people went to the top of the hills to visit the graves at Ching Ming."

Twice a year, at Ching Ming and Chung Yeung, Chinese people in Hong Kong and other parts of southeastern China traditionally visit their ancestors' graves. Ching Ming is in spring during the third month of the lunar calendar, and Chung Yeung is in autumn on the ninth day of the ninth month. In Hong Kong, Ching Ming (lit., "clear and bright") is the more popular of the two fes-tivals. For about three weeks before and two weeks after the actual day of the festival, especially on Sundays when most people take a day off, the roads to the public cemeteries are extremely busy and traffic moves at a snail's pace. During the actual weekend of Ching Ming, official roadblocks are set up at the largest cemeteries and only pedestrians are allowed. Trains and buses are filled to capacity, and taxi and minibus drivers raise their fares. People bring things to burn at the grave site that will be of use to the dead in the afterworld—fruit, meat, sweet cakes, candles, paper money, and other paper offerings.

Ideally, families are buried together at the same graveyard, and on the main day of the festival all important ancestors are paid a visit. But in today's Hong Kong this is rarely the case. Families may spend several days spread out over several weeks in various cemeteries all over Hong Kong and Guangdong vis-iting the graves of mothers, fathers, paternal and maternal grandparents, pater-nal uncles, and sometimes other relatives as well.

At a grave, most people in Hong Kong put the palms of their hands together with the fingers straight and move them up and down and bow. To the peo-ple of Shung Him Tong, the distinction between worshiping and commemo-rating the ancestor is crucial. Several people told me that the popular custom of kowtowing—bowing three times in sequence and making offerings—con-stitutes "worshiping" the ancestor. As Ming Lee explained, this is a heathen and superstitious activity equivalent to worshiping false gods and idols. When Shung Him Tong people visit the cemetery, they kneel and pray at the grave and present flowers as a demonstration of respect for the dead. They emphat-ically insist that this not be confused with worship.[11]

One Tsung Tsin mission pastor explained that Christians "celebrate Ching Ming *in the form of* Easter." The difference between the way Christians and non-Christians celebrate is that non-Christians make offerings to their ances-tors out of fear that, if they do not, the ancestors may cause them harm in the coming year. Christians say they do not believe in the power of ancestors. In-stead, their concern is with remembering their ancestors and recognizing the line of descent. When asked if they celebrate Ching Ming, the people of Shung Him Tong generally say they go to the cemetery on Easter Sunday for Ching Ming festival. Some will say they celebrate Easter *instead* of Ching Ming. To all there is an equivalence: Easter is either equated with or substituted for Ching Ming. Easter Sunday always falls in the span of time in which Ching Ming is celebrated, and Easter and Ching Ming sometimes fall on the same day.

In Shung Him Tong on Easter morning, after the Sunday service, most of the church congregation parades slowly down the dirt road around the back of the village to the cemetery. This includes some who have no ancestors buried there, though a few do not go for that reason. The pastor, standing under the shelter of the large Tsui grave, delivers a short sermon and leads a prayer, and the choir sings a few hymns.

Each family is responsible for the upkeep of its own graves, and by the time of the Easter visit they have usually swept, removed the weeds around the grave, and repainted the inscription on the grave marker. During the Easter visit some people who did not come earlier are seen hastily pulling up weeds and tidying up their family graves. Most visitors bring bouquets of flowers to deposit at each family member's grave, and others are commissioned by friends and relatives abroad to deliver flowers on their behalf. There is a certain status maintained by those who are remembered at this time of year, and pity is expressed for those who have been forgotten, a fact made obvious by the overgrown, neglected appearance of their graves. Some years there is an Easter egg hunt in the cemetery and the tone of the event is very cheerful. Easter is considered a time for reunions, for remembering people, and, as I was told, for the reassuring thought that even if the descendants forget you and neglect your grave, you will be assured an annual visit from the choir.

After Ching Ming, in the monsoon rains and tropical heat, the graves quickly become overgrown with weeds and brush. Most are not cleared again until the following Easter, but Christians do not restrict their visits to Ching Ming and Chung Yeung as do most Chinese in Hong Kong. Some people also visit the grave on the anniversary of the death; other families go at Chung Yeung. Relatives who live overseas are likely to visit graves during the summer holiday or during their Christmas or Chinese New Year visit, despite the popular belief among non-Christians that the lunar new year is a time of renewal when death and related topics should be avoided. Shung Him Tong Christians are aware of such traditions, but in this case, again, they assert that as Christians they need not feel restricted by such proscriptions and superstitions.[12]

Ghosts

Most Chinese I spoke to made a distinction between the spirits of their own dead ancestors and malevolent spirits or ghosts. Ghosts (in Cantonese, *gwai*) are generally thought of as the dead who are not cared for, who died in a tragic way—perhaps too young or violently—and who roam the world at certain times of the year causing trouble (see A. Wolf 1974a:7–9; 1974b:169–76;

Feuchtwang 1974a; Harrell 1974; Wang 1974). While Shung Him Tong Christians claim not to believe in ghosts when asked outright, Christian children still tell stories of ghosts wandering around Chung Him School. Their ghosts suffered the same sorts of deaths as those in conventional Chinese ghost stories. At the school, ghosts are said to be the wandering spirits of those who died at the hands of the Japanese when the school was used as a prison and Japanese headquarters during the Second World War. Among these ghosts, it is rumored, there may even be some vengeful Japanese soldiers who died far from home. One's ancestors, as opposed to ghosts, are generally cared for and therefore are not likely to be malicious spirits unless they are neglected, or died in a terrible way, or left no heirs behind (see A. Wolf 1974b:164; Ahern 1973:199–200). Local non-Christians are also fearful of the ghosts of dead Christians.

In 1987 two brothers who were members of Shung Him Tong died a tragic death. They were farmers and did not live in the village. One brother had climbed into a well to repair an irrigation system. He became trapped by the mud and gases at the bottom of the well and was killed. His brother—in an attempt to rescue him—met with the same fate. Their only other brother had been killed two years earlier when he was struck by lightning. The circumstances of all three deaths were considered particularly horrible and frightening and the brothers were thought by non-Christians to be likely candidates for return as "hungry" ghosts. Even though the deceased were Christian, non-Christian neighbors were particularly concerned that the brothers' ghosts would return because they had died too young (in their late twenties) and "did not want to die," and because their Christian kin performed only Christian rituals. For several days neighbors were seen making offerings at the site of the accident. Thus, to non-Christians, even dead Christians are not exempt from becoming wandering ghosts. Acknowledging the horror of the situation, one older Christian woman said she had seen non-Christian neighbors burning offerings at the site of the well. "If I believed what they do," she said, "I would burn offerings as well."

The Hungry Ghost Festival is the yearly occasion when non-Christians make offerings and set up opera performances to appease and entertain hungry wandering ghosts. Although a major Yu Laan Jit celebration takes place less than a quarter of a mile from the church, church people have no interest in it. On my way back from the festival, en route to the village, I met a young man from the church. Horrified to learn where I had been, he explained to me as patiently as he could that the festival is "the work of the devil," and that only superstitious people participate in it. Christians need not concern themselves with ghosts, only with providing a "comfortable resting place" for the ancestors, remembering them, and paying them due respect. Not observing Yu Laan

Jit is also a statement of Hakka identity. As Mr. C. explained, Yu Laan is strictly a Chaozhou festival, which Hakka learned about only when they moved in among other southern Chinese people.

RITUALS FOR THE LIVING

Christmas

Rituals for the living are primarily Christian but include occasional secularized Chinese traditions. The church year follows the Lutheran calendar, which is divided up into the Christmas cycle running through Advent to the Epiphany, the Easter cycle running through Lent to Pentecost, and "the Time of the Church," which lasts until Advent resumes. Particular hymns and biblical themes and passages correspond with the different church seasons.

Superimposed over the Lutheran calendar is the lunar calendar of Chinese festivals. According to one informant, Chinese festivals are divided into two kinds: "festivals to enjoy oneself and those for the ancestors." In Hong Kong, events from both calendars are marked by public holidays. Christmas and Easter are by far the most important Christian church occasions, while the Chinese New Year is the highlight of the lunar year. Christian holidays are often equated with the most closely corresponding Chinese festivals. For example, Christmas is associated with the winter solstice, Easter with Ching Ming, and to a lesser extent Chung Yeung with All Souls' Day.

"While non-Christians celebrate the winter solstice, Christians celebrate Christmas," several church people pointed out. The winter solstice usually falls on December 21 or 22. In urban areas it is mainly a family event, "a day for staying home, making offerings to the *ancestors,* and enjoying a family dinner" (Law and Ward 1982:83; emphasis in original). In rural areas people can be seen making offerings to sacred trees or rocks, and in some villages this is a day for community members to have a meeting in the ancestral hall (Baker 1968:71, 136).

In Shung Him Tong, Christmas is the most important community occasion; plans for the celebrations begin at least a month before Christmas Day. The youth group arranges a potluck dinner, a party, the caroling schedule, and a talent show or film to attract young people from the neighboring areas on Christmas Night. Sunday school classes rehearse the special Christmas program. In the week before Christmas, the church building is transformed inside and out with Christmas lights, wreaths, a Christmas tree, and ornaments. Over the back wall of the church hall a Christmas tiding is spelled out in English and in Chinese. In 1986 it read, "Joy to the World."

On the Christmas Eve I spent in Shung Him Tong, about two hundred people—dressed more casually than usual—attended church. The children were the center of attention. The lights in the main hall were dimmed and they entered carrying candles and singing "Silent Night" followed by "Away in a Manger." When the children took their seats in the first two rows, the sermon was inaudible over their noise, but they were tolerated for fifteen minutes before being escorted out by the Sunday school teacher. The service was followed by a "tea party" downstairs in the kindergarten classrooms. People crowded into the decorated room to hear a short speech, recite a prayer, partake of refreshments, and participate in the official presentation of gifts to the young people who had done a service for the church such as teaching Sunday school or leading the younger youth groups.

Gift exchanges are not a central part of the Christmas celebration in Shung Him Tong. Presents are generally not exchanged between friends and family members, but little bags of wafers, candies, and cartons of fruit juice are handed out to all who attend church on Christmas Day. This practice attracts young people from the surrounding villages who do not normally attend. There is also a random drawing of gifts by the Sunday school children. These gifts are all given "on behalf of the church" and appear to reward them for their regular attendance and church membership.

On Christmas Eve, the gift presentation is followed by the caroling expedition. It is a serious affair at which only religious Christmas hymns are sung, all in Hakka and always in four-part harmony, to the accompaniment of the pastor's accordion. During my stay, the group went from a government hospital in Fanling to the Jockey Club clinic in Sheung Shui, then to the Tsung Tsin mission home for the elderly in Sha Tin, where many elderly Hakka from the Tsung Tsin mission eagerly awaited their visit, and finally to the Fanling housing estates.

On Christmas Day, energy and excitement soared. Dressy clothes were worn and more than twice the usual crowd—over four hundred people— made its way to the church. The church hall was filled beyond capacity and extra seats were added in the aisles. An overflow of people had to stand outside the door to hear the sermon. In addition to relatives from Hong Kong, Kowloon, and further away, there were many people who attended church only on this occasion, and many who did not belong to the church at all. After the service a large catered banquet was held downstairs in the church for those who had bought tickets, at forty Hong Kong dollars apiece. About half of those who had attended the service, mainly the regular church members, were there.

Twelve people sat around each of the twenty tables, and there was no preplanned seating arrangement. Young people sat together at three tables at one end of the room, as did several young women with children. Few families made a point of sitting together, with the exception of those people who had invited family members who do not usually attend church. Several of the male members of the board of directors did not sit with their families and behaved as hosts, circulating among the guests and proposing toasts at each table with their glasses of soft drinks.

Since Christmas Day is a public holiday, it is a day for reunions and family gatherings throughout Hong Kong. But for the people of Shung Him Tong it is a church as well as a family occasion. While everyone attends the church service, most regular community members also attend the church banquet, but they may also have their own family celebrations, later in the day, at home or in restaurants.

The Chinese New Year

The first of January is not of any great importance to the people of Shung Him Tong, except that it is a public holiday. However, the Chinese New Year—celebrated at the beginning of the lunar year, which falls sometime between the end of January and the first two-thirds of February—is undoubtedly the largest celebration in all of Hong Kong. Preparation for the new year begins in the twelfth month of the old year, but the main celebration begins on New Year's Eve and ends on the fifteenth day of the first month. Most of the activity and celebration takes place during the first five days, after which time many people return to work; the seventh to fourteenth days are less eventful, and then the end of the new year festivities is celebrated on the fifteenth day with the lantern festival.

On the subject of the Chinese New Year in Hong Kong, Ward writes that it is primarily "a family festival focussed on the home" (Law and Ward 1982:27), although at certain times there are crowds at temples and flower markets: "Morally the keynote is renewal. The old year goes and with it go old misfortunes and old wrongs; the new year comes and brings the chance for starting afresh. Socially it signifies reunion, the end of strife, the renewal of harmony. Personally and in business one hopes to pay off one's debts, tidy up all loose ends, and turn over a new leaf" (Law and Ward 1982:17).

Christmas is a major celebration in Shung Him Tong, but for non-Christians in Hong Kong it is largely a secular occasion and a commercial holiday. In the villages surrounding Shung Him Tong and in the nearby market, there is relatively little excitement over Christmas. The Chinese New Year, however, is a major occasion for everyone. A month or two before the new year begins, rows and rows of potted trees and plants are in evidence in nurseries and gardens all over the New Territories. As the end of the old year approaches, small orange and tangerine trees are transplanted and shaded or exposed to the sun in order that the fruit be perfectly golden and ripe. Farmers carefully tend their flowers and peach trees to make sure that they are at the earliest stages of bloom at the beginning of the new year. It is most inauspicious to have blossoms that are past their prime at the new year, as the partially open buds represent the promise of a fruitful and flourishing year to come.

At least two weeks before the end of the year women become especially industrious "renewing the house," an activity comparable to "spring cleaning." As the new year approaches all family members lend a hand painting and whitewashing walls, or at least repainting doorways and window frames, washing cars, and pounding mattresses. On the twenty-fourth day of the twelfth month, non-Christians believe that the kitchen god leaves for heaven to give a report on the family's behavior over the past year. They prepare special sweets for him and burn his image to send it to heaven. The sweets are believed to sweeten his words, or as one Christian put it, non-Christians believe they can "bribe him to say good things about the family."

During the last several days of the old year, the markets are transformed. Streets and alleyways are lined with potted pink, purple, yellow, and red chrysanthemums, peach trees, and orange trees. The shops and hawkers' carts selling incense and other funeral ritual objects are filled with bright red posters and banners—couplets, single lucky characters, door gods, red envelopes for lucky money, red ribbons, and rounded mirrors to decorate altars and doorways—the special new year purchases. Special foods, many of them also served by Christians at the new year, are sold at the dry goods store, such as candied coconut, lotus seeds and roots, and several other types of seeds symbolizing fertility (see Anderson and Anderson 1977:380; E. Anderson 1988). The price of chicken almost doubles as the demand goes up. By the last day of the old year, the market is louder, friendlier, and more crowded than usual. Almost everyone is there because the market and restaurants are closed for the first two days of the new year and because it is believed that no food should be prepared on those days. Outside the shops and houses, tables are set up with candles, incense, cooked rice, and chicken for the gods.

In much of Lung Yeuk Tau, the tables normally used for card games and mahjong are seen on front porches and in front yards laden with offerings. By New Year's Eve, food for the next two days has been prepared; the first banquet is held, and visits are made to temples and to the special, late-night flower market. Firecrackers, although illegal, are constantly heard in the rural areas. That night "lucky papers" are hung to decorate doorways—door gods are affixed to double doors, one large character is mounted over the top of the door, and couplets are arranged on either side—and at some houses outdoor lights are kept on all night.

Observance of the new year in Shung Him Tong is conspicuously different. Although Christians clean their houses and are caught up in the excitement of the new year, they do not have the same competitive attitude and propensity for displays as have other people in Lung Yeuk Tau. One does not see new paint on doors and fences, and lucky red papers do not appear outside their doorways; nor is one struck by the number of peach trees and orange trees. Although special care is put into the flower arrangements at church for New Year's Day, decorations are not given the same attention as at Christmas. Shung Him Tong people do, however, often have new haircuts and wear special or new clothes on the first of the year.

While non-Christians visit temples on New Year's Day, Christians go to church. Next to Christmas, the Chinese New Year draws the largest crowd to the church. The attendance on the morning of New Year's Day in 1988 was about a hundred more people than usual, about a hundred less than at Christmas, and also included a number of overseas visitors. Christmas draws many people from the surrounding villages who do not otherwise ever come to church. Some of these people might consider themselves "Christian" but are not considered such by the regular church members; others, such as my landlady's daughter, attend "for the fun" although they do not consider themselves Christian. At the Chinese New Year, more non-Christians are involved in their own family activities, and church ranks as a low priority.

May, a young Christian woman from Shung Him Tong, explained that the main difference between the way Christians and non-Christians celebrate the new year is "we hold feasts for new year and midautumn festival, but we never *baaisahn* [worship gods]." As she put it: "At midautumn festival when non-Christians have a feast and set out a table of food offerings for the gods, the Christians also look at the moon, eat moon cakes, and have a family feast, but they don't offer food to the gods. At new year it is the same; Christians still *baainihn* [pay new year visits], give out lucky money, but they don't set out a table for the gods or make offerings to the ancestors."

Non-Christians have a number of beliefs regarding the new year that Christians claim they do not share. One is that it is bad luck to mention topics relating to death during the new year celebrations. On the fifth day of the Chinese New Year the church evangelist and I were invited to attend a banquet at the home of a prominent Shung Him Tong family. The conversation turned to the topic of one of the old respected women of the village who had died several years earlier. She had refused to see a doctor or take medicine because "she placed her life in God's hands." Mr. P., the one recounting the event said, "I told her that God had given her intelligence to use to know when to go to a good doctor and take medicine." In the course of the discussion topics touched on included suicide and death. Finally one of Mr. P.'s daughters in her late twenties laughed and said with a tone of concern, "We shouldn't be discussing this at new year!" Her father's response to this was a cheerful, "It doesn't matter, we're Christians!" The evangelist chimed in a little more self-consciously with, "Christians don't follow such beliefs." Indeed, during the first few days of the new year, a few people, mostly those from far away, did go to the cemetery to leave bouquets of flowers and pay their respects to their ancestors.

One of the main activities of the Chinese New Year is *baainihn*, which means paying visits. Customarily, on the first day of the new year a married couple and their children will visit the husband's relatives, and on the second day the wife's. Non-Christians will not pay visits on the third day "because they believe you will get into arguments and fights if you do." Though I was told that "Christians do not believe this and they also *baainihn* on this day," the third day was the only one during the new year celebration on which I received no visits and no invitations, and on which people preferred to stay home and relax. Among Christians and non-Christians, younger people generally pay visits to older ones and present them with boxes of sweets or bags of oranges or other fruit.

People of Shung Him Tong were not in agreement concerning the propriety of Christians using the traditional Chinese New Year greeting of *gung hei faat choih* (congratulations and wishes for increased prosperity). Some disapprove because it refers to a desire for material prosperity. Instead they say *Sannihn faailohk* (lit., "new year happiness" or "Happy New Year"). According to Yee Ling, "Some Christians greet each other with phrases which refer to wealth and prosperity, but the pastor certainly wouldn't." As Mr. C. put it, "We Christians don't say such things, because our rewards are in the next life so we don't worry about wealth in this world." Christian businessmen are likely to say it because of the expectations of their non-Christian associates. According to another man, "Christians aren't supposed to say '*gung hei faat choih*' but many of us want wealth so we say it anyway! The pastor won't say it and neither will many church people."

While greetings at the new year may be a subtle sign of one's religious beliefs, they are also easily adjusted to meet the expectations of different audiences. A person might address church friends and the pastor one way and non-Christian friends and colleagues another. Pictures of door gods, couplets, and lucky papers, however, are eschewed as more concrete symbols of one's identity, as they are visible on the outside of gates and doorways.

As one older, retired Swiss missionary explained to me, he and other Basel missionaries who worked in China during the early part of the century forbade such heathen activities as hanging lucky papers. Today these are conspicuously absent from the doorways of Christian homes in Shung Him Tong. Door gods, Christians told me, echoing the words of the old Swiss missionary, are obviously contrary to Christian monotheistic beliefs. The absence of couplets was more difficult to explain, since some common couplets and single-character papers represent acceptable Christian concepts, particularly those that refer to "blessings" or "peace throughout the seasons." Christians are not prevented from having lucky papers on their doors, but as one man explained, "They have just lost interest in those things." The Swiss missionary's explanation was that although the message may in itself sound Christian enough, the practice is linked to the whole system of Chinese religion, which is contrary to Christianity.

Shung Him Tong Christians are disinterested in couplets not because of their literal meanings but because they see them as markers of religious identity. There is not anything inherently wrong with the message of some couplets—some are admittedly good Christian themes and several people pointed out to me that, in their native villages in Guangdong, couplets were "invented" citing Christian themes—but they are associated with a set of beliefs and values that Christians do not share. Couplets were the topic of several conversations and of the first Sunday sermon of the Chinese New Year. There is nothing wrong with making statements about health, wealth, peace and happiness, said the visiting pastor, but non-Christians only put up the characters asking for peace and blessings because they do not have them. Christians, on the other hand, are "already rich and noble" by virtue of being Christian—they may not have material wealth, but they lead rich and noble lives—unlike the non-Christians who put up such couplets in hopes of becoming wealthy and famous. As most Christians see it, the main problem is with couplets that "deal with money or getting rich" and express a desire for acquiring wealth "without working for it." The couplet "*wong choih jau sau*," for example, expresses a wish that money will come into their hands by indirect means (lit., "indirectly money [wealth] come to hand [received]"). To Tin, Yee Ling, and Mr. C., "indirect means" implies winning at cards, mahjong, or horse races, activities inappropriate for Christians.

Non-Christians put papers at their doorways to attempt to bring luck to their families, or to make statements about their families. In the past, I was told, scholars put obscure learned phrases on their doors to demonstrate that they were educated. When one family built a new house in the village next to Shung Him Tong, its members placed a paper around their doorway that read "*laan gwai tang fong*" (lit., "orchid cassia rise fragrant").[13] Tin explained the couplet to mean that "they were not dependent on their ancestors for their wealth. They were poor before and are now succeeding." The phrase was intended to reflect both what they are and what they hope to be. Likewise, the lack of lucky papers on Christians' doors reflects one facet of their identity.

As with beliefs concerning death pollution, people of Shung Him Tong are vividly aware of many of the non-Christian proscriptions and practices associated with the Chinese New Year. At the same time, they deny the relevance of such beliefs or attempt to define a strict boundary between what is and what is not acceptable Christian behavior. This strong awareness of what Christians do not and should not believe, juxtaposed with frequent attempts to reconcile, delineate, and rationalize Christian and Chinese practices and beliefs, illustrates that there is far more ambiguity regarding these two sets of belief, and the associated identities, than may at first appear.

RITES OF PASSAGE

Baptism, confirmation, marriage, and death in Shung Him Tong are marked by special church rituals, but births are not. In Shung Him Tong, as in other parts of Hong Kong, many believe that a mother should stay at home with her newborn for one month and not receive visitors who are not part of the immediate family (see also Topley 1974:234). The new mother should be fed special foods such as pickled ginger, pig knuckles and tendons cooked with eggs and ginger, and chicken cooked in wine, which are believed to give her strength. Births, particularly those of sons, are often celebrated with a banquet a month after the birth. In the past, the child received his or her name on that day. Besides a possible announcement at the Sunday service, no special or additional church celebrations occur until the time of a child's baptism.

Three or four times a year, groups of three or more people are baptized or confirmed at the end of the Sunday service. On one occasion there were three adults and four children; three of the children were babies and one was a boy about seven years old. Children may be baptized as infants but some parents prefer that their children be baptized when they are old enough to decide for themselves. Most children are confirmed when they are in their early or mid-teens. Adults who wish to join the church must be baptized but need not be confirmed. If they were already baptized at another church of a different denomination and wish to join Shung Him Tong, they need not be baptized again. Instead they take part in a short ceremony that is "like a baptism without the water." One man reminisced that in the 1920s and 1930s there were very large groups baptized at once, and often whole families were baptized together. Today the number of baptisms has decreased (see fig. 1).

Traditionally, all birthdays were celebrated on, and calculated from, the seventh day of the new year, but today in all of Hong Kong individual birthdays have become more important. While birthdays of elders, and men in particular, have long been considered significant by the Chinese, birthday celebrations for the young have only recently become more popular. The church plays a special role in the celebration of young people's birthdays. Youth group members hold two large birthday celebrations a year celebrating all the birthdays of youth group members that fall within a six-month period. As at Christmas, gifts given at these occasions are "from the church" and are distributed at random. Birthdays of individual youth group members are also sometimes recognized with a cake, a few gifts, and a small party. As with most Chinese, birthdays in Shung Him Tong are deemed increasingly important as a person grows older, especially the sixtieth birthday, which marks a complete cycle of the Chinese calendar. After the age of sixty, birthdays are celebrated by the entire extended family. On his ninetieth birthday, one man from the village held a huge celebration to which friends, relatives, and prominent people in Hong Kong were invited. This was considered a particularly extravagant event by any Hong Kong standards.

More than any other occasion, marriage ceremonies come closest to illustrating the dual or perhaps triple system of beliefs that exist in Shung Him Tong. Until recently, a marriage in Shung Him Tong might have included three different ceremonies: a church ceremony, a civil ceremony at the city hall, and a "traditional" Chinese tea ceremony and banquet. A few years ago the minister of Shung Him Tong received the legal right to perform marriage ceremonies so marriage at the city hall is no longer necessary.

During the year I was in Shung Him Tong there were only two weddings, one church and one village. The village wedding was on a Sunday while most people were at church. Because the groom and his family were Christian, although the bride was not, the pastor was invited to come and lead a prayer and hymn and give his blessings after the ceremony. The church wedding I attended resembled in all respects a traditional western church wedding. The bride wore an ornate white lace gown and the groom a tuxedo. A flower girl carried a basket of flowers and a little boy was the ring bearer. The bride's father walked her down the aisle and "gave her away." The minister gave a short sermon and led a prayer. Then the church choir sang, followed by the exchange of vows. The bride and groom placed their hands on a Bible and agreed to the vows and signed the wedding certificate. This was followed by another prayer and a hymn, after which the bride and groom proceeded out of the hall, followed by the minister, both families, the choir, and the guests.

After the ceremony an informal reception was held downstairs in the church. Photography was the main event. Bride and groom posed as they cut the cake and with each of the guests in turn. Following the church wedding, the bride and groom returned to the groom's parents' house for the tea ceremony. Again the photographer was given a central spot from which to record the event. The bride and groom each carried a cup of tea, which they served to his parents. The parents then handed them each a red envelope containing gifts of money or jewelry, told them to treat each other well, took a sip from the cups for the sake of a photograph, and then vacated their seats so the eldest brother and his wife could be served. They too feigned drinking the tea just long enough for a photograph, as did the next brother and his wife. And so it went down the line of descent, with each pair served in the same seats and the photographer busily snapping away. The bride's parents had been served before the church ceremony. Non-Christian brides and grooms kneel at the feet of their parents as they present them with tea, but Shung Him Tong Christians believe they "should not bow or kneel before anyone but God." After the tea ceremony, the bride changed into a red Chinese-style wedding dress and the family set off for the restaurant banquet.

The church ceremony and reception lasted only an hour, and like the tea ceremony, appeared hasty and superficial. The most important consideration appeared to be the photo-taking. While everyone from the church was invited to the church ceremony and reception, only the immediate family attended the tea ceremony; family, some church members, friends, and associates from outside the church community were invited to the banquet.

FENG-SHUI

Feng-shui is a particularly interesting topic to examine with respect to what it says about the identity of Shung Him Tong people. To non-Christians, *feng-shui* is commonly believed to be a "theory of the forces underlying such natural phenomena as hills, watercourses, certain directions, etc. which affect human fate and therefore must be taken into careful consideration in choosing sites for graves, temples, and all buildings" (Law and Ward 1982:90). Reference to *feng-shui* was made many times by Shung Him Tong Christians in connection with such topics as the founding of the village, the beauty of the area surrounding Shung Him Tong, the establishment of the cemetery, graves, and houses, the good or bad fortune of particular people, and the location of the new church.

Several Shung Him Tong people told me that *feng-shui* is a "superstition," implying that it is a false belief, particularly if it is "taken too far" and is believed to be capable of influencing a person's success or prosperity. Others, including one church elder, described *feng-shui* as secular, "scientific" logic, or as an intuitive aesthetic sense that "all Chinese people know." Along with this "rational" and secularized view of *feng-shui* is an attitude of condescension toward those who "take it too far" and treat it as a religion.

Mr. C., a particularly conservative and pious Christian, expressed a very common sense view of *feng-shui*. The topic arose as we were discussing Hakka houses. While we were drinking tea, he began to sketch a horseshoe-shaped Hakka house, the kind he had seen when he was growing up in Wuhua. As he drew the decorations on the outside, he explained that the Hakka were stone carvers while the Chaozhou were wood carvers. Very rich Hakka would have carvings over the front entrance and some along the eaves of the roof. I asked whether such a house had good *feng-shui* and he answered:

Yes, it's very simple. All it has to do with is balance. If I were to situate myself well in front of the house, I would want to see a house which is balanced properly. It's only logical. The house should be a little bit up on a hill but not too high up, and looking out from the house there should be a view, but not an open view. Preferably there should be hills and mountains which surround the view. You don't want it to be too open.

He demonstrated this by seating himself straight and holding his arms out before him: "When I am at my house I should feel like a man looking out and sitting in his throne. Things should all be balanced." Then he fidgeted with one hand as if he imagined some imbalance: "Balance, that's all *feng-shui* is." The Chinese concept of balance, he explained, is connected with ideas of hygiene. By way of contrast he described an apartment in Luen Wo market where there are rows of rooms with few windows as "unhygienic." Old houses, he explained, had thicker walls and the tiles on the roof had air passing through them into the house so they reflected heat away in the summer. New houses have thin walls and can only reflect or repel the heat for a few hours before they absorb it and the whole house gets hot.

Non-Christians consider *feng-shui* an important factor in placing graves. A well-placed grave not only insures proper rest for the dead but can also assure the descendants success, prosperity, and the birth of sons.[14] Several people of Shung Him Tong told me that outsiders believe that Shung Him Tong has very good *feng-shui,* which explains the large horseshoe-shaped graves located on the hill above the village. One is the grave of a multimillionaire who made his fortune in Malaysian mining. Many years ago he is said to have approached Pang Lok Sam to ask whether he could be buried there. As Tin explained, "Of course the villagers, being Christian, couldn't care about *feng-shui,* so they let him build it." Another man from Shung Him Tong told me the tale of one of the newer graves: another rich man asked permission to put his grave on the hill and was refused by the villagers—who as Christians disdained the idea of *feng-shui*—until "he offered to pay every family in the village a hundred Hong Kong dollars, and more to the church elders," after which he was allowed to build the grave.

Like many villagers, a relative of Pang Lok Sam commented on the beauty of the location of the Shung Him cemetery and said that it had good *feng-shui,* explaining that "Pang Lok Sam and all old people back then knew about *feng-shui.* Although he didn't hire a *feng-shui* expert to find the site, I think he knew it had it." The cemetery appears to follow the basic rules of *feng-shui*: it is located in one of the green contours or "veins" of the dragon, to the rear of the village. To the people of Shung Him Tong, the cemetery is in an ideal location that satisfies both those who openly believe in *feng-shui* and those who do not. Everyone agrees that a cemetery should be located on a hill and it should not be too close to the places of the living.

According to the founding legend of the village (see chap. 3), Shung Him Tong is located in a place where the *feng-shui* is very good. As one particularly pious and conservative Christian explained, on a certain level *feng-shui* is just common sense—"something all Chinese know intuitively." Thus it is no surprise that the son of Pastor Ling should have picked a good site: not only did he have an intuitive aesthetic appreciation of *feng-shui,* but he was also a trained engineer involved in surveying for the Kowloon Canton Railway.

The local people were opposed to the Christians settling at Shung Him Tong because their presence was expected to obstruct the locals' own *feng-shui.* But the locals were also afraid to settle there themselves because the site, although considered good, was also potentially hazardous. The Punti were surprised, according to one young woman, that no harm came to the Christians, because part of Shung Him Tong is located along the throat and head of the dragon, while another part sits on top of the pearl that the dragon holds in his mouth. As one Hong Kong *feng-shui* expert explained, "A house on the dragon's head can be risky: living on its brain is good, but a slight miscalculation could put the residents dangerously close to the beast's mouth, the source of strong ch'i [*qi,* energy or cosmic breath] and a huge appetite" (Rossbach 1983:37). Too much *qi* can prove as much of a problem as too little in causing misfortune. In the ideal site, the *qi* flows smoothly and the *yin* and *yang* are balanced (Weller 1987:173–84; Rossbach 1983:28; Feuchtwang 1974b:48–56).

Shung Him Tong is neatly nestled between two low-lying hills to the northeast and the southwest with Dragon Mountain sheltering its back to the southeast and the Phoenix River running across the front southwest to north.[15] The village is oriented in the same direction as the older neighboring villages in Lung Yeuk Tau, which are believed to be oriented to best take advantage of the geomantic features of the area. The village is nestled in the embrace of the hills, which is referred to as the classic *feng-shui* "armchair" formation, or as the "dragon-protecting pearl" (Rossbach 1983:39–40; Freedman 1969, 1979; Knapp 1977:4; Lai 1974; Lip 1979). For Hakka Christians of Shung Him Tong, of course, this is out of practical rather than religious considerations.

Tales of the effect of *feng-shui* on the people of Shung Him Tong continue to circulate. According to one friend from Shung Him Tong, the Punti believe that one church member dug up the pearl from the dragon's mouth when he and his brother built their two houses and that this act brought them bad luck. According to another person the family had bad luck because they severed the tendons in the dragon's feet: "that is why the older brother got very sick and couldn't walk and then he died." Another person disagreed, insisting that it was not the tendons but the pearl that had been dug up; it was the pearl, she said, that "people say brought bad luck." Yet another person explained that the desecration did not cause the brother's death but rather the death of the church member's son, and the fact that he now has only one son. "But," he quickly added, "Christians don't believe this."

The most striking tale of *feng-shui* in Shung Him Tong involves an aborted attempt to build the new church; it is a topic that the villagers are hesitant to bring up because they do not want to "stir up conflicts again." By the late 1960s the church building had become too small and the board began the process of deciding where the new church would be built. Some people wanted the church high up on the hill and others wanted it on level land near the old church. A third group was in favor of putting it on the slope on the west side of the village, but that plan was not popular because the slope was too steep. Those who wanted the church located on the hill between Shung Him Tong and the neighboring village wanted it there, according to Mr. C., because it would be visible from far away and closer to non-Christian villages. Those who favored the old church site wanted it there because it would be more convenient and more easily accessible on foot. Their plan, they said, would also be cheaper because it would not require a new road for transporting construction materials.

The decision was made to build the church on the hill. A new lot, northeast of the village on a small hill overlooking the neighboring non-Christian village, was leased from the government and plans for construction began. As Freedman aptly wrote of *feng-shui* and Chinese architectural aesthetics, "Let one man in a village build a fraction too high; let him make a window or a door that can be interpreted as a threat; and he has a struggle on his hands" (1969:14). The attempt to build the church above the village was interpreted as a literal and figurative attempt by Christians to put themselves "above" their neighbors and to prosper or benefit at the expense of the non-Christian village (cf. Freedman 1979:203; Feuchtwang 1974b:118). According to one government official familiar with the incident, "The Lung Yeuk Tau Tengs were against the church on the hill . . . because they thought the hill was the source of their *feng-shui* and that the church would block it." As Tin explained, "It would be like the people of the church were looking down on them, looking down at their houses."

When on the first day of construction a child from the non-Christian village nearby became seriously ill—and died, according to some—a large group of Punti believed to be from Lung Yeuk Tau organized a roadblock and threw stones to prevent the construction team from passing. Rather than attempt to negotiate with their angry neighbors, the Christians abandoned the hill site and built the new church next to the old one on lower land, a plan that some Christians had favored all along. One man remembers that after this incident several fences were erected and many Shung Him Tong people were afraid to walk through Lung Yeuk Tau at night.

Several Shung Him Tong people explained that "any time the villagers complain about *feng-shui*—not just *feng-shui* but also graves, roads, and buildings—the government doesn't want to stir up trouble with the Punti" and they let them have their way. Like many people in the Hong Kong government, some Shung Him Tong people believe that *feng-shui* beliefs are used by indigenous villagers as a "good excuse to do or not do certain things." In the New Territories government records, there are numerous examples of Punti opposition to construction projects because the *feng-shui* of the region would be disturbed. There are also numerous records of "*feng-shui* complaints" being solved with financial settlements. Shung Him Tong people believe that, although non-Christians may in fact believe in *feng-shui,* they are also well aware of the economic benefits that they can receive through such claims. In the case of the church site, however, even money would not have solved the problem. As Tin explained, they "believed in *feng-shui* and just didn't want the church looking over their shoulders. I believe in *feng-shui* too, but not that it can make you rich or poor." As Freedman has written: "Chinese may cease to believe in and practice his [sic] traditional religion without abandoning his faith in geomancy. Be he Christian or atheist, fung shui retains its meaning and appeal. Geomancy is a 'science' for those who would have it so" (1979:195).

Feng-shui, like the other beliefs outlined in this chapter, demonstrates the way in which the religious beliefs and practices of the people of Shung Him Tong differ significantly from those of their neighbors. While all religious systems have internal contradictions and inconsistencies, what is important in this case is that the ambiguities between the two systems have allowed Hakka Christians to create a rhetoric for arguing that they are Chinese. The Chinese and Christian identities of the people of Shung Him Tong are expressed through their Christian religious practices and the Chinese practices that they attempt to define as secular. Their identity is also expressed in the management of their landscape and the construction of their village. To British administrators, government officials, and European missionaries, the physical appearance of the village communicates—among other things—a concern for Christian orthodoxy. To their non-Christian neighbors, it displays many traditional aesthetic qualities and concern for *feng-shui.*

In their day-to-day lives, through their treatment of ancestors, their celebration of Chinese festivals and rites of passage, and the physical construction of their village, Hakka Christians express their Chinese identity within a constrained framework of acceptable Christian behavior. Yet as we have seen, the Hakka Christian definition of Chinese identity differs from that of non-Christians. Christians attempt to create a Chinese identity divorced from Chinese religious beliefs and practices, and thus they are constantly in a position of having to rationalize and clarify the ambiguities—to draw and redraw boundaries between Christian and Chinese funeral practices, between Ching Ming and Easter, between the aesthetic and superstitious elements of *feng-shui*. Their ancestors are commemorated, not worshiped, and their festivals and rites of passage are reinterpreted as secular or Christian occasions. Similarly, the reinterpretation of *feng-shui* as "common sense" or as a purely aesthetic consideration is carefully spelled out verbally by Hakka Christians because their behavior—the construction of homes, church, and cemetery—suggests that they do subscribe to such a belief.

Although the particular beliefs and practices associated with the care of the dead in Shung Him Tong are not the same as those of non-Christians, the fact remains that these Chinese Christians are also concerned with their ancestors and their own conception of "proper" care. The church cemetery has not so much replaced the family cemetery as it has become a cemetery for the extended "church family." In much the same way, the importance of the church in people's minds has not replaced the importance of family and ancestors but has extended the family to include the entire Hakka Christian church community. Just as a family graveyard maps out the family genealogy, the church cemetery maps out the genealogy of the church community.

In contrast to the "dual" system of beliefs identified by Nash among Bolivian tin miners whose Catholic and "folk" beliefs coexist but are separated or "compartmentalized" in time and space (1979), the system developed by Hakka Christians attempts to separate Christian beliefs from all other religious beliefs and practices, which are rejected outright as false. In other words, Hakka Christians do not practice a syncretic religion that combines elements of Christianity with elements of Buddhism, Taoism, or Chinese popular religion. Nor do they restrict their practice of Christianity to particular contexts— certain times and circumstances. Instead, what they maintain of Chinese non-Christian religion has been transformed into a set of rationalized beliefs and values that they claim are compatible with Christianity. These "secularized" Chinese religious practices are most evident, as we have seen, in the cases of festivals and rites of passage, particularly those concerning death and *feng-shui*, because these are most closely tied to ancestors, genealogy, and history, and therefore to Hakka and Chinese identity.

As the examples above illustrate, Shung Him Tong's attempt to reconcile Chinese and Christian identities by way of rationalizing their respective religious beliefs and practices has not been easy, nor will it be entirely successful so long as Shung Him Tong villagers practice the type of Christianity they do, in which the two sets of beliefs are defined as mutually exclusive. This is not to say that their endeavors have been entirely unsuccessful, either; rather, the process is an ongoing one, as is the process of reconciling Hakka Chinese and Christian identities.

6 Transforming Images of the Hakka

In the province of Kwangtung, three tribes may be distinguished
that differ largely, not only in their language, customs, and
manners, but in character.

A European missionary (Oehler 1922:351)

Hakka are very good people; hardworking, thrifty and practical,
not like the Punti who like to have a good time and are not
hardworking.

A thirty-year-old Hakka woman from Shung Him Tong

The Cantonese were in the plains for longer and are richer and
learned how to not work so hard. . . . [They] think of Hakka as
inferior, uneducated, and aggressive, but the Hakka people have
shown that they are wrong.

A seventy-year-old Hakka man from Shung Him Tong

A friend recently sent me a full-page color advertisement for United Airlines.[1]
The caption reads, "Going for the green in Hong Kong," and beneath it is a
photograph of four people walking across a golf course. The two in the center are clean-cut young men—possibly businessmen, one Asian and one
white—dressed in golf clothes. The other two people, one on either side, each
pulling a heavy load of golf clubs, are the caddies. But these are not ordinary
caddies; they are middle-aged Chinese women wearing baggy black pants,
loose dark blue blouses with high collars, and circular flat straw hats with black
cloth brims that come down around their faces. Both are stocky and wear
sturdy, flat shoes. Far from the common advertising image of women used to
sell cars and other products, these women are not meant to be seductive and
alluring. Nor do they fit the western or orientalist stereotype of the delicate,
submissive, and sexy Asian woman. Instead they are strong, tanned, and hardworking, exotic in a different sense: the stereotypical image of a Hakka
woman.

Despite what is often described as a decline in the overt social or political
relevance of Chinese ethnic identities in Hong Kong, colorful popular images

127

of each group persist. Certain character traits are thought to distinguish one Chinese ethnic group from another, and few people in Hong Kong would fail to identify the sturdy hardworking women in the advertisement described above as stereotypically Hakka. Among the main features I have heard attributed to the Hakka by both Hakka and non-Hakka are their poverty, their honesty, and their propensity for hard work—especially the women. Even Hakka Christians in Shung Him Tong, who say that distinctions other than that drawn between true believers and nonbelievers are divisive, believe, like many others in Hong Kong, that there are certain character traits that distinguish the Hakka.

I was told by several people in Shung Him Tong, for example, that Hakka may be poor, but they strive for upward mobility; they are honest, hardworking, thrifty, and clean, and they value education. In contrast, they depicted non-Hakka as dishonest, lazy, wasteful, and sometimes dirty. Cantonese were described as generally wealthier than Hakka but also likely to be on an economic decline—particularly Punti families—because they are often lazy, immoral, dishonest, corrupt, and frivolous, and they do not value hard work and education. Chaozhou, who were once poor farmers like the Hakka, are now considered economically successful, but several Hakka in Shung Him Tong said that Chaozhou may be dishonest and corrupt, and that they are far more likely to be involved with drug smuggling and other illegal activities than are Hakka. Cantonese and Hokkien boat people, with whom the people of Shung Him Tong have little interaction, I was told are characterized as dirtier, less intelligent, and less educated than other Chinese. These stereotypes are strikingly similar to those that have been recorded by other anthropologists in other parts of Hong Kong (e.g., E. Anderson 1968:98–99; Blake 1975, 1981:45–88).

It is important to note that many of the stereotypes and negative images presented in this chapter were elicited by specific questions and were not part of everyday casual conversations. Most people in Shung Him Tong consider it un-Christian to cast aspersions on other people, and for that reason a lot of the material on the subject was collected in response to such questions as, who are the Hakka? what are the Hakka like? and how are the Hakka different from other Chinese? Often, the answers I received were phrased in such a way as to distance personal view from popular negative stereotypes: "Many people say that the boat people are . . . ."

Stereotypes, in some instances, contain elements of truth, but often they have little or no basis in fact and cannot actually be used to distinguish members of one group from another. My main objective in this chapter is not to examine these stereotypes in any great detail for the extent to which they do or do not reflect Hakka reality in Shung Him Tong. It should be obvious from the preceding chapters that many of these stereotypes do not represent objective truth.

Here, I am more concerned with stereotypes of the Hakka for what they can tell us about the construction of Hakka, Chinese, and Christian identities.

The people I spoke with in Shung Him Tong, when pressed, admitted that many of the characteristics they assign to themselves may be as appropriately ascribed to a non-Hakka as to a Hakka. It is certainly possible, they agreed, to find thrifty, honest, clean, and hardworking non-Hakka, but those people are thought to display Hakka characteristics. When I asked about a very hard-working Cantonese woman who spoke fluent Hakka, Mr. C. jokingly responded, "Perhaps one of her parents was really Hakka?!" Stereotypes of non-Hakka may also fit certain Hakka individuals. In one conversation Yee Ling reluctantly agreed that it is possible to find a Hakka person who "wastes or squanders money." She looked around the restaurant to make sure no one could hear us talking, and then whispered that there were even young Hakka people in the newer part of Shung Him Tong who spent money on drugs and gambling. But these people, she warned me, should in no way be considered typically Hakka. Although many people I spoke to recognized the possible overgeneralization of their characterizations, on another level they also believed that the qualities ascribed to the Hakka exist as social facts.

In previous chapters I have suggested that Hakka of Shung Him Tong consider themselves at once Hakka, Chinese, and Christian, but that being Hakka does not mean that they share a particular Hakka "culture," Hakka customs, or even necessarily Hakka language. What many Shung Him Tong people do share, including those who I describe in the final section of this chapter as "staunch" Hakka and Hakka "skeptics," is a rhetoric of what it means to be Hakka, a sense that there are certain Hakka values and character traits that are embedded in Hakka history. As I describe in the following section, Hakka Christians of Shung Him Tong have constructed an image of Hakka identity that at once transforms negative characterizations of the Hakka into positive ones, identifies them with the Chinese in general, and corresponds to their image of good Christians.

HAKKA CHARACTER

Poverty, History, and Hard Work

Almost everyone in Hong Kong I asked, whether Chinese or non-Chinese, man or woman, young or old, university professor or street hawker, characterized the Hakka as poor. As one nineteenth-century Basel missionary noted: "If you were to ask a thorough-bred Punti about the character of the Hakkas, he would certainly, in the case of his condescending to acknowledge that he ever heard of such people, turn up his nose and tell you that the Hakkas are quite beneath your notice, that they are a kind of semi-barbarians, living in poverty and filth" (Eitel 1867:81). A young Cantonese schoolteacher explained to me as we rode the train from Tai Po to Fanling that she would not want to be Hakka; they are always poor and therefore must sweat and toil. She pointed to the construction workers and the farm laborers outside the window of the train as if to illustrate her point.

Everyone I asked in Shung Him Tong agreed that the Hakka were once very poor, but also indicated that this is no longer the case. As Ming Lee flatly stated, "Nobody is poor in Hong Kong anymore. Everyone has a place to live, education, and enough food." Nor did the people I asked consider the past poverty of the Hakka something negative. As one older man from Shung Him Tong explained, Hakka people are grateful that they were once poor; it is because Hakka have been relatively poorer on the whole than other Chinese that they learned the importance of thrift, frugality, and a simple way of life. Like many other people from Shung Him Tong, this man cited several members of the community as perfect examples: "Those brothers came from a poor family and that is why they learned to work hard." "His ancestors were poor, so they were forced to work very hard." The Ling, Pang, Cheung, and Tsui families were once poor, I was told, but because of the important Hakka traits that they exemplified they are now economically well off.

Hakka positive characteristics—that they are hardworking, honest, frugal, cooperative, and supportive of one another and have "egalitarian" gender roles—are all believed to stem from the fact that they were once poor. These Hakka qualities, another man explained, distinguish them from other Chinese because they are linked to the hardships, migrations, and poverty that only the Hakka experienced. To Hakka Christians, then, Hakka character is explained as having developed in the past and forms part of the collective Hakka memory. Such ideas about the Hakka are reinforced in the telling and retelling of Hakka, local, and family history. The same idea is expressed in the greater Hong Kong Hakka community. As written in the preface of a history of the International Hakka Association in Hong Kong: "There are several special characteristics of our people. . . . First is the frugality and industry of our people. Our forefathers could not have possibly survived the difficult times during their migration, had it not been [for] their power to endure the miseries and hardships of life. These fine qualities have now become our heritage" (Aw 1950:1–2). That the character of the ancestors is thought to have become the Hakka "heritage" implies that there are intrinsic characteristics belonging to all Hakka. Because of this legacy from the time of poverty, even people of Shung Him Tong who are now financially well off, I was told, can maintain their wealth because they continue to express Hakka qualities.

In Chinese peasant proverbs, in passages of Confucian texts, and in the words of the people in Shung Him Tong, we find indications that poverty in and of itself is not necessarily considered a negative thing, nor is wealth necessarily good. As one woman from Shung Him Tong said, it is certainly better to be poor and honest than wealthy and dishonest.[2] When Hakka are described by non-Hakka as poor, however, it does seem to carry negative connotations. The quotation from Eitel cited above implies that Punti were contemptuous of Hakka "poverty and filth." In the case of the Cantonese woman I spoke to on the train, poverty is not as distasteful as the idea that it seems endless and inescapable. The reason this young woman did not want to be Hakka was not only that they are poor but that, despite all their hard work, Hakka remain poor and must continue to "sweat and toil." There are other negative implications associated with this image of inescapable Hakka poverty.

One implication is that poverty is the result of human failings. An overwhelming number of the twentieth-century Chinese peasant proverbs compiled by Arkush (1984, 1990) convey the view widely held by people of Shung Him Tong that, "If man works hard the land will not be lazy" (1984:467). Another such proverb states, "Poverty comes, not from eating or clothing, but from inadequate planning" (1990:319). And still another dictates, "If men are industrious at plowing, and women at weaving, there will be enough to wear and to eat" (1990:322). As Arkush argues, very few of the proverbs he found expressed a fatalistic resignation toward poverty. They suggest that with hard work, frugality, cooperation, and "sufficient effort, properly directed, nothing is impossible" (1984:466–67). Thus, the implication of these proverbs is that the Hakka continue to be poor because they do not work hard.

But such is not the case. Hakka are widely reputed to be very hardworking. The Hakka and non-Hakka I spoke to, including the young woman on the train, shared the general perception of Hakka as industrious. If the image of Hakka poverty is not due to lack of effort or skill, then why does it persist?

While few of the proverbs Arkush found express a strong sense of fatalism— that "life is controlled by supernatural forces" (1984:466)—in this case, fate provides a possible explanation. As C. K. Yang notes, poverty is not necessarily considered a sign of moral or ethical failure, but the misfortunes that often accompany poverty may be. In traditional Buddhist thought, Yang explains, extreme poverty and other misfortunes can be ascribed to sins committed by an individual in this life or in a previous life (1961, 152).[3] This implies that alleged Hakka poverty may stem from the moral failure of individuals or of the Hakka as a whole. Confucian doctrine expresses such wisdom in this phrase: "Exert the utmost of human abilities, and then resign the rest to the decree of Heaven." Likewise, "It is up to man to plan things, but it is up to Heaven to decide their success" (C. Yang 1961:273). If one adheres to such beliefs, and believes also that the Hakka are always poor, then it follows that their misfortune stems from their own lack of effort, or from some supernatural cause. As Harrell explains: "Lots of people display the entrepreneurial virtues of hard work, thrift, frugality, moderate risktaking, and an ability to cooperate with and manipulate others, but not all succeed, in spite of these virtues. . . . When entrepreneurial and moral values fail to explain, fate comes in" (1987:99). If Hakka are poor despite their hard work, then fate, heaven, or some other supernatural cause may be the reason.

All the more insulting to the Hakka than their image of persistent poverty is the implication that the Hakka as a whole—not merely certain individuals—are fated to be poor. Why would such a group of people be fated to always live in poverty? This idea is linked, I suggest, to the ultimate insult: if the Hakka are collectively "not in good grace" or have "failed in their attempts to follow the right path," then they are not good Chinese.

Among many people in Shung Him Tong I found an explicit attempt to combat the negative images of the Hakka. Many people were ready to allay any doubts as to the outstanding moral character of the Hakka by listing numerous examples of famous, wealthy, well-respected, hardworking, patriotic, heroic, egalitarian, and scholarly Hakka from their community and in the broader arena of Chinese history. Most often cited are Dr. Sun Yat-sen, Hong Xiuquan, Deng Xiaoping, Paul Tsui, D. Y. Ling, Luo Xianglin, and Pang Lok Sam, each of whom demonstrate positive Hakka characteristics.

Negative characterizations of the Hakka persist, however. As one Cantonese businessman put it, the Hakka are poor and "don't like to spend money . . . but unlike other Chinese who are careful with their money, they don't get rich." The implication again is that Hakka express the Chinese virtue of frugality but cannot escape their poverty as have other Chinese. Hakka can list all the famous wealthy Hakka they can think of, but it does not weaken such an opinion. The stereotype of the Hakka as poor is so pervasive that wealthy Hakka are rarely thought of or recognized as Hakka, and Hakka outside of Shung Him Tong with ambitions for upward mobility often prefer not to identify themselves as Hakka.

The descriptions of Hakka character I collected in Shung Him Tong clearly are attempts to construct their identity in opposition to the stereotypes that non-Hakka assign to them. Negative qualities such as poverty and stinginess are transformed into positive characteristics: poverty is honorable, and stinginess is in fact thrift. Each of these qualities stands in contrast to the image the Hakka have of the wealth, laziness, corruption, and immorality of non-Hakka.

As described in Chapter 3, several Hakka Christians I spoke to believed that wealthy non-Christians, particularly the Punti Teng of Lung Yeuk Tau, often lack ethics and self-discipline and are therefore doomed to eventual economic decline. Yet by arguing that they themselves maintain the character of the poor even when their economic situation improves, Hakka Christians imply that they can gain financial success without fear of the inevitable "fall into despair within three generations" attributed to the Punti.

Cantonese—particularly shopkeepers—say that the Hakka do not easily part with their money. They interpret Hakka frugality as miserly behavior. The Cantonese, on the other hand, are characterized by the Hakka as wasteful, as evidenced not only by history but also in their day-to-day life. This is clear, I was told by Mrs. P., from the way the Cantonese throw out the stems of the *choisam,* a green leafy vegetable, eating only the leaves, whereas Hakka make use of the whole thing. To illustrate Hakka miserliness, "Pui Yan," a Cantonese woman, explained that her Hakka mother-in-law does not open the boxes of sweets she receives as gifts at the Chinese New Year but recirculates them when she goes to visit others. Although there is obviously nothing essentially Hakka or Cantonese about such practices, they are often interpreted as such.

Thrift, like other Hakka qualities, is said to be part of the Hakka heritage. At a restaurant with Pui Yan and her husband, a Shung Him Tong church member, the conversation seemed to follow a well-rehearsed pattern. The husband explained that the Hakka are very careful with their money.

"Stingy and miserly!" Pui Yan jokingly retorted.

He shook his head in disagreement and immediately shifted the conversation to the topic of his grandfather's frugality. As a boy, when he was very poor, his grandfather always carried his shoes to school and only put them on when he reached the schoolyard so as not to wear them out. But when he was older and had become quite wealthy he was known for his generosity and at the Chinese New Year always gave a hundred Hong Kong dollars to each of his many children and grandchildren.

Another commonly cited characteristic of the Hakka is that they are a tight-knit group with a spirit of cooperation and mutual support. As one Hakka woman put it, "Hakka are supportive of one another and they treat each other as brothers." Another Hakka man recently wrote to me that Hakka are famous for their "stubborn resistance" against invaders or oppressors. Most Hakka in Shung Him Tong would agree with a statement in a Hong Kong Hakka Association publication that the Hakka are known for their strong "spirit of unity and solidarity," which grew out of a need for Hakka forefathers to unite "to overcome difficulties and hindrances that lay before them" (Aw 1950:2). The general consensus among people I spoke to in the village is that in the face of nineteenth-century hardships, the Hakka allied themselves with their Hakka neighbors in order to defend themselves against Punti enemies. The famous ongoing feuds in Meixian and Wuhua between Hakka of different surnames, of which I was told in other conversations, were conveniently omitted in the context of this discussion.

Today there are few if any violent feuds or hostile Punti neighbors. (The conflict over the location of the new church is usually presented as either a Punti/Christian one or as an interpersonal one.) But the legacy of the Hakka forefathers is said to live on: because the Hakka were poor, they learned to co-operate. As the church evangelist explained, "Hakka people are very close-knit and very cooperative with one another; they exhibit much brotherly support." What is often interpreted as cooperation and unity by the Hakka implies ex-clusivity, "clannishness," and hostility to the non-Hakka I spoke to.

As mentioned above, a propensity to work hard is a well-known Chinese characteristic, and an important Hakka characteristic to the Hakka themselves. The Hakka work ethic is reflected in several popular sayings. As I discussed the founding of Shung Him Tong with two older men on different occasions, they both said, "*Hakka jim deihjyu,*" meaning, "Hakka take over and become land-lords." Although I only heard this expression from these two men of Shung Him Tong, both insisted that it is the way they are characterized by non-Hakka. With a mixture of pride and modesty, they admitted that it is true. In the words of one of these men, "The Hakka have the reputation of going through China usurping the land from the wealthy landlords and of working very hard." As he explained, this is how the Hakka were able to make their way in Shung Him Tong surrounded by the powerful Punti Teng lineage. Pas-tor Ling and Pang Lok Sam, he continued, started a mortgage company and gradually bought out Punti property. Like several others, these men contrasted Hakka dedication and hard work with the corruption and laziness that caused the eventual decline of the Teng.

Another popular Chinese phrase one of these men used to describe the Hakka was "*Hakka gaang duhk*" (lit., "Hakka plow study"), which is an abbre-viated version of *Hakka yahn gaang tihn duhk syu* (lit., "Hakka plow fields and study books"). The Hakka, he explained, were able to get ahead because they could do both. They value hard work, whether it be work in the fields or the work of the scholar. This man, like others from Shung Him Tong, expresses pride in his ancestors for having the foresight to attend missionary schools, work very hard, and escape their poverty.

Hakka Women

It has been well documented that Hakka often occupied the poorer, more iso-lated, and less fertile areas of Guangdong and Hong Kong during the nine-teenth and early twentieth centuries, while the Punti, like the Lung Yeuk Tau Teng, occupied the more productive fertile areas (M. Cohen 1968; Leong 1985). As a result of economic hardships, men from some Hakka villages chose to emigrate southward and overseas to find work, while Hakka women were left behind with the children and the elderly. The women tended the fields and participated in "men's" work (see Pratt 1960). But even in nonemigrant villages, according to one Tsung Tsin mission pastor, Hakka women worked at farming—"hoeing and planting seeds while the men would lead the buffaloes and plow the earth"—and thus earned their widespread reputation for hard work.

As Mr. C. explained, Hakka women are taught that they must be able to adapt to different situations and must work hard. At an early age, women of his generation learned the popular phrase, "*Jouhdak gunleuhng, cheutdak tengtong*" (Be an official's wife, come out to the drawing room). He interpreted this to mean that "they must know how to be an important official's wife, as well as cook and clean." They should be able to "talk to important guests," and also "know when to leave the drawing room and do hard work." With their reputation for hard work, Hakka women are often held up as exemplars of Hakka character.

Another Hakka man said that Hakka women are better prepared for hard work than non-Hakka women. This view is widely expressed throughout Hong Kong, where Hakka women have a reputation for hard work whether in the fields, on construction sites or on the golf course. Indeed, some non-Hakka farmers are said to have preferred a Hakka wife because they are believed to be more accustomed to hard work. According to Pasternak, whose research was conducted in Taiwan, "Hakka women everywhere enjoy a reputation as exceptional workers. I was often assured by Hokkien friends as well as by Hakka that Hakka women make exceptional wives for that reason" (1983:25).

Less agreement exists on the topic of Hakka men. Two Hakka women, and two non-Hakka women married to Hakka men, told me that Hakka men are lazy compared to their female counterparts. In the words of one young Hakka woman in Shung Him Tong, "There is one thing which is not so good about Hakka culture and that is that the women work harder than the men . . . but this was in the past." Yee Ling was not convinced that it is a thing of the past. She complained that her father wanted to be treated "like a king" and was too lazy to put toothpaste on his own toothbrush, let alone polish his own shoes. I found among Hakka men in Hong Kong, as Pasternak found among Hakka men in Taiwan, disagreement with the idea that they "spend a lot of time sitting around talking while their wives do all the work," although they are the first to agree that "their women are among China's most industrious" (1983:25).

The high rate of male absenteeism in many Hakka villages might explain such characterizations of Hakka men and women as that written by a nineteenth-century European traveler in Guangdong: "It seems to be mainly the women who do the hard work. They do not bind their feet . . . [and] are strong and erect. . . . [T]he women do all the carrying and heavy work. The men do not even know how to carry water—and probably do not demand that the women give them lessons at it" (In Aijmer 1967:75–76). Eugene Anderson was also told that Hakka "women work while the men sit and sing" in the Castle Peak area of Hong Kong where he conducted research. His explanation is that the men "once had to spend much of their time on guard against attacks, and left gardening and other such work to the women. Now, of course, both sexes work" (1968:98).

Most of the Hakka men I asked in Shung Him Tong insist that they are as hardworking as women, with the exception of "Heung Yee," a Hakka Christian in his forties who said that the one "really terrible thing about Hakka culture" is the way they treat boys: "Hakka spoil boys and give them everything. . . . It is well known that Hakka women are strong and hardworking. They have to be because the spoiled boys won't do any work. The men are so spoilt that the women have to do everything." All the boys from the village where he grew up go to the United Kingdom to be cooks, and "when they come back to Hong Kong they are lazy." Now when he returns to that village the old people there say to him, "You know why you grew up to be a good son? Because you were poor." It is important to note in this case that most members of the village where he grew up, including the "lazy young men," were not Christian. Heung Yee disagrees in part with their explanation. He and his brothers are successful, he says, partly because their parents raised them as Christians and taught them to respect hard work and education. While many Hakka will claim that whether they are rich or poor, male or female, there is seldom a loafer among them, according to one Christian Hakka man; Christianity provides further assurance that Hakka people will stay on the right track.

Related to their ability to work hard is the reputation of Hakka women for never having practiced the custom of foot-binding. The practice of foot-binding was a symbol of female subordination reflecting a woman's virtue and the moral standing of her family. It was a sign of high status—evidence that women did not need to partake in physical labor and rarely left the house. Although foot-binding was at first limited to elite families, by the nineteenth century it was a widespread practice among nonelites as well, with the exception of Hakka women and women in some of the tea- and silk-producing regions of southern China (Anagnost 1989:330). Yee Ling, Mr. C., Mr. P., and other Hakka I spoke to claim—and missionary sources also document—that regardless of their economic or social class, Hakka women's feet were never bound, "even if they were daughters of officials." According to one Hakka man in his seventies, "The other Chinese bound women's feet because they wanted to keep them in the house" and also, he grinned, "because it made women walk in a way which is very charming." But even if a Hakka family rose to a position of wealth and power, Hakka claim, daughters were still not required to bind their feet.

In the early twentieth century, condemned as morally reprehensible, foot-binding became a symbol of the oppression and exploitation of women and of all the ills of Confucian society. Although the Hakka practice of not binding women's feet has obvious practical implications, two people from Shung Him Tong claimed that the Hakka refrained from practicing foot-binding on moral grounds. Twentieth-century Hakka historians such as Luo have helped popularize the Hakka claim that they were the first to oppose foot-binding and to treat women as equals on ethical rather than practical grounds. The fact that Hakka women's feet were never bound has now become a part of the rhetoric used to support the idea that Hakka were ahead of their time and have "always treated women as equal." The official Chinese policy regarding foot-binding one man told me, was inspired by the Hakka. It is also commonly known that the Taipings condemned foot-binding and allowed women in positions of leadership.

In a folk narrative entitled "Why Can Hakka Girls Sing Mountain Songs?" told to Eberhard in Taiwan in the 1970s, a forty-seven-year-old Hakka woman recounted the story of a wealthy governor of Guangdong province who could afford to have whatever he wanted: "In spite of that he never married three wives or [had] four concubines, but lived very well with his old wife." The narrator explained that the man and his wife had "suffered the poverty together" and she had helped earn money for his studies. He never forgot what she had done. As the narrator explained,

> This tells us about the origin of the equality of love of the Hakka women, but it also tells us how the equality of sexes . . . had its origin, and that it is not a hollow word, but that the women with both feet on the ground carry on the problems of the family together with the men. And because Hakka women can live without men, they are not afraid if the men cheat upon them—they just cannot cheat on them. . . . Hakka are people who had to flee from suppression, and their surroundings are all poor, and so they all have to endure together. If one has to suffer, the others will help him, and so the Hakka girls work just as their men do; in contrast to other women, the Hakka women have as the first ones gained their position, and so they also sing songs that the others do not sing (Eberhard 1974:104–5).

This legend reflects Hakka pride at being "the first ones" to "gain the [higher] position of women" and stresses the point that the position of women is directly linked to their hard work and economic contributions to the family. It also reiterates the point that although most Hakka start out poor, when they become wealthy they still remember what it was like to be poor and for that reason they are better people of higher morals.

Although the people of Shung Him Tong take pride in the idea of Hakka gender equality, several young women pointed out to me that common practices in the church community do not substantiate this stereotype. As noted in Chapter 4, women appear on the surface to have equal roles in the church—there are always the same number of men and women who officiate, usher, and take collections at the Sunday service, and there are equal numbers of men and women on the church board. But those who are commemorated and best remembered are often men, and men are thought to be far more influential. In practice, like the "official's wife" described above who must cook and clean and be a good conversationalist with her husband's guests, women in Shung Him Tong perform many more of the "service" roles for the church, such as translating, teaching Sunday school, evangelizing, and working as secretaries.

Cantonese women have the reputation, I was told by a young woman in Shung Him Tong, of being among the most attractive and delicate of all Chinese women. Physical attractiveness—often symbolized by small delicate feet—is not a characteristic commonly associated with the popular image of Hakka women. When another young Hakka woman told me that the last two "Miss Hong Kong" beauty contest winners were Hakka, the statement expressed pride as well as her surprise and did not imply that all Hakka women are beautiful. Although people highlight the fact that Cantonese women are weak and frail in comparison to Hakka women, the physique of Hakka women is not portrayed as a positive aesthetic quality but rather as a practical asset.

Hakka are sometimes depicted as having darker skin than other Chinese—an observation used by non-Hakka to support the nineteenth-century claim that Hakka were descendants of hill tribes rather than pure Chinese. The Hakka, however, associate the possible darker skin of some individuals with the extrinsic factor of exposure to sunlight because they spend more time working outside. Conversely, people who work outside are often assumed to be Hakka. Hard work is also used to explain the "looser, more comfortable clothes of the Hakka" and certain culinary differences. "Hakka eat from larger bowls, and eat bigger portions," one Tsung Tsin mission pastor told me, "because they work hard and are very hungry."

Many of the physical stereotypes of Hakka women are in fact more accurate as class or occupational markers than as ethnic ones. Dark skin, comfortable shoes, muscular builds, and the "Hakka hat" are all indications that people do physical labor outdoors, not that they are necessarily Hakka. Common stereotypes found in daily conversation, on television, and in tourist brochures suggest that these images are of the Hakka, and thus reinforce the impression that all Hakka are poor and working class, and that all poor, outdoor workers must be Hakka.

Christian and Hakka Character

As was shown in Chapter 2, foreign missionaries contributed significantly to the debate on Hakka origins and many of them strongly supported the assertion that Hakka were pure Chinese. European missionaries also lent support to ideas of Hakka "high status" origins and provided the organizational structures—educational facilities and occupational opportunities—that facilitated the formation of a Hakka community. Women who had been raised in mission orphanages or educated in mission schools were married to educated Christian men, thus establishing a stronghold of Hakka Christian leadership, households, communities, and future generations of Hakka Christians. From the mission-educated Hakka emerged a Christian Hakka elite of educators and politicians who would certainly not be considered "country bumpkins" by any standards. These were not the only ways in which Christianity supported Hakka claims. In addition, Christian missionaries provided the Hakka with an ideological model through which they could claim moral superiority over other Chinese. As Christians, the Hakka could look on their heathen neighbors with new disdain.

As was discussed earlier, nineteenth-century Protestant missionaries approached the poorest and most marginal members of Chinese society as those most likely to accept Christianity (cf. Breslin 1980). Although in fact a relatively small number of Hakka converted, Hakka were considered likely converts, and as the missionaries got to know them, it seemed to some as though they were better suited to become Christians than other Chinese. Some missionaries believed that there was something in the character of the Hakka that would make them better Christians or more likely to become Christian than other Chinese. As Moser asserts, "Some early Christian missionaries . . . looked upon the Hakka as candidates for recognition as one of the lost tribes of Israel" (1985:236). Many Hakka Christians today also perceive of themselves as the "chosen" people among the Chinese, a view which many believe the missionaries shared.

Hakka customs and character are now described by some Hakka Christians as though they have always corresponded perfectly with the customs and character of pious Christians. One man's depiction of his ancestors made them appear as though they were in essence Chinese Christians just waiting to be discovered: one might say, proto-Christians.[4] Other people I spoke to thought that conversion to Christianity involved a major shift in values from "uncivilized" paganism to "civilized" Christianity. In either case, the implication among Hakka Christians I spoke to was not only that Hakka make better Christians but also that there are, and have perhaps always been, important similarities between Christian and Hakka character.

Many characteristics that I was told describe the Hakka—such as being honest, hardworking, simple and practical folk—can also be interpreted as Christian or Chinese values. Other features that Hakka Christians described to me as essentially Hakka—such as a moral disdain for begging, prostitution, polygyny, opium smoking, gambling, and foot-binding—are likely to have been invented by Hakka Christians in retrospect, after contact with the missionaries. Although one might argue that some of these "immoral" practices—such as opium smoking and polygyny—might have been less frequent among the Hakka before they converted than among other Chinese, their economic situation was more likely the cause of these "Hakka traits" than pre-Christian piety.

Missionary writings suggest that at least some missionaries became convinced of Hakka superiority. Whether the Hakka convinced them or vice versa, it is clear that the two views reinforced each other. Both assert that Hakka religion was closer to monotheism, that their treatment of women was superior, and that Hakka were more likely to be monogamous than other Chinese. What might have begun as enthusiasm and optimism among European missionaries over their new potential converts gradually became reinterpreted by some missionaries and by the Hakka themselves into reinforcement of their superiority over other Chinese.

Missionaries do not appear to have always categorically considered the Hakka better or more likely candidates for Christianity than other Chinese. But by the end of the nineteenth and early twentieth centuries, the same optimism that characterized Hamberg's writing about the early Taipings was again evident in European missionaries' descriptions of the Hakka, and they became quite the Hakka apologists. Eitel (1867, 1868, 1869) does not suggest that Hakka "Character, Custom and Manners" are generally superior to other Chinese, except perhaps in aspects of the way they treat women and in the more "monotheistic" tendency of their religious beliefs. Like many others, he found the Hakka poor and very hardworking, but he also said that their homes, temples, and ancestral halls were not as clean as those of the Punti (1867:81). After living several years among the Hakka, Eitel shared the view that the Hakka are "an honest and open-hearted set of people" (1867:82) but that

> There is less intelligence among them than there is among the
> Puntis, but there is also less malice, and there is especially less of
> that ridiculous pride with which these Puntis look down upon the
> hated foreign devils [westerners], considering themselves, in spite
> of all the severe lectures they have got, infinitely superior as regards morality, knowledge and power (1867:82).

According to Eitel, the Punti had "intellectual superiority" over the Hakka, and he was frustrated by the fact that Punti "still look down with as much insolence and pride upon us foreigners, as they look down upon those Hakkas" (1867:83).

Another Basel missionary, Lechler, who was "driven out seven times by the Hoklo" before he finally "turned his attention to the Hakka" (Oehler 1922:352), agreed with Eitel's evaluation that "on the whole the Hakkas are not as bigoted as the Puntis" and significantly, "the Gospel has found easier access to them than to the latter" (Lechler 1878:358). Concerning the position of women, Eitel wrote, "To all outward appearance the position of woman seems to be worse among the Hakkas" because she had to do as much heavy outdoor work as men, while Punti women were kept indoors. Non-Hakka women were also more likely to obtain some education and were "cleaner and tidier in their habits" (1867:98). By the end of his discussion, however, Eitel extended his palm to the Hakka because he concluded that "the position of a Hakka woman is certainly more natural and healthy" than those of Punti and Hoklo women, and that they were more likely to have "a happy family life, because it is less hampered by such crying evils as polygamy and female slavery, which nip the growth of affection between man and wife almost in the bud and give little chance for the enjoyment of a quiet and happy home life" (1867:98). But lest he provide too optimistic a view of the Hakka, Eitel also added that the Hakka practice of female infanticide "might appear to justify the imputation of semi-barbarism which Puntis are wont to throw upon them" (1867:98).

Other missionaries such as Lechler and Oehler found the Hakka much more praiseworthy. Oehler observed that "Hakka girls are never sold as second wives or concubines" (1922:352) and that Hakka would rather practice female infanticide—"a custom springing out of the respect in which women are held"—than sell them into slavery (1922:352). To Oehler the Hakka were "healthy, rapidly expanding, active, energetic, and fond of acquiring property. They are a people of the future, unhampered by the prejudices or the easy-going slackness of the old landowners" (1922:352). He also found the Hakka "less clannish" and therefore more approachable by missionaries than either the Punti or Hoklo. These views, significantly, reflect many of the contemporary Hakka characterizations of themselves.

Instead of finding the Hakka less intelligent than the Punti, Oehler, Lechler, and Campbell all remark on the famous Hakka prefecture of Kaying (Meixian), the "abode of scholars, [which] provides the clerks of the court for the majority of the yamens [officials] of China" (Oehler 1922:352). According to Campbell the Hakka had "as high a level of education and culture as can be found in the province" (1912:474). The Hakka demonstrated "political aptitude" and the "military genius of the race" was displayed in their involvement in the Taiping Rebellion (ibid.). Oehler, Lechler, and Campbell, in contrast to Eitel, all mention the extreme cleanliness of the Hakka: "Their custom of daily bathing makes them more cleanly in person . . . than most Chinese" (1912:473). As Blake has pointed out in his study of the New Territories community of Sai Kung, Hakka songs also seem to have many references to bathing (1975:108). The Hakka greeting, "Have you had your bath yet?" (which is still common in Shung Him Tong and in Sai Kung), reflects their concern with cleanliness and purity. They have also been praised for their "love of liberty" (Campbell 1912:473; Oehler 1922:352).

Like these European missionaries, the Hakka of Shung Him Tong I spoke to believed that the Hakka cherish hard work and thrift, qualities that can be interpreted as both traditionally Chinese and Protestant. Several people expressed the Protestant view that an "[u]nwillingness to work is symptomatic of the lack of grace" (Weber [1930] 1958:159), and that poor and hardworking Hakka are far better off than wealthy lazy Cantonese. Their opinions fit well with what Weber wrote in *The Protestant Ethic and the Spirit of Capitalism,* that "even the wealthy shall not eat without working, for even though they do not need to labour to support their own needs, there is God's commandment which they, like the poor, must obey" ([1930] 1958:159–60). This does not mean that the Hakka Christians I spoke with believe that wealth is bad in and of itself, only "in so far as it is a temptation to idleness and sinful enjoyment of life, and its acquisition is bad only when it is with the purpose of later living merrily and without care" (ibid., 163). As Mr. P. explained, the poor are far more likely to avoid immoral temptations than the wealthy. In contrast to the relatively ascetic Hakka, non–Hakka are thought to place more value on leisure activities and the conspicuous pleasures of this world that wealth can provide. Several Hakka Christians shared "the highest ethical appreciation of the sober, middle-class, self-made man" that Weber describes ([1930] 1958:163). It is not an overgeneralization to suggest that many Hakka of Shung Him Tong view themselves as sober and self-made, as opposed to the ostentatious, idle, and sinful Punti.

The Hakka of Hong Kong, however, do not share—either among themselves or among outsiders—the popular Hong Kong Chinese or Protestant reputation for business success. Shung Him Tong is considered more "middle class" and educated than most Hong Kong "villages," but it is not known for its thriving entrepreneurial enterprises. Pang Lok Sam's mortgage company, which in its day was fairly prosperous, is rarely spoken of except by Pang's relatives. One of Heung Yee's brothers, a man in his early forties, explained that there are not many Hakka who are famous in business because it often requires immoral or unethical behavior. He expressed the traditional Chinese preference for advancement through academic achievement or government service (see Skinner 1976:343). Like other Hakka Christians, this man explained that in order to be successful in business—as in local politics—one must be willing to be dishonest. The few businessmen of Shung Him Tong, including Mr. P., claimed that being Hakka is in no way an advantage in their work, and to be a good Christian and a good businessman at the same time presents a dilemma. Two men who were not as successful in commerce as they would like to be explained to me that it is because they are good Christians.

Instead of expressing pride in commercial success, the people of Shung Him Tong claim achievements in the fields of education, politics, and civil service— fields traditionally held in high esteem by both the Chinese and the church community. Although the Protestant ethic equates business success with grace and salvation, wealth for the people of Shung Him Tong is often a sign of corruption. They believe and are reassured by the fact that their reward will come later.

The connection between hard work and moral and ethical behavior is clear in depictions of Hakka women. As Mr. C. explained, because Hakka women are not afraid to work hard, they are never prostitutes, or beggars. When I asked him if the old beggar woman who he spoke to in Hakka at the train station was Hakka, he was visibly flustered. On another occasion he had described her black head cloth and woven band as things that only Hakka women would wear. In an attempt to reconcile his statements he said that she is from a Hakka region of China but that her behavior is very unusual for a Hakka woman.

Rather than beg or become prostitutes, Mr. C. also explained, Hakka women prefer to become servants or even construction workers. Hakka from Shung Him Tong often gave credit to a dedicated and hardworking ancestor— surprisingly often a mother, grandmother, or great-grandmother—for his or her conversion to Christianity. One church elder's mother, for example, became a widow when he was eight years old and went to ask the missionaries for work. As the story is told, she was not afraid of hard work so she became their domestic servant. The missionaries realized that she was honest and hardworking, so they taught her about Christianity. This is a common scenario in the biographies of Hakka women converts in the Basel Mission Archives. Work among the missionaries became an important option for widows, female orphans, and unmarried women. People of Shung Him Tong cited many examples of women who were widowed or never married, who went to work for the mission or became Bible women or evangelists.[5] These women are also presented as models of Hakka character.

Gender and the Chinese Work Ethic

Shung Him Tong people believe that Hakka character entails an ethic of hard work, frugality, and diligence that can be rationalized as good Christian behavior. These qualities are also widely described as Chinese by both Chinese and western writers (for sources see Harrell 1985:204–9). In an article that attempts to go beyond this common stereotype of hardworking Chinese, Harrell defines what he calls an "entrepreneurial ethic" widely held by many Chinese, which helps to explain why in practice *not* all Chinese work hard. Particularly important to the present study is that Harrell's concept of an "entrepreneurial ethic" is not narrowly restricted to those involved in business or commerce but can apply as well to peasant farmers, scholars, preachers, or any other occupation. He writes, "By entrepreneurship I mean the investment of one's resources (land, labor, and/or capital) in a long-term quest to improve the material well-being and security of some group to which one belongs and with which one identifies" (1985:216). In other words, farmers or scholars—including those who enter mission schools—can express an entrepreneurial ethic as well as those involved in marketing and business because they share a common goal: their efforts can directly benefit the long-term interests of their families. This entrepreneurial ethic is future-oriented; its aim is not merely to make quick money but to "to establish hedges and defenses against loss," and thus frugality is also important (1985:216). In contrast to the Protestant attitude that one must work hard only because it is good to work hard, the Chinese attitude, Harrell argues, comes into play "when they see possible long-term benefits, in terms of improved material conditions and/or security, for a group [such as a kin group] with which they identify" (1985:217).[6]

This entrepreneurial ethic was applicable, according to Harrell, to just about every man in traditional China because he could see the clear connection between his hard work and the benefits and security of his family. But in modern capitalist Chinese society there are situations in which an ethic of hard work is not found because, as in a large factory in Taiwan in the 1960s cited by Harrell, workers knew that no amount of effort or hard work would enable them to get ahead.

Chinese women, Harrell speculates, were socialized with the same values as men but have less motivation to work hard because of their "structural position" in society. He writes, "I would propose that it is simply because of the patrilocal family system that the entrepreneurial ethic did not make as much sense for women, particularly young women, in traditional or modern capitalist Chinese society" (1985:221). For unmarried women it made little sense to work hard, according to Harrell, since they would marry out of the family; and for married women, the primary entrepreneurial strategy was to motivate sons to work hard for the family. This also explains, to Harrell, why nineteenth-century texts do not describe Chinese women as hardworking.

Harrell's article raises some important issues for this study. First, it suggests that the Hakka image of diligence, frugality, and hard work is congruent with a broader Chinese work ethic. It also fits, on the surface, with Protestant values, although the underlying motivation for hard work is different. Second,

Harrell's broader definition of "entrepreneurial" enables us to explain how Hakka can display an entrepreneurial ethic but not necessarily be involved in commerce. Finally, Harrell's paper raises several questions with regard to Hakka gender roles (see Basu 1991a).

The widespread reputation of hardworking Hakka women—and the not quite so widespread reputation of lazy Hakka men—recorded by many nineteenth-century observers and still expressed today is quite the reverse of the wider pattern that Harrell describes. According to Harrell's line of argument, since Hakka women in the nineteenth century did indeed appear motivated to work hard, their structural position within society must not have been the same as that of other Chinese women; in other words, Hakka women must have worked hard because, unlike other Chinese women, they believed they could contribute to the future economic security of their families. However, this was not the case. Hakka women also married into their husband's families, and therefore a patrilocal postmarital residence pattern cannot provide an adequate explanation.

It is still possible, however, to argue that the position of women within their families is an important factor, because the position of Hakka women within their families may have been somewhat different from that of other Chinese women (see also E. Johnson 1992). As mentioned earlier, Hakka women during the nineteenth century were less likely to have bound feet than Cantonese women, and they were more likely than other women to work outside of the home and to contribute to the family income by participating in farm work and marketing (see Blake 1981:51–59; Basu 1991a). These differences not only account for the different stereotype of Hakka women but also help to explain why, as Harrell suggests, nineteenth-century western observers did not describe other Chinese women as hardworking. Because of their active role in the public sphere, Hakka women were more likely to be observed doing hard work. Non-Hakka women were more likely to be restricted to the domestic sphere, where their diligence would be less visible to outside observers. Furthermore, it may be possible to argue that Hakka women were symbolically better integrated into their husband's families than Cantonese women. This assertion demands further substantiation, but one Hong Kong study suggests that Hakka women generally have more active and prominent roles in kinship rituals than their Cantonese counterparts (E. Johnson 1992). If, as these factors suggest, the family position of Hakka women was in fact different from that of other Chinese women, and they felt they "belonged" to the family more than other Chinese women, then this would help to explain their greater motivation to contribute to it economically through hard work.

As the material above repeatedly illustrates, hard work is of central importance to Hakka self-definition. Hard work is a Chinese virtue, a Hakka virtue, and a Christian virtue. Chinese tradition dictates that hard work be performed in order to better the future situation of the family or some other group. As Protestants, the people of Shung Him Tong are taught that poverty is not a bad thing and that they should enjoy hard work for its own sake.

After a friend in Shung Him Tong explained for the fifth or sixth time that the Hakka are honest and hardworking, I finally asked him if the Cantonese were not as well. "Of course Cantonese parents teach their children to be honest and hardworking," he answered, "but the Hakka are even more likely to be so because of their history. They have had to be to survive."

"And what about Christians?" I asked.

He thought for a moment, and then answered, "Well, the Cantonese may be honest and hardworking, the Hakka are even more so, and the Hakka Christians would be even more likely to be."

STAUNCH HAKKA AND HAKKA SKEPTICS

In Shung Him Tong, those who consider Hakka identity very important and those who find it irrelevant share many of the same ideas about Hakka character and its distinctive traits. These shared ideas have been shaped by the Hakka church community and the greater Hong Kong Hakka community, but they also reflect an attempt to influence the more widespread image of the Hakka.

In this final section I draw together some materials that have been cited earlier to describe several Hakka Christian individuals whose lives and attitudes demonstrate different degrees of interest in, awareness of, and commitment to their Hakka identity. The people I shall describe fall between two extremes found among the people of Shung Him Tong, which I shall refer to as "staunch" Hakka and "skeptical" Hakka.

Many individuals are inconsistent in their views. For example, in one conversation a church board member told me that Hakka identity is very important, the backbone of the community, and something to be proud of, but in another discussion he espoused the view that Hakka exclusivity is wrong and goes against the teachings of Christianity.

It is also important to stress that even though people disagree on the current relevance of Hakka identity, and many think it is diminishing, there is very little disagreement among Hakka Christians on the issue of who the Hakka are, and the various characterizations of the Hakka. As I have asserted in previous chapters, Hakka ethnicity is relevant to the lives of the people of Shung Him Tong, even for those who do not consider it important. Ethnic conflicts may be rare, but Hakka identity still underlies many of the social patterns and ideological constructs of the people of Shung Him Tong.

Staunch Hakka actively espouse the importance of Hakka identity and are vehemently opposed to allowing the younger generation to forget that they are Hakka. They are proud of being Hakka and are described by others in the community as "very Hakka." Among those who best illustrate this view are the Hakka historian Luo Xianglin, the early village leader Pang Lok Sam, and church board member Mr. C. Luo has been referred to as "Mr. Hakka" (M. Cohen 1988, personal communication); Pang was portrayed by one Hong Kong government official as "the King of Hakkas" (Hong Kong Government 1955); and Mr. C., in the words of several young villagers, is someone who "knows everything about the Hakka."

Luo commuted from Hong Kong Island to Shung Him Tong every Sunday for over twenty years to attend Sunday services at the Hakka church. He was a respected church member who served as an advisor to the church kindergarten and as an elder of the church until his death in 1978. Luo was known among Hakka worldwide as a Hakka advocate and spokesperson. It is not a coincidence that such a person was in part a product of Shung Him Tong. He wrote numerous books about the Hakka, about Chinese history, and about the church and Hong Kong Hakka Association that are widely cited in commemorative volumes of Hakka organizations worldwide. The genealogies he collected from members of the church became part of the evidence he cited in his writings on Hakka history and migrations.

According to Luo's daughter, being Hakka was for her father "a way to be Chinese despite being Christian." His interest and involvement in the Hakka reached well beyond the bounds of Shung Him Tong. As a leader in the Luo family association, he initiated a project to establish an ancestral hall in Lo Uk village in the New Territories for the surname Luo that would be acceptable to both Christians and non-Christians. Generous donations were received from many overseas Luo Christians and the hall was designed so that on one side non-Christians could worship and make offerings to their ancestors, and on the other Christians could pray and demonstrate their respect to Christian ancestors. His daughter explained that he was willing to give up ancestor worship but reluctant to forsake the ancestral hall as a memorial, as a place to honor both Christian and non-Christian ancestors, and as a place to demonstrate filial piety. He was acutely aware that ancestral tablets were concrete representations of the connection with the past, and expressions of Chinese identity. Likewise, he understood that the Shung Him Tong cemetery and its grave markers serve as a genealogy of the community, a substitute for an ancestral hall and tablets, and a reflection of the history of the community.

Pang Lok Sam, who died in 1947, is also remembered as a respected and important member of the community. He is also depicted by many Hakka in

Shung Him Tong and the surrounding regions as a staunch Hakka. Pang was less reflexive concerning his Hakka identity than was Luo. To him, Hakka identity was not a subject for debate but a matter of pride and allegiance. A Hong Kong government official referred to Pang as the King of Hakkas because of his role in New Territories politics both as a founder of the Heung Yee Kuk and as an advocate for Hakka Christians and non-Christians. He helped to establish the local Hakka school, the Hakka Christian cemetery, and Shung Him Church. Pang also founded Luen Wo Tong for Hakka throughout the Fanling region, and like Luo was a well-known member of the Hong Kong Hakka Association. For many years he was a preacher at several different Hakka churches. I was told by two young people from Lung Yeuk Tau that Hakka people from all over Hong Kong went to Pang for help in resolving local feuds and conflicts. A young Hakka non-Christian brother and sister from a Lung Yeuk Tau village described how Pang had been invited to help settle a feud in their family many years ago over the inheritance and rights of two wives in a polygynous marriage.

Hakka Christians such as Pang Lok Sam maintained through their actions that Chinese and Christian beliefs and identities could be reconciled. Although a strict and pious Christian, Pang had a distinct idea about which Chinese practices and customs represented important continuities between the past and the present. The most important, perhaps, was his tribute to the ancestors in the form of a genealogical history of Shung Him Tong, which demonstrated not only how the Hakka community was established and the conflicts in which they were victorious but also the genealogical histories of the Hakka households and their unquestionably Chinese origins (see chap. 3).

Pang was known as a very strict father and a pious Christian. As one close relative explained, before they went to bed each night he would lecture his children on some moral issue: his opposition to birth control; his desire that they marry Hakka spouses; or his favorite subject, that they should not strive to be rich. If God allowed them to become wealthy, he told them, they should appreciate it and not waste their money. If they became poor, then they should learn to become even more frugal.

He was also a filial son and arranged for his father's bones to be transported from Baoan to Shung Him Tong for burial. Although there was no ancestral altar in the main hall of his house, he arranged furniture, ornaments, and portraits of himself and other family members in a special way and dictated in his will that nothing in the hall be changed without the unanimous consent of his descendants. His concern for continuing the line of descent was traditionally Chinese. Although he had twelve children, four daughters and eight sons, one of his sons died young and without an heir. Pang arranged that one of his grandsons be adopted so as to continue that branch of the family. Pang was instrumental in founding the Shung Him Tong community cemetery, yet he selected his own private site with a Chinese-style grave on the opposite hillside, which he hoped would serve as an exclusive family site. Each of these actions represents a conscious connection to the past, and an assertion of his Chinese identity.

Today there are still several people in Shung Him Tong who can be considered staunch Hakka. They are mostly among the older generation of men in the community and are people who are very active in the church. Mr. C.'s daughter explained to me that her father would love to tell me everything about the Hakka, because his children had heard his stories many times and were tired of them. Mr. C. is in his early seventies and prides himself on the fact that his grown children all speak Hakka at home. He explained that it is important for people to study the Hakka:

> Hakka have different culture and traditions. The Hakka language, history, and the customs of the people are different because they are hardworking and honest. Cantonese are lazier because they were richer. Cantonese think of Hakka as inferior, uneducated, and aggressive, but Hakka people have shown that they are wrong. Fifty years ago it used to be like that. Other people may try to be good and honest and hardworking, but Hakka people have had to be. For example in Shung Him Tong at first it was all poor farmers. They didn't let people bully them but they got together and organized to resist other people. They got education and built a church and a school. The other people in the area have no such organizations. The Hakka people would farm and dig and build buildings and work very hard and show that they are not the way other people think of them. Other people don't have the same capabilities as Hakka people. They might smoke opium and gamble away their money. They can't hold on to their money because they are weak.

Particularly noteworthy is the fact that he explains the success of the settlers of Shung Him Tong in terms of their Hakka, rather than their Christian, identity.

Like many members of the older generation, Mr. C. was not born in Hong Kong; he was born and raised in a small village in Meizhou. His mother—the sister of Pang Lok Sam's wife, and also the sister of the first Tsui to settle in Shung Him Tong—became widowed when he was young and was trained as an evangelist by the Basel missionaries. He prides himself not only on his own Basel mission ancestry, but also on that of his wife. Both of them are related to Cheung Fuk Hing and Tsui Fuk Kwong, the first converts in the region of Wuhua. He first came to Hong Kong with his uncle Tsui Yan Sam in 1928 when he was fourteen. It was only after he arrived in Hong Kong that he said he began to realize what it meant to be Hakka. He joined the Hakka association and the Hakka church.

Mr. C. attended Wah Yan College in Hong Kong and was later hired as an interpreter for the British army in Hong Kong. During the Japanese war, in the 1940s, he worked with the British Army Aid Group as an interpreter training Chinese soldiers. At that time he went to Hunan, where he was surprised to find many people with whom he could communicate in Hakka. From then until his retirement, he worked for a large international import-export firm based in Hong Kong. Mr. C. is considered a dedicated church member and has been very active in the organization of the church. Among his many duties, he has served on the church board, as headmaster and codirector of the kindergarten, and on the cemetery planning committee, and has taught a Hakka reading and writing class for church members. He collects written versions of Hakka mountain songs and is an avid scholar of Hakka and church history.

Among the people who are more staunch Hakka in Shung Him Tong today are those who say they attend Shung Him Church *because* it is Hakka, who insist that the sermons or at least part of the services be spoken in Hakka, and who say that the church should help the young people maintain or improve their spoken Hakka skills. They tell their children about the Hakka, and believe they instill Hakka values in them. Many are very knowledgeable regarding Hakka history and take great pleasure in telling stories about the Hakka past. However, the knowledge of Hakka history, character, and customs is not limited to the staunch Hakka.

The image of the skeptical Hakka comes across best in an interview I conducted with Mr. T., a Hakka Catholic who has several relatives in Shung Him Tong today but who spent only a few years of his childhood in the village. His father, who was Pang Lok Sam's brother-in-law, built a house in Shung Him Tong. Mr. T. received a university education in England, attained a high rank in the Hong Kong government, and lives in a posh apartment in an exclusive neighborhood on Hong Kong Island. Several people from Shung Him Tong cited Mr. T. as an example of a "successful Hakka," a man who is wealthy, educated, and well known. He does not think of himself as Hakka, or as a member of the Shung Him Tong community. When I explained to him that my research focuses on the Hakka, he responded, "Why not study the Chaozhou? They're much more interesting." Asked why he thought so, he replied, "They are much more successful. Hakka who become successful are no longer Hakka." From the very start of our conversation, it was clear that he did not consider Hakka identity important, or that he would not admit its importance to me. He did not teach his children to speak Hakka or expect them to marry Hakka. He did, however, know a great deal about Hakka history and origins, and although he had not read Luo's books, he knew of them and knew their content. Given the connection between Hakka consciousness and member-ship in Shung Him Tong, it is not surprising or insignificant that this man is Catholic. He does not attend Shung Him Church, does not consider himself a part of the community, and does not share the Hakka pride of many of the church leaders and elders.

Few of the Hakka women I met would qualify as either staunch Hakka or as Hakka skeptics, although they were often held up as exemplifying Hakka traits or as the bearers of Hakka tradition. Their reputation for hard work and strict morals, the food they cook and the clothes they wear, served as popular symbols of Hakka identity, but it was primarily men who seemed most out-spoken in their concern with the continuity and definitions of the Hakka. Men in particular focused on village genealogies and broader Hakka history. It is not that the women did not define themselves as Hakka; rather, older women were less reflexive with regard to Hakka identity, and younger ones, like younger men, seemed far less interested in Hakka and community history. Discussions with older Hakka women concerning Hakka identity often started with them identifying themselves as Hakka and describing certain Hakka characteristics, foods, or customs, but less often reflecting on ethnic conflicts or Hakka his-tory. Young women, like young men, usually identified themselves as Hakka and told me about Hakka character, but either echoed the evangelist's position that Hakka identity was not important to the community or said they were not sure how much it mattered.

A young woman in her early twenties, whom I will call "Yan Ying," is a good example. She has an older sister who went to Europe a few years ago af-ter she was married to a church member who works for a restaurant overseas. Her older brother works as a mechanic in a nearby town and hopes one day to become a pastor if he can afford the schooling. Her younger brother works in a small factory, and her sister attends secondary school. Her parents were once both farmers, but now her father, who does not like to work much, does some construction work in Kowloon. Her mother, who likes her work, is a janitor in a factory. Yan Ying does most of the cooking and cleaning for her family, and two nights a week she attends night school, where she studies art and design. One older board member described her as very hardworking and pious. She attends church regularly, attends the Hakka language class, belongs to the choir, and helps with the Sunday school and youth groups. Her younger siblings prefer to speak Cantonese at home, so her family does not speak Hakka as much as they once did. She considers herself Hakka and thinks that Hakka are good, hardworking people. She hopes to marry someone who is Christian from the Tsung Tsin churches and perhaps also Hakka, but she has resisted the attempts older women have made to "introduce" her to young men. She likes that Shung Him Tong is a Hakka church, but like other young people, she expressed some concern that this feature might exclude others. Many women I met were like Yan Ying, neither staunch Hakka nor Hakka skeptics.

In discussions about the future of Shung Him Church and the community, the difference between skeptical and staunch Hakka becomes most evident. To the staunch Hakka, the future of the church and community is in attracting more Hakka people as new church members. They correctly argue that, as long as it is a Hakka church, Hakka people will be more likely to join. As the skeptics are quick to point out, in the words of a European missionary, "God does not shine one day on the Hakka, one day on the Punti, and one day on the Chaozhou. To God they are all brothers." In other words, pointing out distinctions between ethnic groups serves to reinforce them, is divisive, and serves to exclude non-Hakka from the church. This creates a paradox of which many Shung Him Tong church members are well aware: the strength of the church at present is that it is a Hakka church. Most members attend because they grew up there, because they know people there, and because the sermons are delivered in Hakka. The goal of the church members, however, is to attract more people to the church. An increasing number of the residents of the surrounding areas are not Hakka, or are Hakka who consider their Hakka identity unimportant and at present do not seem interested in joining a Hakka church.

The problem was clearly illustrated by a businessman, Mr. P., born and raised in Shung Him Tong, who was an excellent source of information on the community, and who is a member of a prominent church family. In a plan for the development of the village, he suggested building a "middle-class" condominium complex. The project would not only make him wealthy, he said, but would also attract the better educated, wealthier "managerial" class, who would come to work at the new industrial estate adjacent to Shung Him Tong. When I commented on this plan, saying that the new residents may not be Hakka, he laughed and said that was unimportant. What was important was that it would provide hundreds of new souls for the evangelist to save. "If God is willing," he added, "my plan will succeed." His businessman's point of view is rationalized and very much supported by his Protestant ethic—the idea, as Tawney put it, that

> Labour is not merely an economic means: it is a spiritual end.
> Covetousness, if a danger to the soul, is a less formidable menace
> than sloth. So far from poverty being meritorious, it is a duty to
> choose the more profitable occupation. So far from there being an
> inevitable conflict between money-making and piety, they are
> natural allies, for the virtues incumbent on the elect—diligence,
> thrift, sobriety, prudence—are the most reliable passport to com-
> mercial prosperity (Tawney in Weber 1958:3).

Thus if, as described above, most Hakka Christians consider business success incompatible with Christian ethics, some at least think it better to evangelize by way of commercial growth and prosperity than to preserve an ethnic identity based on frugality.

The younger generations, in their twenties to forties, like most people in the community, usually fall somewhere between the staunch and the skeptical points of view. One university-educated man in his forties said:

> I admire the hard work and struggle to make a living of the Hakka .... In the past the Hakka lived on the less well-to-do, less fertile land . . . and they have somehow developed a kind of diligence. So would you say diligence is a trait of the Hakka or not? I don't know if it's really a trait or if it's only a myth. But observing and thinking about my grandmother, I somehow have the idea that they are hardworking and they are straightforward people, they aren't as prone to deception. . . . Maybe this is the mark of being country people, of living a very simple life.

According to Yee Ling, the young schoolteacher in her thirties who grew up in Shung Him Tong and who faithfully attends church each week, "To the people of Shung Him Tong, being Hakka is something to be proud of." She is not sure if the same holds true for Hakka outside of the church, however, because most people she knows from school and work are Cantonese: "Hakka people are . . . hardworking, thrifty, and practical, not like the Punti who like to have a good time. . . . When they [the Punti] make money they just become opium addicts, in contrast to people like my grandfather who were poor and saved a little bit of money so he could buy some land." As the comments of the man and woman above reflect, younger people often view Hakka identity as something exhibited by their grandparents' generation. People in their teens and twenties, like Yan Ying and Ming Lee, the factory worker described in Chapter 4, usually identify themselves as Hakka and have some sense of what that means, but they know relatively little about Hakka history and Hakka-Punti conflicts.

Christianity plays a far more obvious role in the lives of most members of the younger generation—particularly those under thirty—than does Hakka identity. They consciously think of their friends as Christian, but often take for granted that they are also Hakka. Christianity is a far more common topic of conversation—in fact, to them it is a burning issue. They believe it their duty to approach all friends and acquaintances to try to convince them to become Christian, but they seldom discuss Hakka identity. Most of the people they know outside the community do not speak Hakka, and even among themselves they often speak Cantonese. Although all the youth group members I knew said it did not matter if they married someone Hakka, at least eight of the ten people I know who have been married since I left Shung Him Tong have married other Hakka church members. It is thus possible that as they get older they will become more interested in their Hakka identity. At present they find Hakka identity irrelevant to the pressing concerns of "modernity"; but this does not mean that Hakka identity will not become a modern concern.

Unlike the young people in the village today, Luo and Pang, and to a lesser extent Mr. C., were influenced by the memory and the experience of Hakka-Punti conflicts and ethnic discrimination. They knew firsthand that Shung Him Tong would never have been established without unity in the Hakka community. There are few young people in Shung Him Tong today who appear to be as staunch Hakka as Pang, Luo, and Mr. C., but this does not mean that Hakka identity is necessarily diminishing or disappearing. As I have argued earlier, the more blatant instrumental aspects of Hakka ethnicity have certainly diminished over the past few decades, but Hakka identity is a far more complicated, less predictable issue.

It is likely that the young people in Shung Him Tong will become increasingly aware of the line of continuity between past and future generations, and the history and future of the community, as they grow older. From conversations with older members of the community, from sermons, from the church newsletters and commemorative issues describing church history, from Hakka songs that have been converted to hymns, from jokes and stereotypes, from the occasional Hakka language class, and from church celebrations and banquets, the Hakka of Shung Him Tong continue to learn about themselves. One final example will serve to illustrate this point.

The 140th Anniversary

The 140th anniversary of the arrival of the first Basel missionaries in Hong Kong was no small event. It was celebrated by members of the Tsung Tsin mission churches throughout the year of 1987 with special services, performances, and banquets, the opening celebration at the Sha Tin home for the elderly, the thirtieth anniversary celebration of the kindergarten, the opening of two new child care centers, retreats, and workshops. Months of planning and preparation were involved. People like Mr. C., the Shung Him Tong pastor, the church board members, and their counterparts at other Tsung Tsin mission churches and schools helped to organize the programs, prepare speeches, write special commemorative publications, arrange numerous rehearsals, and organize invitations for special guests. Members of the missionwide choir, including several of the best vocalists from each church, convened each week to rehearse for the occasion. A poster was designed depicting four missionaries—two from the Basel mission and two from the Rhenish mission—standing at the bow of a ship, its white sail emblazoned with a large red cross, making its way across the sea to China.

The highlights of the celebrations were a variety show on a Friday evening, March 20, and a Tsung Tsin missionwide thanksgiving service and banquet on Sunday, March 22, the Sunday closest to the date when Basel missionaries had arrived in Hong Kong 140 years earlier. Among the special guests in attendance at these events were fourteen official representatives from the Hakka church of Taiwan, eight delegates from the Hakka Basel mission of Malaysia in Sabah, two pastors from Hakka Chinese churches in Canada, and about eight representatives from the Basel mission in Switzerland. Officials from other Hong Kong and Macao churches and seminaries, and from the Hong Kong government, were also in attendance as honored guests.

The variety show was held at the huge Baptist college auditorium in Kowloon. Entire sections of the hall were roped off for members from each of the fifteen churches, for the VIPs, and for the parents and friends of the children who were performing, most of whom did not belong to the churches. The pastors of the Tsung Tsin mission churches and the president of the mission, Simon P. K. Sit, sat along the front row of the stage. The program began with a silent prayer, a Bible reading, a hymn, and another prayer, this last led by Mr. Sit, a Tsung Tsin church pastor, and a headmaster of one of the mission schools. Mr. Sit presented a brief history of the church in which he described how the German and Swiss missionaries had set sail from Europe 140 years earlier, their six-month trip at sea, and their arrival on March 19, 1847, which ultimately resulted in the Hakka church with its present membership of eight thousand.

The variety show consisted of hours of seemingly endless performances of acrobatics and song-and-dance routines by Tsung Tsin mission schoolchildren, who were dressed in stereotypical Chinese silk pajamas, in Swiss costumes, and even in chicken costumes hatching from huge eggshells. There were also dramatic performances, some of them depicting the history and work of the mission: the boat crossing the sea with the four missionaries; a group of young troublemakers who discovered Christianity and were reformed. Halfway through the program, after almost two hours, the former secretary of the Asia division of the Basel mission in Switzerland passed out commemorative silk flags to each school headmaster. After that, the audience slowly departed, though the performances continued.

On Sunday, Shung Him Tong held its 11:00 A.M. service as usual, but people were more dressed up, and there were several overseas guests in attendance. The bishop of the Hakka church in Malaysia, a former pastor for the Hong Kong Tsung Tsin mission, delivered the sermon in Hakka, and the former secretary of the Asia division of the Basel mission gave the benediction and led a prayer. He was also fluent in Hakka.

After the service, everyone rushed home for a quick meal before leaving in a fleet of cars and chartered bus for the 3:00 P.M. joint church service on Hong Kong Island. (Another bus arrived later to transport those who chose only to attend the banquet.) Close to a hundred people from Shung Him Tong, young and old, men and women, attended the service, and I was later told by one proud young woman that Shung Him Tong had had more representatives there than any other church, despite the greater distance they had to travel.

Another Shung Him Tong church member who worked on a financial committee for the whole affair told me that, as of two weeks before the event, individuals from Shung Him Tong had contributed more money to the event than had members of any other Tsung Tsin mission church. Still, he pointed out, this fact would probably just stir up the competitive spirit of the other churches. As it turned out, Shung Him Tong people bought an average number of tickets to the banquet, and the donation from the church was also about average.

The service was held at the Tsung Tsin mission church in Shau Kei Wan. It was the largest and newest church, built on the site of one of the first Basel mission churches in Hong Kong. Arrangements of flowers lined the entrance-way, each with a ribbon inscribed with messages from various well-wishers. Among them were Chung Chi College at the Chinese University of Hong Kong, the Lutheran Church Association of Hong Kong, the Archdiocese of Hong Kong and Macao, the Rhenish mission, the Protestant Church Association of Hong Kong, the Chinese Christian Organization for World Evangelism, the World Hakka Evangelical Association, and many others. In the main church hall extra pews had been added, and people overflowed into the aisles. The pastor's wife and several others from Shung Him Tong served as ushers, and many of the young people waved to us from the choir.

The service was conducted by foreign visitors and the highest Tsung Tsin mission officials, but the pastor and the chairman of the board from Shung Him Tong also played a small role. Mr. C., Mr. P., and several other board members took front-row seats with the Swiss guests.

Language was an issue that caused awkwardness, amusement, and some dissatisfaction throughout the afternoon and evening. It had been determined ahead of time that the main parts of the service should be conducted, as much as possible, in Cantonese and English because of the media presence, and for the sake of the local Hong Kong VIPs. Several board members from Shung Him Tong, as well as representatives from Basel, expressed some disappointment at this decision. One man from Shung Him Tong thought it more important to consider the guests from Malaysia and Taiwan who spoke Hakka but not Cantonese. Mr. Sit began the service with an announcement that, "although this is a Hakka mission, we will use Cantonese today." The Swiss pastor from Basel, who spoke fluent Hakka and no Cantonese, was asked to deliver his sermon in English rather than Hakka. As one Shung Him Tong board member explained to me later, somewhat illogically, this was because he was there to represent Switzerland. The main sermon, by this Swiss pastor, outlined some history of the mission and raised questions about its future after 1997 and its link to other Chinese churches. Another long speech was made by a Tsung Tsin mission high official who was once a student of Luo Xianglin. He painstakingly listed the numbers of converts made and new mission stations, schools, and hospitals opened in Hakka regions each year since 1847, until he was cut off at the turn of the century because time was running short.

The pastor from Shung Him Tong read a Bible passage in faltering Cantonese, and the women sitting next to me worked hard to stifle their giggles. There was a short speech in Cantonese from the president of the Lutheran Church Association of Hong Kong. The same bishop who had spoken in Shung Him Tong that morning delivered a short speech in Hakka, which was translated into Cantonese, and the head of the World Hakka Evangelical Association, a man from Taiwan, also spoke in Hakka. After a few more messages of thanks and congratulations from pastors or officials from the Tsung Tsin Mission—delivered in German or Hakka, depending on to whom they were primarily directed toward—people finally made their way in droves to the restaurant for the celebration banquet.

The tone of the banquet was much less formal, and many who had not attended the service were there. There were about a thousand places reserved, and again Shung Him Tong church members made an impressive showing, enough to fill two large buses on the return trip to the village. I was seated at a table that included nine other people from Shung Him Tong, five of whom—including Tin, Pui Yan, and her husband—I knew quite well. Shortly after we were all seated and introduced, one young woman said that of all the tables, I had been seated at the wrong one. This was, they all joked, "the Chaozhou table." Of the ten of us, five were Chaozhou, one Cantonese, and only three Hakka. Two of the Chaozhou couples, an older couple and their son and daughter-in-law, were long-time church members who spoke Hakka. One woman was Cantonese and was there with her husband, who was related to the Shung Him Tong Tsuis. Another young woman was a descendant of Pang Lok Sam, and her cousin was there with his wife, who was also of Chaozhou descent.

In contrast to the church service, most of the speeches and entertainment at the banquet were lighthearted and mostly in Hakka. As one man explained to me later, there were many jokes about the language "because we are a Hakka church and like to hear Hakka used." At one point, the Swiss guests were asked to sing some folk songs in their native tongue. One chose a Swiss folk song, and another sang in French. Following their comical and unre-hearsed performances, the brother of the Shung Him Tong pastor, also a pas-tor at a Tsung Tsin mission church, was pushed to the microphone and urged to sing a Hakka mountain song. This he graciously declined, saying that they can only be sung in the hills while one works; instead he sang a lullaby in Hakka, which he said he learned from the German missionaries when he was a child. Everyone laughed and applauded loudly.

As one course of the banquet followed another, one of the Tsung Tsin mis-sion officials stood at the microphone and pointed toward the crowd, saying, "Here we are, Hakka, Cantonese, Germans, and Swiss, and yet it is *still* a Hakka church!" Mr. P. was in a jolly mood and came to our table to repeat a joke that he found especially amusing: When one of the old Swiss women mis-sionaries was in Yuen Long, someone asked her when she would learn to speak Cantonese since she was so fluent in Hakka. She replied that she had no in-tention of learning Cantonese, "because doesn't everyone in heaven speak Hakka?" The non-Hakka at our table laughed and one Chaozhou man was quick to inform us that in his family they also speak Hakka.

7 Our Beloved Hakka People

In the preceding chapters I have described the decline in use of Hakka language in Shung Him Tong, the absence of practices or customs that can be labeled "Hakka," and the ambivalence toward Hakka identity among some people, particularly youth. In addition, I have noted that Shung Him Tong has not attracted many new church members in recent years, that some people have left the church, and that many of its older members have settled overseas. However, I maintain that these factors do not necessarily mean that Shung Him Tong will not survive as a community, or that Hakka identity is simply dying out. Membership has not decreased significantly over the past few years. Some new members have joined, and old members marry and raise their children in the church. A pattern of emigration has existed since the village was founded. With the approach of 1997 this process has merely accelerated. As of 1987, however, there were still some church members who could not afford to leave; some who could afford to go but said they had no intention of emigrating; and others who were planning to leave only temporarily until they attain permanent residence status or citizenship elsewhere. The significant point, however, is that emigration opens up contact between the provincial church and the wider Hakka Christian community. Of the emigrants from Shung Him Tong that I was able to trace, the vast majority continue to attend Hakka churches abroad, maintain contact with friends and relatives in the village, and continue to return for visits. So, true to their name, Hakka continue to move on. But the community, despite the appearance of disintegration, is not losing its identity.

An Irish Catholic priest who teaches at one Hong Kong school unequivocally told me when I began my research that "no one is Hakka anymore, or if they are, they'll never tell you." As we have seen, in Shung Him Tong this is certainly not the case. Some Shung Him Tong people express doubt or concern as to the ongoing importance of Hakka identity, but this does not mean that we should unconditionally conclude that Hakka identity is becoming obsolete.[1] The economic and political relevance of Hakka ethnicity, as we have seen, varies according to time and place. During the late nineteenth century and the first four decades of the twentieth century, the material advantages associated with belonging to the Hakka church community were substantial. These advantages enabled the people of Shung Him Tong to build houses, schools, a church, and a cemetery and to achieve their goals in the face of opposition from Punti and wealthy Cantonese. But despite a recent decrease in its explicit political and economic relevance, Hakka identity and distinctiveness in Shung Him Tong has not diminished—though it has changed.

In certain situations, the political and economic relevance of Hakka identity is evident (see Basu 1991b; Blake 1975, 1981; Martin 1992; Oxfeld 1993) and can be used to support the instrumentalist view of ethnicity. But such a perspective sheds little light on the contemporary situation of Hakka Christians in Shung Him Tong. The relevance of Hakka identity in Shung Him Tong is not due to its association with traditional occupational niches or contemporary economic concerns. If, as instrumentalists have suggested, ethnicity is to be seen as competition over scarce resources, then the resources are potential Hakka converts and the symbols of Hakka identity.

Although an instrumentalist model does not explain the persistence of Hakka identity or the form it has taken in contemporary Shung Him Tong, it does help to explain why Hakka identity is downplayed in other contexts. In many parts of Hong Kong, as in San Francisco's Chinatown, Hakka believe that Cantonese identity or a generic "Chinese" identity is of greater advantage than Hakka identity in business and commerce. As one Chinese American woman explained, her father never told anyone, including his children, that he was Hakka until after he had retired from his work in San Francisco's Chinatown fish industry. His business networks were not among Hakka people and he believed it would be disadvantageous for his colleagues to know he was Hakka.

Hakka identity is still immediately relevant in Shung Him Tong—and to some extent in the other Hakka churches in Hong Kong and elsewhere—because it is considered an intrinsic factor in the identity of the community. As I have argued in previous chapters, Hakka identity persists in Shung Him Tong because of the way it has been historically constituted and paired with Christianity.

Although only a small proportion of Hakka converted to Christianity during the nineteenth century, their numbers were significant enough for missionaries and Hakka Christians themselves to assert that Hakka converted in greater numbers than other Chinese. In the aftermath of the Taiping Rebellion and the Hakka-Punti wars, Hakka were discriminated against regardless of whether they were directly involved in the rebellion, and many turned to the Basel Missionary Society for support, education, and refuge.

In some cases, turning to the missionaries was likely to have been considered a last resort in an effort for individuals to help their families escape poverty, starvation, and homelessness. Such is the case of the poor, weak, abused, unwanted, and physically handicapped Hakka converts whose biographies are recorded in the Basel Mission Archives (1868a, 1868b, 1874, 1885, 1889; see Appendix 1). Poverty and deprivation were certainly important factors in the conversion of many Hakka, but such an explanation overlooks a number of other important factors that attracted the Hakka to the Basel mission and that resulted from this association.

The fact that the Basel mission was a Hakka church whose missionaries were more receptive to the Hakka and more knowledgeable about them, and who even idealized the Hakka—sometimes exhibiting their own "Hakka pride"—is certain to have played a role in attracting Hakka to their ranks as opposed to those of other missions. Hakka quickly became aware that the Basel mission welcomed them, recruited them as mission workers, and directed its evangelizing efforts in South China almost exclusively toward them. This was different from the Catholic mission in the region, which was not an exclusively Hakka mission. As one man from Shung Him Tong explained, in his native region of Wuhua there was a Catholic mission that had become associated with one particular group of villages. When the Basel missionaries arrived, his grandfather and the other villagers celebrated, because now they too had a group of missionaries to call their own. The Basel mission became known as the "Hakka church," providing—as did the Society of God Worshipers (Kuhn 1977)—an organizational structure drawing on ethnicity, not surname or native place, as one of the main organizing factors.[2]

For the people of Shung Him Tong and many other Basel mission converts and their descendants, Christianity did not serve as a way to escape Hakka ethnic identity but as a way to preserve and celebrate it. Within the context of the church, the meaning of Hakka identity was certainly adjusted, transformed, and to some extent consolidated. But as the case of Shung Him Tong illustrates, there was no question but that the community was conceived of as integrally Hakka, Chinese, and Christian. This community created a degree of Hakka consciousness and reflexivity not commonly found among other Hakka in Hong Kong.[3]

One important factor that explains the persistence of Hakka identity in Shung Him Tong is that the village has always been labeled by Punti, foreign missionaries, government officials, and non-Christian Hakka as a Hakka Christian community. It is thus difficult for Hakka Christians to escape their Hakka identity within the narrow context of Lung Yeuk Tau. Instead, they have taken the alternative route of trying to transform the image of the Hakka. One central feature of Hakka identity in Shung Him Tong is that it entails a reconstruction, or at least a positive reassertion, of the meaning of Hakka identity, rooted in historical examples that at once claim Hakka *and* Chinese identity. To some extent, this has been the goal of both Christian and non-Christian Hakka leaders and intellectuals. But Hakka Christians such as Pang Lok Sam and Luo Xianglin were in an ideal position to reinvent their identity.

With their better economic and educational situation, Hakka Christian intellectuals have actively advocated a positive Hakka image within their immediate community as well as through their broader ties to the international Hakka community. Their own social and economic positions contradicted the stereotype that Hakka were poor, uneducated, and backward, and so the positive Hakka image took hold. Hakka claims to moral superiority over non-Hakka were reinforced by their belief in proper Christian behavior. History demonstrates Hakka ability to compete with the local Punti, and to establish themselves as respectable, educated, and even elite members of Hong Kong society. The 140th anniversary celebration is a vivid example of a "ritualized" enactment and public production of many of these points as well as an illustration of the broader connection Shung Him Tong has with other Hakka churches, associations, and communities in Taiwan, Canada, Malaysia, and elsewhere.

Non-Hakka in Lung Yeuk Tau and other parts of Hong Kong may still hold on to negative images of the Hakka. Thus many Hakka, including some who grew up in Shung Him Tong but who no longer live there or attend the church, appear to be less committed to their Hakka identities than those who remain connected with the village and a Hakka church. For some it is more meaningful to assimilate into the broader identity of Hong Kong Chinese.

For those who live in Shung Him Tong or belong to the church, to conceive of themselves as Hakka is in part to assert that they are also Chinese. This they do by claiming their legitimate genealogical and blood relations and also by adhering to what they conceive of as "proper" Chinese rules of behavior. What many Chinese lineages aim to do with their genealogies—namely, claim authenticity and status as pure Chinese—Luo and other Hakka historians have attempted to do for all the Hakka. On occasions such as the anniversary of the church, the celebration of the construction of the new church building, and the anniversary of the Tsung Tsin mission, commemorative booklets are published that include articles on the history of the church. The church histories all draw on Pang's history of the community, which in turn draws on individual family histories and genealogies. Similarly, Luo's history of the Hakka draws on Shung Him Tong history. Conversely, the Hakka past is reflected and reproduced in church history, and consequently the identity of Hakka Christians is situated and well-rooted in a Hakka Chinese past. As one nineteenth-century missionary suggested, Hakka history is "nothing else than an outline history of the *Chinese* in general" (Piton 1873:225; emphasis in original). The identity of Shung Him Tong Hakka Christians, then, is represented in their various nested histories: they are at once Chinese, Hakka, and Shung Him Tong Christians.

The Chinese identity of Hakka Christians is maintained because the church provides a situation in which the concept of descent and genealogy is reinforced. While the people of Shung Him Tong do not have ancestral halls, they do have a cemetery where the names of the ancestors are preserved and where genealogies are recorded. In a sense, their identity is inscribed in the physical formulation of their community. The village spatial organization commemorates and preserves the connection between past and present. While Hakka Christians of Shung Him Tong may be viewed by their non-Christian neighbors as "unorthodox" Chinese, the Hakka of Shung Him Tong adapt "orthodox" rules of filial piety and ancestor worship into secular expressions of respect and commemoration in everyday life (cf. Liu 1990). Like many other Chinese, some Hakka Christians of Shung Him Tong maintain contact with their Christian and non-Christian kin in the People's Republic of China. They preserve genealogies and express faith in moral righteousness as key issues in their claim to Chinese identity, but they do so as Christians.

The people of Shung Him Tong maintain their Hakka, Chinese, and Christian identities, but not without some ambivalence. During the Chinese New Year in 1987 I was invited to share a meal with a prominent Shung Him Tong family. The young woman of the house greeted me and, when I presented her with a box of sweets and a bag of oranges, she commented that I had "learned Chinese customs very well." She proceeded to offer me a variety of colorful new year snacks—candied fruits and seeds—from the special partitioned bowl designed for this occasion. Among its contents were lotus seeds, which she encouraged me to eat because they symbolize fertility and the prospective birth of many sons. During the meal the family explained the symbolic significance of the various dishes as bestowing longevity, success in business, stability in marriage, and so on. As the evening progressed the family described various new year "superstitions," and the young woman's father commented that I would find few traditional Chinese customs in Shung Him Tong, "because," he said, "we are not Chinese and we are not European. We are somewhere in between."

This statement can be interpreted in a number of ways. On one level it indicates his ambivalence toward his Chinese identity. It also illustrates that the people of Shung Him Tong are in an unusual marginal position—they are neither Chinese nor western, but something in between. His statement expresses a point I have tried to emphasize in this book, that combining Hakka, Chinese, and Christian identities is not straightforward and does not result in an entirely comfortable fusion, but rather one that is constantly reasserted and renegotiated within the context of the church and village.

A conversation I had with a Swiss missionary is also illustrative. We were discussing the disapproval several Shung Him Tong people expressed toward their non–Christian neighbors' religious practices—things like making offerings to the gods, worshiping at temples, setting up ancestral altars in their homes, and even hanging lucky papers at the Chinese New Year. The missionary voiced with regret his belief that the early missionaries, in their zeal to establish the church without "indigenizing" it, caused Hakka Christians to "become ashamed of being Chinese."

Unlike the Swiss missionary, I did not come to this conclusion. The people of Shung Him Tong may be "ashamed" or "embarrassed" by certain Chinese customs, but they are proud of being Chinese. Their criticism and rejection of certain non-Christian religious practices—those they cannot reconcile with their Christian beliefs—in part allows them to retain other Chinese beliefs and practices and thus maintain their Chinese identity. Beliefs and practices such as *feng-shui* and filial piety are rationalized and retained despite the Christian orthodoxy that the people of Shung Him Tong have inherited from the early Basel missionaries.

The relationship between Christian and Chinese practices, like that between Chinese and Christian identities, has not been free of tension. It has required that Hakka Christians continue to define and redefine, to justify and rationalize their Hakka, Chinese, and Christian practices. This process hinges, I have argued, on Hakka identity and the construction of its relationship to Christianity and Chinese identity. A Hakka Chinese missionary from Taiwan in the 1970s wrote that the relative failure of Protestant missions among the Hakka in Taiwan has been because "'becoming Christian' has come to mean 'leaving our beloved Hakka people'" (Liao 1972:7). In Shung Him Tong, and to some extent in other related Hakka churches, one can argue just the opposite.

Early Converts

LI TSIN KAU

The following account of the life of Li Tsin Kau serves to illustrate the impact of his association with Hong Xiuquan on his life and how it brought him and his family into contact with the Basel mission. As Smith explains:

> The services rendered by the several generations of the Li family to the congregations and schools of the Basel Missionary Society well repaid the initial interest and attention which the young Li Tsin-kau had been given when he first turned up in Hong Kong in 1853 as one displaced because of his connection with the leader of the Taiping movement (1985:227).

Although Li Tsin Kau's descendants were not involved in the establishment of Shung Him Tong, they do have certain connections with the village. Like many residents of Shung Him Tong, Li's sons attended the Basel Missionary Society Boys' School in Lilang, and three of them married women who had attended the mission-run girls' school. His youngest son, Li Shin En, was baptized in Hong Kong in 1859 and served as a catechist at the Hakka church in Sai Ying Pun, Hong Kong, from 1883 to 1888, married the daughter of Shung Him Tong's founder, Pastor Ling Kai Lin. The couple formed part of the large group of Hakka Christians and friends and relatives of the Taipings who emigrated to Sabah, North Borneo. There, under the auspices of the Basel mission, Li organized a Hakka congregation (Smith 1985:227).

The following outline of Li Tsin Kau's life draws primarily from two archival reports in the Basel mission. One was written by Rudolf Lechler (Basel Mission Archives 1868a), and the other is a revised version of Lechler's report written by Li's youngest son, Li Shin En (Basel Mission Archives 1885; see also Smith 1985:77–82).

Lechler's biography of Li Tsin Kau is one of many biographies and reports on Chinese converts sent back to mission headquarters in Switzerland to communicate the work the missionaries had accomplished and to ensure the continued support of the mission. Most of the biographies follow a similar structure, depicting the life and religious beliefs of the convert before conversion, the events leading up to the conversion, and the person's role within the Christian community. I was unable to find similar autobiographies for Shung Him Tong converts, in part because Shung Him Church was considered relatively independent of the "parent mission," having been organized by well-established and respected Chinese Basel converts, and in part because the interior of China was of greater interest to European missionaries.

According to Lechler and Li Shin En, Li Tsin Kau was born in 1823 in the village of Wo Kuk Liang, Tschang Yen district, Guangdong province. He worked as a farmer and was also the village teacher. He studied from the time he was eight years old until he was fifteen, so he knew how to read and write and was familiar with the Chinese classics. When he was twenty years old he married and became the head of his household. The following year his first son was born, followed by three more sons and two daughters.

One of Li's uncles, his father's brother, was a devout Buddhist and Li also became interested in Buddhism despite his family's objections. He was vegetarian and recited Buddhist prayers. Once he went with his uncle to visit a Buddhist temple and to see the depictions of the torments of hell. The scene that made the deepest impression on Li was of a man who was sentenced to death before the celestial court when the Goddess of Mercy came and saved him.

According to Lechler and Li Shin En, Li Tsin Kau was introverted, modest, and kind, and was considered a man of strong moral character. He faithfully worshiped his ancestors and the idols. He had been raised very strictly and upheld the morals his father had taught him. Some of his comrades thought that Li's good character influenced them to avoid engaging in such immoral activities as gambling, drinking, smoking opium, and prostitution. He usually admonished them for eating the meat of cows and dogs because such animals are friends of humankind. Li Tsin Kau believed that the moral philosophies of Confucius and Mencius were the best rules to live by; Buddhist philosophies also provided him with comfort concerning death.

Hong Xiuquan had been a well-known teacher in the home of Li's maternal grandparents, and Li's father and Hong were good friends. Li Tsin Kau often heard his father speak of Hong and his wonderful visions. When Hong came to Li's village they would discuss the moral and political decline of the country. As Li Tsin Kau explained to Lechler, when the villagers heard Hong's views, he won their hearts; they thought that their prayers had been answered by heaven and that he had been chosen to bring better times.

Hong and Li discussed fasting and vegetarianism, and Hong said that eating meat could not be bad or God would not have provided animals. Hong also criticized ancestor worship and said that the idols were all false. Hong told Li about the power of God and about his mission to destroy the idols. Li heard Hong speak of Jesus, their brother in heaven who would forgive their sins. As Li explained to Lechler, there was much more that Hong taught him, but mainly he remembered the idea of God being stronger than the idols. Li was interested in Hong because he preached about good people who worshiped a wise God. Hong promised the Chinese people a better life—but Li's association with Hong later thrust him and his family into misery.

When Hong was in Guangxi, Li attempted to reach him, but the authorities frustrated his efforts and he returned home. A few years later, when his following was forty-five hundred strong, Hong wrote to Li's father urging them to join him in Guangxi. Again, Li attempted to join Hong, but the government forces learned of the plan, and the group was forced to disperse and flee. Li's father and his uncle were arrested and taken away. Li believed that they died in prison. His wife fled with their children to her father's home. His mother was hidden by friends. Like many other "friends and relatives of the leaders of the Taipings [who] were rooted out of their native districts and at the same time cut off from the troops of the rebellion" (Smith 1985:77), Li was forced to flee. He went first to Macao and the region surrounding Hong Kong, where he worked for over a year as a *feng-shui* expert.

Li was about to try to return home in 1852 when he met Hong Rengan, a relative of Hong Xiuquan who later became an important Taiping leader, and together they headed back to Hong Kong. From there they hoped to go to Nanjing where Hong had a good foothold. On their way, Hong Rengan stopped in Buji where he received instruction for baptism by the Basel missionary Hamberg. Hong Rengan and several others were baptized by Hamberg and afterward returned with him to Hong Kong. Li explained that Brother Hamberg worked with Hong Rengan because he hoped that he would influence Hong Xiuquan.

Shortly after, Li and two of his friends also met Hamberg in Hong Kong. They were all well received and Hamberg spent much time preparing them for baptism. Meanwhile, Hamberg wrote *The Visions of Hung-Siu-Tshuen and Origin of the Kwang-si Insurrection* (1854) based on what Hong Rengan told him. Hamberg hoped that the proceeds from the book would enable him to finance the four men's voyage to Nanjing. Lechler also returned to Hong Kong and assisted Hamberg with the lessons. As Lechler recounted, Li did not make exceptional progress with his studies. He was concerned only with the ninth commandment and the topic of lies. He thought that, for the most part, he lived righteously and had learned all he needed to long ago from Hong Xiuquan, who had taught him that God was true and that the idols were false. His main regret was that he had not been able to reach Hong in Nanjing. It was only because Rengan told him that the baptism he had received from Hong was no good that he decided to be baptized again after three months of training. As Lechler wrote, Li was baptized but had not yet realized true happiness.

In April 1854 Li and Hong Rengan had an opportunity to travel to Nanjing by way of Shanghai, but they did not reach their destination. In Shanghai, with Hamberg's letter of introduction, they were able to stay in the mission hospital. But, as Smith explains, they ran into a friend and allowed him to stay in their room. The friend left his opium pipe on the bed, and when the missionaries discovered it, the three men were forced to leave (1985:80).

Li and Hong then had a falling out because Li accused Hong of lust and carelessness. Meanwhile the news of Hamberg's death reached Shanghai and there was no way for them to reach Nanjing. As Li explained to Lechler, "I had no friend on earth, no money to get back to Hong Kong, and I thought that I would die there in misery." At that point, his life took a turn. As Li Shin En recounted, his father began to pray fervently; he considered himself a wretched sinner, but thanked the Lord for his mercy. His inner change was followed by an external sign: he rose from his prayer and saw a light and was convinced that "the Lord has his own plans for me." The Lord moved the hospital missionary to have mercy on Li Tsin Kau and gave him enough money to get back to Hong Kong. There he met Lechler, who gave him money to return home. After he visited his family he became a mission helper in Buji. In 1856 Lechler brought Li with him to Hong Kong, where he worked first at a mission hospital and then as Lechler's mission helper.

When Hong Rengan finally reached Nanjing in 1858 he wrote to Li urging him to come. Li set off for Nanjing, but then decided to turn back because he began to think that Hong Xuiquan was deceived by the devil. As Li is said to have written to Rengan, he realized that Hong's vision was wrong. Hong saw God as an angry old man in a black gown; but Li knew that he was dressed in white and was not an angry old man but a reconciled, loving father.

The remainder of Li Shin En's account of his father's life describes his commitment to the Basel mission, his role in raising his children to be staunch Christians, and his illness and death in 1885.

Having accepted the Lord's will, Li was inspired to teach the gospel to his family, so in 1858 he returned home where he found his loved ones impoverished by the war. He thanked God that they had survived and he was convinced that they should all follow the Lord. But because they could not be openly Christian there, they moved to Hong Kong. In 1859 his wife and children were baptized and became members of the Hakka Basel mission church in Sai Ying Pun.

Li urged his children to attend sermons. He organized evening prayers in his house and taught his children that it is better to be honest and poor than to be dishonest and rich, and that he had never seen a happy dishonest man. If his children wanted to celebrate his birthday, he said, they should spend it praying and doing penance. He was a strict teacher and often used the rod. As Li Shin En wrote, one could blame Li Tsin Kau for his use of the rod except that all his children say that they are thankful for their father's discipline. His motto was that it is better to be without children than to have naughty ones. The chastened child was reminded that in punishment he or she was experiencing the father's love.

Li was ill for several years before he died in 1885. He had worked for the mission for over twenty years, and several of his children continued to do so.

TSANG FUK MING

The first convert from Wuhua, which was then named Changle, was Cheung Fuk Hing from Zhangcun, and it was he who spread the gospel to his relative Tsui Fuk Kwong from Zhankeng Hang, the second convert in Wuhua. Cheung and Tsui were both closely related to the Tsuis and a branch of Cheungs who belong to Shung Him Tong. Tsui Fuk Kwong is largely credited with the conversion of Tsang Fuk Ming, the subject of a report written by the missionary Jacob Leonhardt to the mission headquarters in Basel (Basel Mission Archives 1889).

As Leonhardt wrote, a hundred souls were baptized in 1862 in Zhangcun. Among them were sixty-five from Nyenhang which was later to become an important mission station and the site of the middle school attended by Pang Lok Sam and several generations of the family of Pastor Ling Kai Lin. Among this first group to be baptized was Tsang Fuk Ming, who was in his sixties at the time.

Tsang Fuk Ming was one of three brothers. Of them he was the one who most resembled his father; even as a "heathen," Leonhardt points out, he was a modest, quiet person who held his parents in high esteem and who had a good reputation. His older brother followed in his grandfather's footsteps and became a geomancer or *feng-shui* expert, his younger brother was a farmer, and Fuk Ming did some farming and also worked as a doctor, although he had had no opportunity to go to school. He worshiped the idols because he respected them and not out of personal greed. He did not smoke opium and lived a modest life as a result, said Leonhardt, of the piety that came from the bottom of his heart. He was one of the "pious heathens" who were "made of truth," which is to say that he was closer to the truth and therefore more willing to listen to the gospel.

In 1854 Tsang Fuk Ming first learned about Christianity from a man who worked with him named Tsui who was a cousin of Tsui Fuk Kwong. Tsui told Tsang about the Lord who created heaven and earth, that the idols were nothing, about the Ten Commandments, and that Christ, God's son, was sent to save humankind. Although Tsui's preaching lacked eloquence, Tsang felt that he was telling the truth, so he asked him to invite Tsui Fuk Kwong to tell them more. Tsui Fuk Kwong came in 1855 and they prayed and discussed the commandments all night long. Many years later, Tsang Fuk Ming's son recalled to Leonhardt how as a boy he would sit up late with his father and listen to the endless conversations.

It was not easy for the early converts. Several lost their livestock and their houses were plundered. As a leader among the converts, Tsui Fuk Kwong was particularly mistreated. Because he was a doctor, Tsang Fuk Ming's life was easier than that of many Christians.

At the end of the 1850s, Tsang Fuk Ming and his relatives decided to expand their house. When they finished, the kitchen was struck by lightning and their non-Christian relatives thought it was a consequence of Fuk Ming's Christian beliefs. The lightning did not do much damage, and at least one Christian relative felt that it was a beneficent act on the Lord's part: he cleaned the house of evil spirits.

The non-Christians both feared and hated the Christians, whom they believed drove away their deities. Tsang Fuk Ming told Leonhardt that once, when he walked past a temple where people were asking advice of a spirit medium, the spirit in possession told the people that he could no longer answer their questions because of Fuk Ming's presence.

At that time there was still no chapel in the area. Sometimes the Christians met in homes; sometimes they went to see Cheung Fuk Hing or Tsui Fuk Kwong in their villages. Christians only met when it was dark so as not to "aggravate the heathen." Cheung Fuk Hing played an important role in spreading the gospel, so when Philip Winnes appeared as the first European missionary in the region in 1862, he was greeted by Tsang Fuk Ming and a number of other candidates for baptism. As Leonhardt put it, they were a flock just waiting for the shepherd.

Tsang Fuk Ming was an active Christian. Although his father had been opposed to Christianity at first, Fuk Ming managed to convert him. When they lived in different villages, Fuk Ming visited him every Sunday to discuss the gospel and praise the Lord. When his father died at 101 in 1875, he was buried against his will in a "heathen-style" burial because the majority of the family was not Christian. Fuk Ming saw his wife and most of his eight children become Christian, but he was dismayed that all his friends and family did not convert. He wanted salvation for all because he knew the fate of those who do not believe.

One day after the sermon he met his Christian son in the marketplace. Fuk Ming cursed his laxity because he feared for his salvation. It was said that he himself did not know laxity, did not desire worldly things, and refused the pleasures of this life. That is why he hated such lack of discipline in others and was particularly strict to members of his family: his severity was the answer to God's love.

When Tsang Fuk Ming died in 1889, both Christians and non-Christians attended his funeral. He stipulated in his will that he have a Christian burial and that the rest of his money be used so that his grandchildren could attend mission school. His non-Christian relatives dared not question his will because his Christian son accepted it. Disregarding the traditional belief that rain on a coffin throws the family of the deceased into disorder, Leonhardt ordered that the coffin be taken to the cemetery in the rain. No one dared to intervene, and the procession moved on as they sang and prayed.

Tsang Fuk Ming's seventh son succeeded him as a church elder. Fuk Ming's grandson also became a preacher, as did his great grandson, who was for many years the pastor at the Hakka church in Sai Ying Pun, Hong Kong.

The Families of Shung Him Tong in 1932

Most family histories of early Shung Him Tong villagers begin with a geneal-ogy, followed by an account of their conversion to Christianity and their rea-sons for moving to Shung Him Tong. In these histories, several patterns emerge: most of the settlers were Christian before they arrived, and those who were not converted shortly after arrival; the first settlers were mostly from the Baoan re-gion of Guangdong and all were Hakka; and, in almost all cases, disturbances in their native villages spurred their emigration to the reputedly more peaceful, British-governed New Territories. Almost all of the histories stress the positive factors of moving to a Christian village.

LING KAI LIN (see fig. 2)

There are several sources on the history of the Ling family, the most detailed of which was written by Ling Sin Yuen, the eldest son of Kai Lin, and is in-cluded in the Pang volume (see Pang 1934; Luo 1965; Lin[g] 1974). Some relatives of Ling Kai Lin in Hong Kong provided helpful information, and I was also able to obtain several articles about the family written by Lin[g] Dou Yeung, the son of Ling Sin Yuen.[1] Although he lived in the United States, Ling Dou Yeung was still an elder of Shung Him Church in 1987.

Ling Sin Yuen begins his family history by recounting the belief that if a person does not know his ancestors he will be worse than an animal, and that one should trace his family history as far back as possible. He traces the Ling history back to Kat in Jiangxi province, Cheung who moved to Meixian in Guangdong province, and Yat Lam who moved to Buji, Baoan. Ling Kai Lin is the fifth-generation descendant of Yat Lam; the first four were Yuk Bun, Wan Choi, Chiu Shui, and Chun Ko. Chun Ko was the father of Kai Lin. Chun Ko was a "simple and honest" person who "worshiped idols" until he was forty, when he learned of Christianity from the Basel missionary Hamberg.

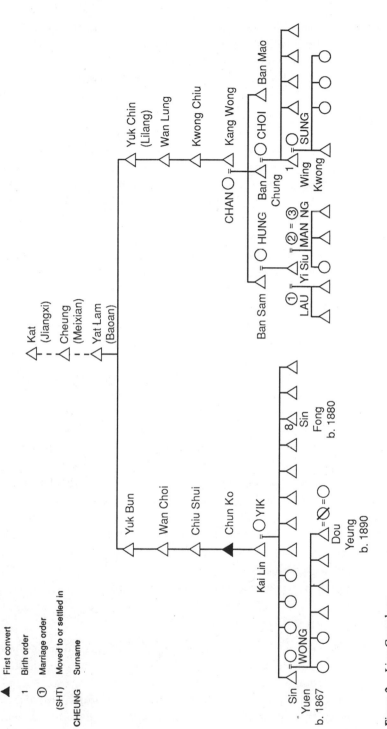

Figure 2. Ling Genealogy.

He then "left the idols and became devoted to the true God. He and his family were baptized and became Christians" (Pang 1934:39).

However, hatred of Christianity grew among the villagers and Christians suffered persecution. The missionaries were expelled from the village, so they left for Lilang, where they established a school and taught the Bible. Kai Lin entered that school and after graduation went with his wife to Zhangcun in Wuhua, where he worked for twelve years. Later, concerned for his parents because he had no brothers who could take care of them, Kai Lin applied to return to his native village. He wanted to "look after his parents and fulfill his duty as a son" (Pang 1934:40). His application for a transfer was approved, but when he reached home the plans had been changed and he was sent to Chang Shan Kou. At that time he wrote the following poem expressing his sadness at leaving his parents, and his commitment to his calling:

> Just as I unload my saddle at my native village
> Then I must lead my horse to Chang Shan.
> If not to spread truth and obey divine orders,
> How could I leave my home and my father's face?

According to Ling Sin Yuen, Kai Lin's aspiration to sacrifice himself to others and transform his filial piety into loyalty to God was clearly revealed in the poem (ibid.).

Kai Lin stayed in Chang Shan Kou for three months and then was sent to Guzhu, where a new church was being built. After living there for six years, he went back to Lilang, where he devoted himself to the church for another thirty-six years. In the words of Sin Yuen, Kai Lin raised his children and worked for the church, endured hardships, and spared no effort in performing his duty. At fifty-seven he retired and returned home, but his passion for helping others never left him. He raised enough money to build a church and school in his village, but he was not happy there because it was not a peaceful place. He "founded" Shung Him Tong in 1903 and thereafter enjoyed a peaceful life in Lung Yeuk Tau, returning to his native village only for visits. In 1918, at age seventy-four, he returned to his native place, where he died and was buried. His wife (surname Yik) died in Shung Him Tong at the age of ninety in 1932 and was one of the first people to be buried in the Shung Him Tong cemetery.

LING BAN CHUNG (*see fig. 2*)

The family of Ling Ban Chung was poorer, less educated, and did not become Christian until much later than Ling Kai Lin's family. They became Christian after coming to Shung Him Tong and worked mostly as farmers.

Ling Ban Chung's genealogy branches, like Ling Kai Lin's, from that of their common ancestor, Ling Yat Lam, who moved within Guangdong province from Meixian to Buji, Baoan. Yat Lam's sons were Yuk Bun and Yuk Chin. Yuk Bun was Kai Lin's great-great-grandfather and Yuk Chin was Ban Chung's. Yuk Chin moved to Lilang and was the father of Wan Lung. Wan Lung's son was Kwong Chiu, and Kwong Chiu's son was Kang Wong. Kang Wong married a woman whose surname was Chan and their three sons were Ban Sam, Ban Chung, and Ban Mao. It is not clear whether Ban Sam and Ban Chung were Christian but several members of the following generation credit Pastor Ling Kai Lin with their conversion.

Ban Chung was from Lilang, Baoan. He heard about Lung Yeuk Tau from a neighbor, and in 1898 moved with his family to Ma Wat village in Lung Yeuk Tau. In 1899 the Lung Yeuk Tau Teng protested against the British acquisition of the New Territories, and during the disturbances Ling returned briefly to Lilang. But within the next few years he returned to Lung Yeuk Tau and settled in Shung Him Tong.

PANG LOK SAM (*see fig. 3*)

Pang Lok Sam begins his family history with his great-grandfather Sing Fu and his great-grandmother (surnamed Ho), who lived as farmers in Longhua, Baoan. His grandfather and grandmother (surnamed Cheung) ran a business, and his father and mother (surnamed Wong) worked in the Longhua market.[2] Pang Lok Sam's parents learned of Christianity, and in 1879 they were baptized nearby in the Langkou church. Pang Lok Sam was born in 1875 and baptized when he was four years old. When he was eight, his father died and his mother began to work as a housekeeper for Basel missionaries. He went on to mission-run schools: primary school in Lilang, secondary school in Wuhua, and then Lilang Seminary, from which he graduated in 1896 and took up missionary work. In 1899 he married Tsui Dou Leung from Zhankeng, Wuhua, with whom he had twelve children. After working two years at the Zhankeng church, Pang Lok Sam was transferred to a church in Zijin. In 1901 his youngest brother died. His mother was heartbroken, and to console her he applied to the mission for a transfer to Baoan to be closer to her. He was transferred to Tai Po and later Sha Tau Kok in the New Territories. In 1905 he began to preach in Shung Him Tong but also continued to work in Tai Po, Nam Wa Po, and Sha Tau Kok.

Pang played an active role in the development of the village and in New Territories politics and was involved in the founding of the Heung Yee Kuk. He was personal friends with Sir Cecil Clementi during the latter's years as district officer and later his governorship. Pang was awarded the Coronation Medal (Ingrams 1952:170), and was also one of the originators of the plan for establishing the Luen Wo market in Fanling. Before the market was

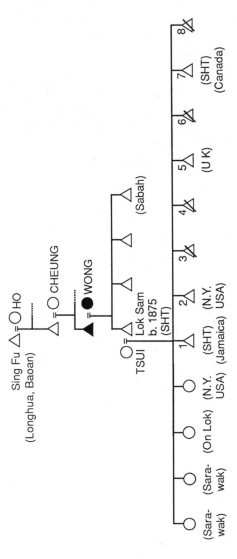

Figure 3. Pang Genealogy.

established, people from Fanling did their marketing in Sheung Shui at Shek Wu Hui. But the fees collected from vegetable hawkers were spent on social welfare projects in the Sheung Shui area and did not benefit the people of Fanling. The Luen Wo market was completed in the early 1950s and is run primarily by the Punti Pang of Fanling. Pang died in 1947 and did not live to see the market fully developed.

It was because of Pang that the family of Tsui Yan Sau decided to settle in Shung Him Tong. Pang's wife was the sister of Yan Sau, making Tsui and Pang brothers-in-law. Tsui was a direct descendant of the first Basel mission convert in Wuhua.

TSUI DOU LEUNG (*see fig. 4*)

The Tsuis all trace their ancestors back to the district of Wuhua in Guangdong. Chung Lai moved from the town of Wuhua to the nearby village of Zhankeng. Fuen Po was born in the ninth generation after Chung Lai. When Fuen Po heard of the mission station in Zhangcun, Wuhua, he went there to learn more about God. At that time many people were opposed to Christians and considered Chinese converts to be followers of the barbarians. Fuen Po was baptized in Zhangcun and, despite ill treatment from his neighbors, stuck to his beliefs.

Fuen Po worked as a farmer and had four sons and two daughters. His sons were Wung Nam, Wung Cheung, Wung Kwong, and Wung Mo. The fourth son, Wung Mo, baptized "Dou Leung," studied at missionary schools, later graduated from the seminary in Lilang, and went to teach at a mission school in Meixian. Dou Leung had eleven children, several of whom settled in Shung Him Tong. After Dou Leung resigned from teaching, he went to Xingning to "do business" and then to Hong Kong to expand the business.

Dou Leung brought his son Yan Sau with him to Hong Kong and began to raise pigs on the southeastern side of the island. When Yan Sau was about ten years old, while playing on the beach, he met some Catholic priests who taught at Saint Joseph's College. They invited Yan Sau to attend classes at St. Joseph's, where he converted to Catholicism, finished secondary school, and taught for several years after his graduation. Yan Sau married the daughter of his father's close Basel mission coworker; the marriage had been arranged when he was a child. Although Yan Sau was Catholic, his wife remained Protestant and became a model elder of Shung Him Tong (Cheung 1984). In 1919 Yan Sau founded Wah Yan College, one of the most renowned schools in Hong Kong. In 1924 Tsui asked his brother-in-law Pang to help him find a place to build a house. Sehk Louh, the Tsui's house, was built in 1925 and

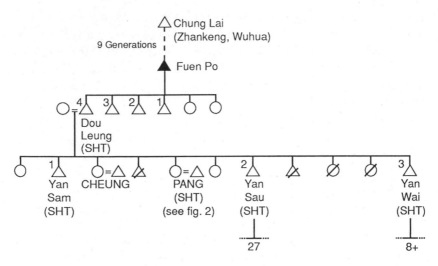

Figure 4. Tsui Dou Leung Genealogy.

Dou Leung came to live there with Yan Sau's family. In 1926, Yan Sau's younger brother, Yan Wai, brought his wife and children to Shung Him Tong and worked for his brother as a teacher at Wah Yan College. Later, the family of Yan Sam—Yan Sau and Yan Wai's eldest brother—also settled in Shung Him Tong.

TSUI KWONG CHUNG AND TSUI KWONG WING
(*see fig. 5*)

Tsui Kwong Chung's and Tsui Kwong Wing's families were both from Zhankeng, Wuhua. Their common ancestor was Man Ho, who had five sons. The third son, Fa, had a grandson named Shuen Shung; Shuen Shung's son was Kiu Sin; Kiu Sin was the father of Kwong Chung.

Kwong Chung was not happy with life in his native village so he applied to his great-uncle Tsui Yan Sau to come and work as a janitor at Wah Yan College. In 1928 he brought his wife (surname Cheung) and his son Shui Kun and his son's wife to Hong Kong. A few years later he decided he would some-day like to live in Shung Him Tong. He discussed the matter with his cousin Kwong Wing, who was already living in the Fanling area and, with the help of Pang, they built houses there in 1931. Kwong Chung and his family were Christian.

Kwong Wing's great-great-grandfather was Pit Fat. His son was Sin Hong. Sin Hong's son was Yuek Sut and Yeuk Sut's sons were Kwong Wing and Kwong Yuet. All of Yuek Sut's descendants were Christian, and they all

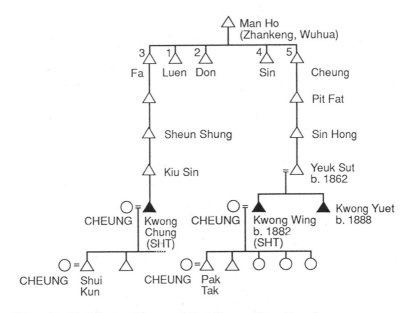

Figure 5.   Tsui Kwong Chung and Tsui Kwong Wing Genealogy.

worked in Wuhua as farmers. After 1910 a feud broke out between them and a Cheung family: "The two families fought with guns and after that my family began to decline. . . . The situation was not good; there were often robberies; the government was corrupt; the gentry persecuted us; and the village was small and crowded . . . and there was no fertile land" (in Pang 1934:101). Kwong Wing went to work for the missionary school in Lilang, and during the summers he worked as a servant for Pang Lok Sam. When the school was relocated in Xingning, Kwong Wing hoped to move to Shung Him Tong and was promised Pang's help. In 1925, Kwong Wing started off to Wuhua to fetch his family, but on his way through Ping Shan in the New Territories he was robbed. He returned to Lung Yeuk Tau, where he borrowed money from Pang and rented a house and some land to farm in Po Kat Tsai. When his family arrived, he continued farming there for six years until 1931, when he moved to Shung Him Tong with his cousin Kwong Chung.

CHEUNG WO BAN (*see fig. 6*)

Cheung Ka Yuen moved from a village near Boluo, Huizhou district, to Pa Mon village, in Baoan. Later he moved from Pa Mon to Ma Hom, also in Baoan. Cheung Wo Ban's great-uncle Kong Ban was baptized by Basel missionary Lechler. Wo Ban's father To Po was also Christian; thus, at age

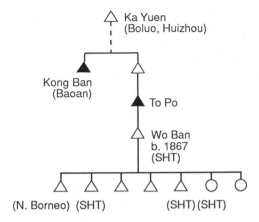

Figure 6.   Cheung Wo Ban Genealogy.

ten, Wo Ban entered the missionary school in Lilang. At sixteen he went to secondary school in Wuhua, and at twenty attended Lilang Seminary. In 1890, when he was twenty-three, he was sent to work as a missionary in Zijin. He remained there until 1899 when he was sent to Kwai Chung, Baoan, and then to teach at the Langkou school in Lilang. He remained there for nine and a half years until he was sent to Shung Him Tong in 1913.

Cheung did missionary work in Shung Him Tong and was the first teacher at Chung Him School. By the time he had been in Shung Him Tong a few years, he had no desire to return to his native village, which was poor and remote. Many of his relatives had already emigrated to Sabah, so instead of returning to Baoan, he decided to settle permanently in Shung Him Tong, and in 1928 he built a house there.

Wo Ban's eldest son worked in the government office in Sabah, North Borneo. His second son was a minister; his third son was a teacher; his fourth son worked for a mining company; and his fifth son worked in the Hong Kong British Government Lands Office.

CHEUK HING KO (*see fig.* 7)

Like Pang, Cheuk Hing Ko was from Longhua, Baoan. His ancestors moved there from Sai Lam, Wuhua. Hing Ko's grandfather had four sons, the second of whom he called Wah Sing, who in turn had a son named Hing Ko. Wah Sing was converted by Rhenish missionaries who had established a station in Langkou. Hing Ko attended a Rhenish mission school and then opened a shop in Shen Zhen. Later he moved back to Longhua and opened a grocery and medicine shop and a mortgage company. Business went well but one day his

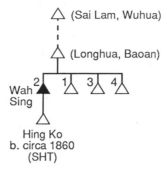

shop was burglarized, so he moved to Sai Ying Pun, Hong Kong. After some time he returned to Longhua, but did not feel safe there. He had heard of Shung Him Tong because he knew of Pang Lok Sam and Ling Sin Yuen and knew that, like him, they were Christian. In 1917 he built a house in Shung Him Tong and traveled back and forth between there and Longhua. He died in the 1920s and in 1931 only two of his daughters and his youngest son remained in Shung Him Tong.

YAO DOU ON (*see fig. 8*)

Yao Dou On was a native of Huiyang. As a child he came to Hong Kong with his mother and attended the Sham Shui Po charity school. He became Christian and after graduation went to work on a customs ship. He became known as Iron Man for resisting corruption on the ship. Yao's wife (surname Wong) was the sister of the wife of Ling Sin Yuen. While Dou On lived with his wife, daughter, and three sons in Sham Shui Po, Rev. Ling Sin Yuen worked at the Basel mission church there. Yao Dou On mentioned to Ling that they would like to live in the country, and Ling recommended that they move to one of the vacant houses in Shung Him Tong. They moved there in 1927.

CHAN CHEONG WO (*see fig. 9*)

Today there are many families of the surname Chan living in Shung Him Tong, but most are not related to those who were there in the early period of village history.

Chan Man Sing and Chan Chin Kung's ancestors had lived in Baoan in a place called Lilang for many generations before the family members scattered to other regions. Cheong Wo moved to Tsz Tong village in Lung Yeuk Tau and later to Shung Him Tong. He had two sons, Yuk Chuen (Choi?) and

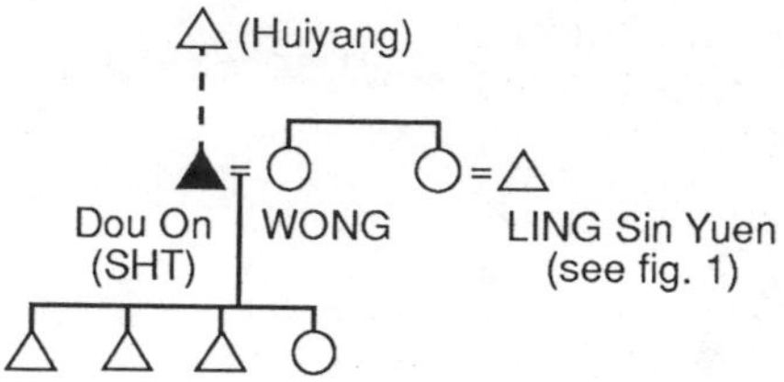

△ (Huiyang)

▲ = ○   ○ = △
Dou On │ WONG   LING Sin Yuen
(SHT)   (see fig. 1)

△ △ △ ○

Figure 8.   Yao Dou On Genealogy.

Kwai Choi. Yuk Chuen married a woman named Wong who gave birth to a daughter and then died. He then married a woman named Tsang and they had two sons and three daughters. All of them became Christian. Kwai Choi went to America and was baptized there. He married a woman named Lo and they had five sons. After Lo died, he returned with his children to Shung Him Tong. He remarried a woman by the name of Yao and they had a son and a daughter. By 1930 two of the sons had gone to America and the others lived in Shung Him Tong.

TSANG TING FAI (*see fig. 10*)

Along with the Cheuks and Chans, the Tsangs are no longer represented among the present residents of Shung Him Tong. Tsang Ting Fai's ancestors were from Wuhua, but at the beginning of the Qing dynasty (1644) some family members moved to Huiyang. Yat Kin moved to a village in Longgang. There he raised a family, started an ancestral hall, and farmed the land. He married a woman named Lam with whom he had three sons, each of whom lived in separate houses in the same village. The eldest son, Lap Bun, married a

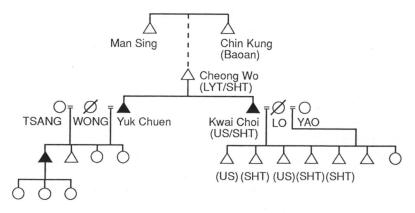

Figure 9.   Chan Cheong Wo Genealogy.

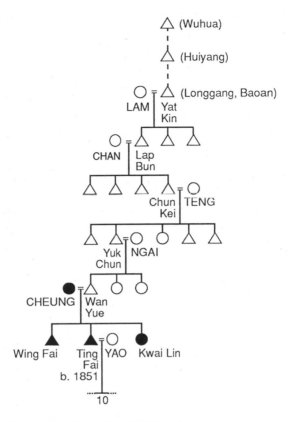

Figure 10. Tsang Ting Fai Genealogy.

woman surnamed Chan and had four sons. The youngest son, Chun Kei, married a woman named Teng and had four sons and a daughter. Yuk Chun, the second son, married a woman named Ngai and they had a son and two daughters. Yuk Chun's son, Wan Yue, married a Cheung and had two sons and a daughter. The sons were Wing Fai and Ting Fai, and the daughter was named Kwai Lin.

From the time the family moved to Huiyang the Tsangs were farmers. Ting Fai was born in 1851, a chaotic time of war, floods, and famine. His father died in 1865 and he and his brother were forced to discontinue their studies. At that time he and his brother, sister, and mother all became Christian. When the period of mourning for his father was over, they removed the altar and the idols from their home. In 1866 they were baptized at a Berlin mission church by the Basel missionary Hamberg. The following year Ting Fai's brother died, so at seventeen he went with his mother and sister to

Canton to continue his studies. He attended On Tak Theological Seminary and in 1876, when he was twenty-five years old, went to work as a missionary. He was introduced to a woman of the surname Yao, whom he later married at the Basel mission church in Sai Ying Pun; the ceremony was performed by Rev. Lechler. In 1880 Ting Fai went to Hawaii as a missionary and also did some business.

Ting Fai had seven sons and three daughters. After his mother died in 1902 he decided to return to his native village to preach the gospel, since few of the people there believed in Christianity. Within a year eight families had converted. He rebuilt his family's graves and built a road to connect his home with the nearby church. Then in 1903 he returned to Hawaii. On the ship en route to Hawaii he met Dr. Sun Yat-sen. In Hawaii in 1904 he began to work for the Yuet Han railroad project and also became involved in stock investment. When the fall of the Qing dynasty was imminent in 1909, the shareholders of the Kwong Mei Company requested that he return to China. In 1921 he returned to Hawaii for the third time. The following year he returned to his native village to build a house for his retirement. Three months after construction was complete, three of his kinsmen in the village were killed, and soon after five of his relatives were beaten. Many of his relatives then left for Malaysia, and Ting Fai moved to Shung Him Tong, where his good friends Pang, Ling, and Cheung had houses.

Notes

CHAPTER 1: WHO ARE THE HAKKA?

1. The name of the village literally means respect or worship (Shung) with humility or modesty (Him) hall or church (Tong). The "village of humble worship" is a loose translation found in Ingrams (1952) and used by several informants. I have chosen not to disguise the name of the village because I draw on numerous village histories and church publications in which the name is evident.

2. In this work, I do not use individuals' real names, except for those of authors and public figures, and those that appear in Pang's volume (1934).

3. For an excellent summary of various approaches to the study of ethnicity see Bentley (1983). See also Bentley (1987:24–27) for descriptions of the instrumentalist (e.g., A. Cohen 1969; Despres 1967; Young 1983) and primordialist (e.g., DeVos 1975, 1983; Geertz 1973a; Isaacs 1975; Keyes 1976) models of ethnicity.

4. There are also Basel mission partner churches in Cameroon, Nigeria, Kenya, the Sudan, Zaire, Bolivia, Chile, and Peru. On the history of the Basel mission see Hermann (1911), Jenkins (1989), MacGillivray ([1907] 1979), Oehler (1922), Schlatter (1916), Schultze (1916), Voskamp (1914), Witschi (1965, 1970), and Yu (1987).

5. There has been significant research conducted in Hakka communities in Hong Kong and Taiwan. Noteworthy are the studies by Berkowitz et al. (1969), Bracey (1966), E. Johnson (1975, 1976a, 1976b, 1984, 1988, 1992), G. Johnson (1971), and Pratt (1960) in Hong Kong. M. Cohen (1976), Lamley (1981), and Pasternak (1972, 1983) have written about the Hakka in Taiwan. Hayes has also conducted extensive research in several Hong Kong Hakka communities (1977, 1983). See also J. Hsieh (1980, 1985), Ng (1968), and Strauch (1984). Most studies of the Hakka, however, do not treat Hakka identity as variable, situational, or problematic but as a sociological given. An important exception is the excellent study of Sai Kung by Blake (1975, 1981).

CHAPTER 2: HISTORY AND THE CONSTRUCTION OF HAKKA IDENTITY

1. "Min" is the term used to refer to the "minnan" languages of Fujian. "Yue" is the term used to refer to the Cantonese dialects.

2. Lechler (1878) and Luo Xianglin (1933) assert that "Hakka religion" is no different from that of other Chinese. This supports Luo's underlying point that Hakka are Chinese. Eitel (1867, 1868, 1869) and Bohr (1980) suggest some differences including a tendency toward monotheism, less emphasis on the worship of state-sanctioned deities, and less emphasis on Buddhist than Taoist beliefs. These observations do not suggest the existence of a "Hakka religion" but instead are likely to point to some of the vast regional differences in "Chinese religion." Certain aspects of Hakka ancestor worship do seem to differ from other Chinese groups. See Chuang (1990) for a comparison of Hakka and Hokkien ancestor worship in Taiwan, and E. Johnson (1992) for a comparison of Hakka and Punti ancestor worship in Hong Kong.

3. As described in n. 6 below, linguistic sources I have found do not support the idea that Hakka is closer to Mandarin than Yue or Min, yet this view is still popular among most Hakka. As one Hakka member of the United States Hakka Federation recently wrote to me in a letter, "Chinese linguistic experts have proved that Hakka dialect was ancient Mandarin. While Mandarin in Central China has changed . . . the Hakka dialect did not change because they lived in remote places and had few contacts with other people."

4. The exact dates of the five migrations vary from source to source. Leong places the first migration at 317–874 A.D., the second at 874–1276, the third at 1276–1682, the fourth at 1682–1867, and the fifth beginning in 1867 (1980:6).

5. European missionary Charles Piton also argued that Hakka have been immigrants

> only since the end of the Chang Dynasty, when, for a period of 53 years, there were not less than 13 emperors of 5 different dynasties who consecutively had an ephemeral sway over China. During those times of trouble a great number of Chinese emigrated into the South, which being more remote from the scene of the struggles, enjoyed a comparative state of peace; and the descendants of these emigrants are the *Hakkas* of today (1873:225–26).

6. Hashimoto writes that the Hakka assertion of their origins in the Central Plains of China is "largely supported by various historical as well as linguistic evidence" (1973:1). See also Moser (1985), Sagart (1982), and P. Yang (1967). Norman (1988:222) and Ramsey (1987:111) identify Hakka as part of the "southern group" of Chinese languages because, although there are some unmistakably northern features, they consider Hakka to be more closely related to the other southern dialects around them. Norman says that the fact that Hakka language belongs to the "southern group" indicates that "these [Hakka] dialects have developed from a variety of Chinese that has been present in South China since Han and Sanguo times (first to third centuries AD)" (1988:222). Norman's linguistic evidence suggests an even earlier migration than Luo's earliest wave, one that is more compatible with what Hsieh and Eitel classify as the first period of migration. As Ramsey and Norman explain, the assertion that one often hears among Hakka, that their language is closer to Mandarin than is Cantonese, is not supported by linguistic studies.

7. An overwhelming amount has been written on the Taiping Rebellion. For a historical analysis of the Taiping, see Kuhn (1978). For material on the documents of the Taipings, see the monumental collection translated by Michael (1966, 1971). For a collection of early English-language documents about the God Worshipers and the Taiping Rebellion, see Clarke and Gregory (1982). For more on Hong, the leader

of the Taiping Rebellion, see the Basel missionary Hamberg's biography of Hong (1854) as told to him by Hong's cousin. For a closer look at the religious issues and beliefs of the Taipings, see Boardman (1952), Bohr (1978), Wagner (1982), and Shih (1967). See Boardman (1962) and Newbern (1953) for a discussion of the millenarian aspects of the Taiping Rebellion, and Smith (1976) for what became of some Taiping "family and friends." Teng (1962) reviews key books and articles written about the Taiping Rebellion by Chinese, English, French, German, Japanese, and Russian authors.

8. According to Luo, Sun Yat-sen was Hakka (1933: chaps. 7, 8; 1965:388–96). This point has been questioned by Tan (1963, cited in Erbaugh 1992). Sun came from a family that considered itself Cantonese, in "a county where Hakka nearby were looked down upon" (Moser 1985:247). According to Moser, when Sun opposed the binding of his sister's feet, his mother responded, "Would you have her as a stranger [Hakka] or as one of us?" (Linebarger [1925] 1969, cited in Moser 1985:247). Sun also is said to have learned of the Taiping Rebellion from an old Hakka man who had participated in it and who spoke Hakka fluently (Moser 1985:247). According to one Hakka informant in the United States, "It is a well established fact that Dr. Sun Yat-sen was a Hakka. . . . Dr. Sun Yat-sen himself said he's Hakka."

9. Teng (1971:49) puts the number of converts at almost two thousand, while I. Hsu (1978) estimates the figure to be over three thousand. At its height, Kuhn asserts that the Taiping movement numbered about two million (1977:351).

10. Yu (1987) notes that Ling Kai Lin, the founder of Shung Him Tong, is reputed to have told his grandson, who then told Luo Xianglin, that he was baptized by Hamberg along with Hong Xiuquan. This is unlikely, but it is possible that Ling was baptized with Li Tsin Kau or possibly Hong Rengan.

11. The Taiping Rebellion is now hailed as an early display of *Chinese,* not Hakka, nationalism, and as a precursor of the Chinese Revolution, which was strongly opposed to foreign interference and domination. Teng refers to the Taiping as "a gigantic cthnic movement to overthrow the foreign Manchu dynasty," but he uses the term "ethnic" to refer to Chinese, not Hakka (1971:vii).

12. An attempt to minimize the distinction between Chinese subethnic groups in order to unify the Han Chinese majority is evidenced in the government policy of the People's Republic of China. There, Mandarin—the native language of an estimated 70 percent of mainlanders—has become the national language. The "national minorities" are displayed as the exotic "other" in contrast to the unified image of Han Chinese, which includes the estimated Hakka population of thirty-five million. In an attempt to reinforce the solidarity of the Han Chinese, as Erbaugh has observed, Chinese publications rarely mention whether a person is Hakka, although Hakka represent a disproportionately high number in the Chinese government (1992).

13. The translation into English from the Chinese version that Nakagawa used reads:

> The Hakkas are surely a branch of the people of the Middle Field, and quite a characteristic, robust, and outstanding one, at that. The fact that their progenitors, although compelled to migrate, came from the Middle Field can be ascertained by the following evidences: their respect for their own stock; their high morale as warriors; their deserving self-reliance. Mark my words, the

Hakkas are sure to intensify their influence in due course of development and to exalt the people of China (Nakagawa 1975:209).

The original source reads quite differently:

The Hakkas are certainly a very distinct and virile strain of the Chinese race. The circumstances of their origin and migrations go far to account for their pride of race and martial spirit. Probably they never had the custom of foot-binding. It is safe to predict that Hakkas will play an increasingly important part in the progress and elevation of the Chinese people (Campbell 1912:480).

CHAPTER 3: SHUNG HIM TONG:
THE IMAGINED COMMUNITY

1. The term "Punti" is sometimes translated to mean "indigenous" or "native" but does not usually refer to the pre-Chinese (pre-Han) inhabitants. "Punti" is used in several different ways depending on the context and the person using the term. The most common uses are as follows. (1) It is used by Cantonese speakers to refer to the descendants of Cantonese-speaking people who lived in the New Territories before the British. This includes those who successfully "passed" as Cantonese. (2) It is used to refer to the Chinese people who were in the New Territories before the British, regardless of whether they were Hakka speakers or Cantonese speakers. (3) It is used very broadly to refer to people who are not "recent immigrants" to the New Territories. This generally means people who arrived before the late 1940s. Punti can be juxtaposed to Hakka in some cases, and can include Hakka in others. In most cases, however, the term refers to pre-British Yue-speaking inhabitants.

2. As Faure defines it, the Cantonese term *heung* (*xiang*) can be used to describe a cluster of villages so close that they appear to merge together, as a larger community including villages and village clusters, or to describe a "cluster in which each village forms a distinct unit," as in Lung Yeuk Tau, also known as Lung Shan Heung (1986:181).

3. Anthropological research has been conducted among several of the higher-order lineages in the New Territories. See R. Watson (1985, 1982) for information on the Teng of Ha Tsuen; Potter on the Teng of Ping Shan (1968); J. Watson on the Man (1975); Baker on the Liao (1968); and Faure (1986) on Eastern New Territories lineages, especially Teng and Pang.

4. It is interesting to note the early censuses used language as the means of distinguishing between Hakka and Punti (Hong Kong Government 1911). Later censuses (1962, 1966) still distinguished between "usual language," but in this case it was between Hakka and Cantonese (the Punti language, strictly speaking is not the same as Cantonese—the language spoken in Canton—is not often understood by Cantonese speakers, and is sometimes mistaken for Hakka). In the 1971 census, language is given as a factor of place of origin. In the 1981 census there is no category of language, only place of origin defined so broadly as to include all of Guangdong in one category; thus, it is impossible to determine the size of the Hakka population as their "place of origin" is the same as that of the Cantonese. Census data for 1971 and 1981 suggest that

there are far more Chaozhou than Hakka. This is misleading as most Hakka have been in Hong Kong far longer than the Chaozhou and therefore their "usual language" is often Cantonese. The bulk of the Chaozhou population live in urban areas, while many Hakka remain in the rural New Territories (see Sparks 1976a, 1976b).

5. The official boundary of Shung Him Tong, used for administrative purposes and for population census information, stretches over a far wider area than the "social" boundary of Shung Him Tong. The fact that there are at least two ideas about what is meant by Shung Him Tong becomes clear with the following example: the official population of Shung Him Tong is thirteen hundred, and this number is used to determine the number of village representatives to which Shung Him Tong is entitled. But church members say that "almost everyone in Shung Him Tong village goes to church" and that "95 percent of the people in Shung Him Tong are Christian and all are Hakka." During the year I attended Shung Him Tong Sunday services, less than two hundred people attended church each week, and many were from outside of Shung Him Tong, even with its boundaries most broadly defined. Shung Him Tong, as it is represented in this study, is the Shung Him Tong of Hakka Christians. The question of who is considered to "belong" to the community is addressed in the following chapter.

6. This is an unpublished address presented by K. M. A. Barnett while serving as District Commissioner of the New Territories, now held at the Colonial Secretariat Library, Hong Kong.

7. See Pasternak (1983:12–26) for an example of the unwelcome reception of Hakka in Taiwan.

8. The manuscript was compiled by Pang Lok Sam in 1934. It was later mimeographed. A photocopy of a mimeographed copy is in the Chinese collection of the Hong Kong University Library. It is handwritten and poorly duplicated so not all parts are legible.

9. It is unclear whether the immigrants were accompanied by their families. Women and children are rarely mentioned in the history of the village or in the family genealogies. Daughters may be listed but their names are rarely recorded, nor are those of their husbands and children.

10. It is not clear whether the tenant farmers Ling and Chan who Ling Kai Lin invited to farm his land are the families of Ling Ban Chung, Ling Ban Sum, Chan Yuk Choi, and Chan Kwai Choi.

11. One informant was quick to tell me that the earlier name of Shung Him Tong meaning "Always Prosper" need not refer to material wealth, but could also mean "spiritual wealth," or an increasing number of believers.

12. See Baker (1968:36–37) for an example of the dislike of Christians in Sheung Shui.

13. The Hong Kong property of the Basel mission had been transferred to the Hong Kong church during World War I, but the Tsung Tsin mission, or the "Hakka church," did not gain its independence until 1928. When the Germans lost the war, Tsung Tsin mission became independent largely for economic reasons. The Basel mission churches in China were not affected by the war as were their churches in Africa, India, and Hong Kong, since the German missionaries who belonged to the Basel mission were allowed to remain (see Pang 1934; also Jenkins 1989).

14. According to W. Lo (1965:95–96, 113), in imperial China the Punti often prevented recent Hakka immigrants from registering with the local government so that they would not be eligible "to participate in the local civil service examination, for which each district had a fixed quota." As early as 1789 a separate quota was set up for the Hakka in certain parts of Guangdong in an attempt to reduce the "conflicts between the minority groups and the rest of the population" (Chang 1955:81). See Lun Ng (1984) concerning village education in the New Territories region during the Qing dynasty.

15. In a government memo (Hong Kong Government 1923), the colonial secretary inquired of the north district officer whether the school was to be a commercial or a philanthropic venture. The north district officer responded:

> Mr. Pang has collected subscriptions from the local Hakka community for the purchase of the land and building of a school, after that the school will be dependent on fee and government aid. There will probably be about 40 pupils paying HK$5 or HK$6 per annum. This will scarcely pay the salary of the teacher . . . so there is unlikely to be any commercial profit. I believe this to be a genuine case and worthy of assistance.

16. It is difficult to generalize about where Hakka non-Christians sided in these disputes. In some cases Hakka non-Christians turned to the powerful Hakka Christian leaders for support in their own disagreements with Punti villagers. In the case of the dispute with On Lok described in this chapter, local Hakka might well have sided with the people of Shung Him Tong because, like the Lung Yeuk Tau Punti, they could also benefit from the new path through On Lok. In other conflicts that were specifically between Hakka Christians and Punti, such as in the conflict over the new church site described in Chapter 5, most local non-Christian Hakka appear to have attempted to remain neutral rather than risk offending their Punti neighbors.

17. According to the European missionary,

> On the night of the sixteenth of this month, as I was studying at Chung Him School, I heard about fifteen shots coming from the direction of On Lok village. All the people in the room were stunned and knew not what to do. Others in the village were so frightened that they closed their doors and dared not go out. On the night of the seventeenth, Mr. Kwong, a detective, visited Pang Lok Sam to investigate the shots fired the previous night. It had been reported to him that some Shung Him Tong villagers had wanted to destroy the barricade set up at the Shung Him bridge, that On Lok villagers had had to fire to warn them, and that Pang Lok Sam and our villagers had fired back. After hearing this, Pang Lok Sam wanted to establish his innocence, so he presented his two rifles and pistol together with the 150 bullets to the Sheung Shui police station for examination. The bullets had been registered before the incident took place and all of them were accounted for; solid evidence that Pang Lok Sam did not fire at 7:30 P.M. on the sixteenth (in Pang 1934:19).

CHAPTER 4: THE HAKKA CHURCH COMMUNITY AND DAILY LIFE

1. The stereotypical round, flat "Hakka hat" with black fringes is never seen in church.

2. Since I left Shung Him Tong in 1987, two young Hakka people from the village have made plans to enter theological seminaries.

3. Shung Him Tong also resembles the early Basel mission in its rejection of the ecumenical movement. Tsung Tsin mission is instead affiliated with the Lutheran church.

4. See also Liao (1972) for an explanation of the "failure" of Protestant missionaries among the Hakka in Taiwan, which he says was in part because becoming Christian was equated with giving up Hakka identity.

5. The Cantonese term Geiduktouh (Jidutu), meaning "Christian," is almost exclusively used to refer to Protestants, while the Cantonese term Tinjyugaau (Tianzhujiao) refers only to Catholics. Some Shung Him Tong people do not believe that Catholics worship the same God. This idea is reinforced by the fact that Protestants generally translate God in Cantonese as Seuhngdai (Shangdi), while Roman Catholics generally use the Cantonese term Tinjyu (Tianzhu). The fact that Catholic and Protestant Bibles originate from different European translations of earlier texts and translate such basic terms as "God" and "Christ" in different ways has contributed to the impression that these are vastly different religions. Many people I spoke to also were highly critical of the fact that Catholics "worship saints" and that their nuns "resemble" Buddhist ones.

CHAPTER 5: CHRISTIAN SOULS AND CHINESE SPIRITS

1. In a study of urban resettlement of a Hakka village in Hong Kong, Berkowitz demonstrates the adaptability of Chinese religion: gods who were not needed in the new setting were sent back to heaven, while others were assigned new duties (1969). See also Harrell (1974:204).

Similarly, Francis Hsu cites a letter written to a Beijing newspaper in 1947 in response to a request for personal experiences that relate to "how to conquer poverty." The person who answered wrote that becoming Catholic was "in short . . . one of the ways of meeting an emergency. Just get baptized and don't worry about the rest. . . . Another way out is to go to the Relief Department of the Bureau of Social Welfare" (1981:272).

2. J. Watson outlines the following structures of Chinese funerary rites: In the "performative domain" are (1) "public notification of death by wailing and other expressions of grief"; (2) donning of the appropriate white attire for mourners; (3) "ritualized bathing of the corpse"; (4) "the transfer of food, money and goods from the living to the dead"; (5) "the preparation and installation of a soul tablet for the dead"; (6) "the ritualized use of money and employment of professionals" who perform ritual services; (7) "music to accompany the corpse and settle the spirit"; (8) "sealing the corpse in an airtight coffin"; and (9) "expulsion of the coffin from the community" (1988:12–15). In the ideological domain, the Chinese believe (1) in a continuity and similarity between this world and the next; (2) that there is no radical dualism between body and soul; (3) that after death there continue to be reciprocal relations between the living and the dead; and (4) that there must be a balance between the sexes even in death—thus the practice of posthumous or ghost marriages (1988:8–11). Watson stresses that the practices associated with death rituals were standardized and absolute, while the belief system was "loosely organized at best and rarely enforced" (1988:10).

3. As Whyte puts it, "In the enduring stress on the strong links and obligations between family members which persist beyond the grave, if not the ritual structure,

modern Chinese urbanites can still express their essential Chineseness" (1988:316). The same can be said for the people of Shung Him Tong.

4. Baker describes the persecution of Christians in a village in Sheung Shui, several miles from Shung Him Tong, as follows:

> In 1909 the first convert in the village was made, but this "evoked strong opposition which took the form of persecution and entailed suffering for the truth's sake." . . . The villagers generally are strongly opposed to Christianity now well represented in their midst, and they have been successful in driving out one family whose house has been closed up *by the officials* . . . and we believe sold (Baker 1968:36–37; emphasis in original).

5. By arguing that what is essential to Chineseness is not religious, they are constructing an identity that bears important similarities to the secular Chinese identity in the People's Republic of China (Whyte 1988). Also see Whyte for a discussion of the importance of "proper" burial practices and the redefinition of what is deemed proper in the People's Republic of China (1988:314).

6. Like the residents of Ch'inan, Taiwan, described by Ahern, the people of Shung Him Tong I spoke to did not consider the crowdedness of the public cemetery a drawback (1973:188).

7. Pang's grave was built on a site that he selected on his own private land before the rules were as strictly enforced as they are today. Pang's wife, however, is buried in the Shung Him cemetery. It is noteworthy that despite Pang's role in establishing the cemetery, he was not buried there. His horseshoe-shaped grave, covered with a shelter and adorned with red painted crosses, overlooks the Shung Him cemetery from the opposing hill. Some speculate that having his own spot conveyed more honor, others that he wanted the same rights as the Punti in the area, and still others that he might have thought the spot would be more permanent since it was on his own family property.

8. Photographs play an increasingly important part in funerals and weddings. When someone has died, photographs of the person in the home are often turned around for a few days, as Christians explain, out of respect. Another explanation not expressed by Chinese Christians stems from the Chinese belief that a photograph can capture one's soul and must be removed to allow the soul to travel to the afterworld.

9. Simple yarn flowers may be an adaptation of the proscription against wearing "fine" clothes such as silk. Although several detailed studies of mourning grades exist, I have found no explanation of the significance of the green color of the yarn flowers. As A. Wolf (1970, 189–207) found in Taiwan, rough cloth is worn by the closest relations, white by a generation further removed, dark blue by the great grandsons' generation, red by the following generation, and yellow by the next. These colors indicate increasing genealogical distance from the deceased. Wolf also describes a practice of placing a dead man in his coffin with coins in his pocket. Just before the burial the coins are removed and the children and grandchildren tie them to their wrists. The children generally use a white string and the grandchildren use a blue string (1970:199). It seems possible that these practices are related to the blue and green yarn flowers. As Wolf explains, blue is a "middle point on the scale, halfway between the

extremes of joy [symbolized by red or yellow] and sorrow [the rough hemp fabric]" (1970:191).

10. As Ahern describes in Taiwan, red steamed cakes are passed out to funeral guests because red acts "as a prophylactic to ward off any danger from lingering contact with ghosts" (1973:174).

11. In Hong Kong it is acceptable for Catholics to bow to graves, but people of Shung Him Tong generally do not. Catholics, I was told, usually go on All Saints' Day in November, near Chung Yeung, rather than at Easter or Ching Ming.

12. People from Shung Him Tong did not seem to be aware that in some parts of China graves are visited as part of the lunar new year celebration or on the last day of the old year.

13. A looser interpretation might be that "flowers come up and have a fragrant smell."

14. Much has been written on this subject. See, for example, Ahern (1973), Freedman (1966, 1979), and Weller (1987).

15. The typical *feng-shui* site for a village, town, or city is facing south. "South," however, is always defined by the direction the site is facing:

> The front of the site is always the south and all south stands for, and
> front is symbolic for south even if it has proved impracticable really to face
> due south. It [the site] should always have an unhindered view. Likewise
> the back of a site is always the north and should be blocked, left is always the
> east and all it stands for, right is always a symbol for the west (Feuchtwang
> 1974b:2).

CHAPTER 6: TRANSFORMING IMAGES OF THE HAKKA

1. Thanks to Lesley Sharp for calling this to my attention.

2. Confucius is reputed to have said, "Having only coarse food to eat, plain water to drink, and a bent arm for a pillow, one can still find happiness therein. Riches and honour acquired by unrighteous means are to me as drifting clouds" (*Analects* 7:15 in de Bary 1960:22).

3. As the Confucian *Analects* suggest, "Poverty and low station are what people dislike; but if one ends up with them by not complying with the Moral Way, he cannot get rid of them" (*Analects* 4:5 in Jochim 1986:124).

4. See, for example, Basel missionary Leonhardt's description in Appendix 1 of the Christian convert Tsang Fuk Ming before he became Christian. According to Leonhardt, Tsang was one of the "pious heathens" who were "closer to the truth."

5. These occupations are still considered valid options for unmarried women in Shung Him Tong. One young woman was told by her parents that she ought not marry because of her past psychological problems, which they feared were hereditary. Instead, she considered the option of becoming an evangelist.

6. This also helps to explain why charity and gifts of money were not as desirable to early converts as work and educational opportunities.

CHAPTER 7: OUR BELOVED HAKKA PEOPLE

1. Hakka identity in Taiwan provides an important lesson. As little as a decade ago, Hakka identity there appeared to be on the decline, but it has since made a striking comeback. Before 1986, Martin writes, ethnic consciousness in Taiwan was such that scholars "rightly collapsed the different ethnic origins of the Taiwanese population" and depicted Taiwan's Hakka, Hokkien, and aborigines all as native Taiwanese (1992:2). Today, Taiwan Hakka have organized into an active political movement. Martin asserts it is "no longer possible to discuss ethnicity in Taiwan without distinguishing Hokkien, Hakka and aborigines from one another" (1992:2).

2. That a nontraditional association has become the basis for the perpetuation and transformation of Hakka identity is not what some scholars might expect. J. Hsieh provides us with an interesting point of contrast. His work among Huizhuo Hakka associations in Hong Kong suggests that because Chinese voluntary organizations are based on traditional principles of locality, kinship, and occupation, they "not only constitute a modernizing agency for better adaptation to modern situations, but also work as a mechanism for perpetuating and preserving Hakka tradition" (1985:157). In accord with the point made by Shack in his work among ethnic groups in Ethiopia (1973), the case of Hakka Christians shows that ethnic identity can also persist and be perpetuated by nontraditional urban voluntary associations.

3. Just as the Hausa who live in Yoruba towns in Nigeria and who have adopted the Tijaniya religion to strengthen their identity (A. Cohen 1969), so the Hakka Christians described in this book have taken on a "new" religious identity to strengthen their ethnic identity. The difference between Cohen's study and my own is that Cohen uses the Hausa case to support an instrumentalist argument that ethnicity persists because it serves economic interests.

APPENDIX 2: THE FAMILIES OF SHUNG HIM TONG IN 1932

1. Some of the Lings spell their name "Ling" and others such as Dou Yeung spell it "Lin." I have chosen the spelling "Ling" in order to distinguish it with another surname more commonly spelled "Lin." Dou Yeung also commonly writes his name "Do Yang," following the Mandarin pronunciation. Lin Tschong Hin is another name for Pastor Ling Kai Lin.

2. The Chinese word for "business" (*shengyi*) can refer to anything from a shop or a mortgage company to hawking on the street or raising pigs. It can also be roughly translated as "project."

Glossary of Chinese Terms

Entries in the glossary are arranged in alphabetical order according to the first term in the entry. Cantonese terms are marked (C), the romanization of Basel Mission Archives material is marked (BMA), and Mandarin terms in pinyin are marked with an asterisk (*). Unmarked personal and place names follow the Hong Kong usage (see Note on Romanization).

baainihn (C) (*bainian**)　拜年

baaisahn (C) (*baishen**)　拜神

Baoan*　寶安

*bendi** (see Punti)

Boluo*　博羅

Buji* (BMA: Pokat)　布吉

Chan　陳

Chang Shan Kou*　長山口

Changle* (BMA: Tschonglok)　長樂

Chaozhou*　潮州

Cheuk　卓

Cheung (BMA: Tschong)　張

Cheung Fuk Hing　張復興

Cheung Hing Tong (Chang Xing Tang*)　長興堂

Cheung Wo Ban　張和彬

Ching Ming　清明

choisam (C)　菜心

Chong Hom Tong　松磡塘

Chung Yeung　重陽

Dongguan*　東莞

Fanling　粉嶺

*feng-shui**　風水

Fujian* (Fukien)　福建

gatyi (C)　吉儀

gau (enough) (C)　夠

gau (nine) (C)   九

Geiduktouh (C) (Jidutu*)   基督徒

Guangdong* (Kwangtung)   廣東

Guangxi*   廣西

Guangzhou* (Canton)   廣州

gung hei faat choih (C)   恭喜發財

Guzhu*   古竹

gwai (C)   鬼

Ha Tsuen   厦村

Hakka (*kejia**)   客家

Hakka gaang duhk (C)   客家耕讀

Hakka jim deihjyu (C)   客家佔地主

Hakka yahn gaang tihn duhk syu (C)   客家人耕田讀書

Han*   漢

Henan*   河南

heung (C) (*xiang**)   鄉

Heung Yee Kuk   鄉議局

Hong Rengan*   洪仁玕

Hong Xiuquan*   洪秀全

Huizhou*   惠州

Jiangxi*   江西

Jiaying* (BMA: Kaying)   嘉應

jouhdak gunleuhng, cheutdak tengtong (C)   做得官娘出得廳堂

Kam Tin   錦田

ke*   客

kejia* (see Hakka)

Kexi Datonghui* (United Hakka Association)   客系大同會

Kong (Gong)   江

Kowloon   九龍

laan gwai tang fong (C)   蘭桂騰芳

Langkou*   浪口

Lantau   爛頭（大嶼山）

li* (ritual; proper conduct)   禮

*li** (measure of distance)　里

Li　李

Li Shin En　李承恩

Li Tsin Kau　李正高

lihksi jaahpgwaan (C)　歷史習慣

Lilang* (BMA: Lilong)　李朗

Ling　凌

Ling Ban Chung　凌品忠

Ling Dou Yeung (Lin Do Yang)　凌道揚

Ling Kai Lin　凌啟蓮

Ling Sin Yuen　凌善元

Lo Uk　羅屋

Lo Wai　老圍

Longhua*　龍（花）華

Luen On Tong　聯安堂

Luen Wo　聯和

Luen Wo Tong　聯和堂

Lung Shan　龍山

Lung Yeuk Tau　龍躍頭

Luo Xianglin* (C: Lo Heung Lam)　羅香林

Ma Wat Tsuen　麻笏村

Ma Wat Wai　麻笏圍

Meilin* (BMA: Moilim)　梅林

Meixian*　梅縣

Meizhou*　梅州

Min*　閩

*minzu**　民族

Nam Wa Po　南華莆

Nyenhang (see Yuankengli*)

On Lok　安樂

Pang　彭

Pang Lok Sam　彭樂三

Ping Shan　屏山

Po Kat Tsai　布吉仔

Punti (*bendi**)　本地

*qi** (*ch'i*)　氣

Sai Kung　西貢

Sai Ying Pun　西營盤

San Uk Tsuen　新屋村

San Wai　新圍

Sannihn faailohk (C)　新年快樂

Sehk Louh (C)　石廬

sei (to die) (C)　死

sei (four) (C)　四

Seuhngdai (C) (Shangdi*)　上帝

Sha Tau Kok　沙頭角

Sha Tin　沙田

Sham Shui Po　深水埔

Shanxi*　山西

Shau Kei Wan　筲箕灣

Shek Wu Hui　石湖墟

Shen Zhen*　深圳

*shengyi**　生意

Sheung Shui　上水

Shung Him Tong　崇謙堂

Sichuan*　四川

Tai Po　大埔

Teng* (C: Dahng)　鄧

Tinjyu (C) (Tianzhu*)　天主

Tinjyugaau (C) (Tianzhujiao*)　天主教

Tsang (BMA: Tschang)　曾

Tsang Fuk Ming　曾復明

Tsui (BMA: Tschi)　徐

Tsui Dou Leung　徐道良

Tsui Fuk Kwong　徐復光

Tsui Yan Sam　徐仁深

Tsui Yan Sam　徐仁深

Tsui Yan Sau　徐仁壽

Tsung Tsin Association　崇正會（館）

Tsung Tsin mission　崇真會

Tsz Tong Tsuen　祠堂村

tujia*　土家

Tung Kok Wai　東閣圍

Wing Ning Tsuen　永寧村

Wing Ning Wai　永寧圍

wong choih jau sau (C)　橫財就手

Wuhua*　五華（花）

xiang* (see *heung*)　鄉

Xinan*　新安

Xingning*　興寧

yahn leuih hohk (C)　人類學

Yao (Yau)　丘，邱

Yao Dou On　丘道安

Yu Laan Jit (C)　盂蘭節

Yuankengli* (BMA: Nyenhangli)　元坑（源坑）裡

Yue*　粵

Yuen Long　元朗

Zhangcun* (BMA: Tschongtschuen)　樟村

Zhankeng* (BMA: Tsim Hang)　粘坑

Zijin*　紫金

zu*　族

Bibliography

ARCHIVAL SOURCES

Basel Mission Archives

1868a   "Biographie des Li Tschin Kau" (Biography of Li Tsin Kau). A-1.6, no. 9.

1868b   "Drei Neue Kamaraden" (Three new converts). A-1.6, no. 38.

1874   "Biographie von Wong En Kau" (Biography of Wong En Kau). A-1.9, no. 34.

1885   "Das Leben des Verstorbenen Li Tschin Kau erzhalt von seinem Sohn" (Life of the late Li Tsin Kau as told by his son). A-1.19, no. 38.

1889   "Biographie von Tschong Fuk Min" (Biography of Tsang Fuk Ming). A-1.23, no. 99.

1899   Lin Tschong Hin. Request for leave of absence (in German). A-1.33, no. 64.

1900   Lin Tschong Hin. Request for resignation (in German). A-1.34, no. 61.

Hong Kong Government

1905   New Territories Crown Block Lease.

1911   "Report on the Census of the Colony for 1911." *Hong Kong Sessional Papers, 1909–1912*. Hong Kong: Government Printer.

1923   *Colonial Secretariat Office Report*, CSO file no. 1923/1797 [October 23].

1930   *Colonial Secretariat Office Report*, CSO file no. 1930/5374 [April 29].

1931   *Colonial Secretariat Office Report*, CSO file no. 1931/4840, [April 21].

1955   "Politics in the New Territories." Unpublished address by K. M. A. Barnett. Government Secretariat Office.

1960   *A Gazetteer of Place Names in Hong Kong, Kowloon and the New Territories*. Hong Kong: Government Printer.

1962   *Report on the 1961 Census*. Hong Kong: Government Printer.

1966   *Census*. Hong Kong: Government Printer.

1971   *Census*. Hong Kong: Government Printer.

1981   *Census, Main Report*. Hong Kong: Government Printer.

1983   *Hong Kong Island, Lantau and the Outlying Islands.* Vol. 1 of *Hong Kong Streets and Places: The Official Guide.* Hong Kong: Government Printer.
1985   *Kowloon and the New Territories.* Vol. 2 of *Hong Kong Streets and Places: The Official Guide.* Hong Kong: Government Printer.

BOOKS AND ARTICLES

Ahern, Emily M.
1973   *The Cult of the Dead in a Chinese Village.* Stanford: Stanford University Press.
Aijmer, Goran.
1967   "Expansion and Extension in Hakka Society." *Journal of the Hong Kong Branch of the Royal Asiatic Society* 7:42–79.
Anagnost, Ann.
1989   "Transformations of Gender in Modern China." In *Gender and Anthropology: Critical Reviews for Research and Teaching.* Sandra Morgen, ed. Washington, D.C.: American Anthropological Association, 313–42.
Anderson, Benedict.
1983   *Imagined Communities: Reflections on the Origins and Spread of Nationalism.* New York: Verso Press.
Anderson, Eugene N.
1968   "Prejudice and Ethnic Stereotypes in Rural Hong Kong." *Kroeber Anthropological Society Papers* 37:90–107.
1988   *The Food of China.* New Haven: Yale University Press.
Anderson, E. N., Jr., and Marja L. Anderson.
1977   "Modern China: South." In *Food in Chinese Culture: Anthropological and Historical Perspectives.* K. C. Chang, ed. New Haven: Yale University Press, 317–82.
Arkush, R. David.
1984   "If Man Works Hard the Land Will Not Be Lazy: Entrepreneurial Values in North Chinese Peasant Proverbs." *Modern China* 10, no. 4:461–79.
1990   "Orthodoxy and Heterodoxy in Twentieth Century Chinese Peasant Proverbs." In *Orthodoxy in Late Imperial China.* Kwang-Ching Liu, ed. Berkeley: University of California Press, 311–31.
Aw Boon Haw.
1950   "Preface." In *Xianggang Chongzheng conghui sanshih zhounian jinian tekan* (Hong Kong Tsung Tsin Association thirtieth anniversary special publication). Hong Kong: Tsung Tsin Association, 1–2.
Baker, Hugh.
1966   "The Five Great Clans of the New Territories." *Journal of the Hong Kong Branch of the Royal Asiatic Society* 6:25–47.
1968   *A Chinese Lineage Village: Sheung Shui.* London: Frank Cass.
Balfour, S. F.
[1940] 1970   "Hong Kong Before the British." *Journal of the Hong Kong Branch of the Royal Asiatic Society* 10:134–79.

Barnett, K. M. A.

1964   "Hong Kong Before the Chinese: The Frame, the Puzzle and the Missing Pieces." *Journal of the Hong Kong Branch of the Royal Asiatic Society*. 4:42–67.

Barth, Fredrik.

1969   "Introduction." In *Ethnic Groups and Boundaries: The Social Organization of Culture Difference*. Fredrik Barth, ed. Boston: Little and Brown, 9–38.

Basu, Ellen Oxfeld (see also Ellen Oxfeld).

1991a   "The Sexual Division of Labor and the Organization of Family and Firm in an Overseas Chinese Community." *American Ethnologist* 18, no. 4:700–718.

1991b   "Profit, Loss and Fate: The Entrepreneurial Ethic and the Practice of Gambling in an Overseas Community." *Modern China* 17, no. 2:227–59.

Bentley, G. Carter.

1981   *Ethnicity and Nationality: A Bibliographic Guide*. Seattle: University of Washington Press.

1983   "Theoretical Perspectives on Ethnicity and Nationality." *Sage Race Relations Abstracts* 8, nos. 2:1–53, 3:1–26.

1987   "Ethnicity and Practice." *Comparative Studies in Society and History* 29, no. 1:24–55.

Berkowitz, Morris I., Frederick P. Brandauer, and John H. Reed.

1969   *Folk Religion in an Urban Setting: A Study of Hakka Villagers in Transition*. Hong Kong: Christian Study Centre on Chinese Religion and Culture.

Berreman, Gerald D.

1979   "Self, Situation, and Escape from Stigmatized Ethnic Identity." In *Caste and Other Inequities: Essays on Inequality*. Gerald D. Berreman, ed. Meerut: Folklore Institute, 164–68.

Blake, C. Fred.

1975   *Negotiating Ethnolinguistic Symbols in a Chinese Market Town*. Ph.D. diss., University of Illinois at Urbana-Champaign.

1981   *Ethnic Groups and Social Change in a Hong Kong Market Town*. Asian Studies at Hawaii, no. 27. Honolulu: University Press of Hawaii.

Boardman, Eugene P.

1952   *Christian Influence Upon the Ideology of the Taiping Rebellion, 1851–1864*. Madison: University of Wisconsin Press.

1962   "Millenary Aspects of the Taiping Rebellion." In *Millennial Dreams in Action: Essays in Comparative Study*. Sylvia Thrupp, ed. Comparative Studies in Society and History, supp. 2. The Hague: Mouton and Company, 70–79.

Bohr, Paul Richard.

1978   *The Politics of Eschatology: Hung Hsiu-Ch'uan and the Rise of the Taipings, 1837–1853*. Ph.D. diss., University of California at Davis.

1980   "The Hakka and the Heavenly Kingdom: Ethnicity and Religion in the Rise of the Taiping Rebellion." *China Notes* (Fall) 133–36.

Bracey, Dorothy Heid.
1966   *The Effects of Emigration on a Hakka Village*. Ph.D. diss., Harvard
              University.
Breslin, Thomas.
1980   *China, American Catholicism, and the Missionary*. University Park: Penn-
              sylvania State University Press.
Bruner, Edward M.
1986   "Ethnography as Narrative." In *The Anthropology of Experience*. Victor
              Turner and Edward M. Bruner, eds. Urbana: University of Illinois
              Press, 139–55.
Campbell, George.
1912   "Origin and Migration of the Hakkas." *The Chinese Recorder and Mis-
              sionary Journal* 43:473–80.
Chang, Chung-li.
1955   *The Chinese Gentry: Studies on Their Role in Nineteenth Century Chinese
              Society*. Seattle: University of Washington Press.
Char, Tin Yuke, and C. H. Kwok.
1969   *The Hakka Chinese, Their Origins and Folk Songs*. San Francisco: Jade
              Mountain Press.
Cheung Sui Wing.
1984   "Jidujiao Xianggang Chongzhenhui Fenling Chongqiantang huishi"
              (History of Tsung Tsin Mission's Shung Him Church, Fanling, Hong
              Kong). In *Chongqiantang* (Shung Him Church). Kowloon: Lai Hung
              Publishing Company, 1–5.
Chuang Ying-chang.
1990   "A Comparison of Hokkien and Hakka Ancestor Worship." *Bulletin
              of the Institute of Ethnology: Academia Sinica* 69 (Spring): 133–60.
Clarke, Prescott, and J. S. Gregory.
1982   *Western Reports on the Taiping: A Selection of Documents*. Hawaii: Uni-
              versity Press of Hawaii.
Clifford, James, and George E. Marcus, eds.
1986   *Writing Culture: The Poetics and Politics of Ethnography*. Berkeley: Uni-
              versity of California Press.
Cohen, Abner.
1969   *Custom and Politics in Urban Africa: A Study of Hausa Migrants in Yoruba
              Towns*. Berkeley: University of California Press.
1974   "Introduction: The Lessons of Ethnicity." In *Urban Ethnicity*. Abner
              Cohen, ed. ASA Monographs, no. 12. London: Tavistock Publica-
              tions, ix–xxiv.
Cohen, Myron.
1968   "The Hakka or 'Guest People': Dialect as a Sociocultural Variable in
              Southeastern China." *Ethnohistory* 15, no. 3:237–92.
1976   *House United, House Divided: The Chinese Family in Taiwan*. New
              York: Columbia University Press.
Cohen, Paul A.
1963   *China and Christianity: The Missionary Movement and the Growth of Chi-
              nese Antiforeignism, 1860–1870*. Cambridge, Massachusetts: Harvard
              University Press.

Constable, Nicole.
    1991   "History and the Construction of Hakka Identity." Unpublished typescript.
    1992   "Hakka Christian Expressions of Hakka Identity." In *Guest People: Studies of Hakka Chinese Identity*. Nicole Constable, ed. Unpublished typescript.

de Bary, Wm. Theodore.
    1960   *Sources of Chinese Tradition*. New York: Columbia University Press.
    1975   *The Unfolding of Neo-Confucianism*. New York: Columbia University Press.

de Groot, J. J. M.
    [1892] 1964   *The Religious System of China,* Vol. 1, book 1. Taipei, Taiwan: Literature House.
    [1897] 1964   *The Religious System of China,* Vol. 3, book 1. Taipei, Taiwan: Literature House.

Despres, Leo A.
    1967   *Cultural Pluralism and Nationalism Politics in British Guiana*. Chicago: Rand McNally.

DeVos, George.
    1975   "Ethnicity: Vessel of Meaning and Emblem of Contrast." In *Ethnic Identity: Cultural Continuities and Change*. George DeVos and Lola Romanucci-Ross, eds. Palo Alto, California: Mayfield Publishing Company, 363–90.
    1983   "Ethnic Identity and Minority Status: Some Psycho-Cultural Considerations." In *Identity: Personal and Socio-Cultural: A Symposium*. Anita Jacobson-Widding, ed. Atlantic Highlands, New Jersey: Humanities Press.

Eberhard, Wolfram.
    1952   *Chinese Festivals*. New York: Henry Schuman.
    1974   *Studies in Hakka Folktales*. Taipei: Chinese Association for Folklore.

Eitel, E. J.
    1867   "Ethnographical Sketches of the Hakka Chinese." *Notes and Queries on China and Japan* 1 nos. 4:37–40, 5:49–50, 6:65–67, 7:81–83, 8:97–99, 9:113–14, 10:128–30, 11:145–46, 12:161–63.
    1868   "Ethnographical Sketches of the Hakka Chinese." *Notes and Queries on China and Japan* 2, nos. 2:145–47, 11:167–69.
    1869   "Ethnographical Sketches of the Hakka Chinese." *Notes and Queries on China and Japan* 3, no. 1:1–3. Revised editions in *China Review* 2 (1873–74): 160–64, 20 (1891–92): 263–67.

Erbaugh, Mary S.
    1992   "The Secret History of the Hakkas: The Chinese Revolution as a Hakka Enterprise." *China Quarterly* (December) no. 132:937–68.

Faure, David.
    1986   *The Structure of Rural Chinese Society: Lineage and Village in the Eastern New Territories, Hong Kong*. New York: Oxford University Press.

Feuchtwang, Stephan.
    1974a   "Domestic and Communal Worship in Taiwan." In *Religion and Ritual in Chinese Society*. Arthur P. Wolf, ed. Stanford: Stanford University Press, 105–29.

1974b   *An Anthropological Analysis of Chinese Geomancy.* Vientiane, Laos: Vithagna.

Freedman, Maurice.
1958   *Lineage Organization in Southeastern China.* London School of Economics Monographs on Social Anthropology, no. 18. London: Althone Press.
1966   *Chinese Lineage and Society: Fukien and Kwangtung.* London School of Economics Monographs on Social Anthropology, no. 33. London: Althone Press.
1969   "Geomancy: Presidential Address 1968." *Proceedings of the Royal Anthropological Institute of Great Britain and Ireland for 1968.* London: Royal Anthropological Institute of Great Britain and Ireland.
1979   "Chinese Geomancy: Some Observations in Hong Kong." In *The Study of Chinese Society: Essays by Maurice Freedman.* Stanford: Stanford University Press, 189–211.

Geertz, Clifford.
1973a   "The Integrative Revolution: Primordial Sentiments and Civil Politics in New States." In *The Interpretation of Cultures: Selected Essays by Clifford Geertz.* New York: Basic Books, 255–310.
1973b   "Deep Play: Notes on the Balinese Cockfight." In *The Interpretation of Cultures: Selected Essays by Clifford Geertz.* New York: Basic Books, 412–53.

Gernet, Jacques.
1985   *China and the Christian Impact: A Conflict of Cultures.* Cambridge: Cambridge University Press.

Guldin, Greg.
1977   " 'Little Fujian (Fukien)': Sub-Neighborhood and Community in North Point, Hong Kong." *Journal of the Hong Kong Branch of the Royal Asiatic Society* 17:112–30.

Hamberg, Theodore.
1854   *The Visions of Hung-Siu-Tshuen and Origin of the Kwang-si Insurrection.* Hong Kong: China Mail Office.

Harrell, Stevan.
1974   "When a Ghost Becomes a God." In *Religion and Ritual in Chinese Society.* Arthur P. Wolf, ed. Stanford: Stanford University Press, 193–206.
1985   "Why do the Chinese Work So Hard: Reflections on an Entrepreneurial Ethic." *Modern China* 11, no. 2:203–26.
1987   "The Concept of Fate in Chinese Folk Ideology." *Modern China* 13, no. 1:90–109.
1990   "From *Xiedou* to *Yijun,* The Decline of Ethnicity in Northern Taiwan, 1885–1895." *Late Imperial China* 11, no. 1:99–127.

Hashimoto, Mantaro J.
1973   *The Hakka Dialect: A Linguistic Study of Its Phonology, Syntax, and Lexicon.* Cambridge: Cambridge University Press.

Hayes, James.
1962   "The Pattern of Life in the New Territories in 1898." *Journal of the Hong Kong Branch of the Royal Asiatic Society* 2:75–102.

1977   *The Hong Kong Region: 1850–1911: Institutions and Leadership in Town and Countryside*. Hamden, Connecticut: Archon Books.

1983   *The Rural Communities of Hong Kong: Studies and Themes*. Hong Kong: Oxford University Press.

1984   "The Nature of Village Life." In *From Village to City: Studies in the Traditional Roots of Hong Kong Society*. David Faure, James Hayes, and Alan Birch, eds. Hong Kong: Centre of Asian Studies, University of Hong Kong, 55–72.

Hermann, H.

1911   "The Work of German Missions in China." *The China Mission Year Book* 2:257–69.

Ho Ping-ti.

1959   *Studies on the Population of China, 1368–1953*. Cambridge, Massachusetts: Harvard University Press.

Hobsbawm, Eric.

1983   "Introduction: Inventing Traditions." In *The Invention of Tradition*. Eric Hobsbawm and Terence Ranger, eds. New York: Cambridge University Press, 1–14.

Hsieh, Jiann.

1980   "Persistence and Preservation of Hakka Culture in Urban Situations: A Preliminary Study of Voluntary Associations of the Waichow Hakka in Hong Kong." *Journal of the Hong Kong Branch of the Royal Asiatic Society* 20:34–53.

1985   "An Old Bottle With a New Brew: The Waichow Hakkas' Associations in Hong Kong." *Human Organization* 44, no. 2:154–61.

Hsieh Ting-yu (see also Char, Tin Yuke).

1929   "Origins and Migrations of the Hakkas." *The Chinese Social and Political Science Review* 13, no. 220:208–28.

Hsu, Francis L. K.

1948   *Under the Ancestors' Shadow: Chinese Culture and Personality*. New York: Columbia University Press.

1981   *Americans and Chinese: Passage to Differences*. Honolulu: University of Hawaii Press.

Hsu, Immanuel C. Y.

1978   *The Rise of Modern China*. Third ed. New York: Oxford University Press.

Huang, Parker Po-fei.

1970   *Cantonese Dictionary: Cantonese-English, English-Cantonese*. New Haven: Yale University Press.

Ingrams, Harold.

1952   *Hong Kong*. London: Her Majesty's Stationery Office.

Isaacs, Harold.

1975   *Idols of the Tribe: Group Identity and Political Change*. New York: Harper and Row.

Jenkins, Paul.

1982   "Mission History—A Manifesto." In *Research Bulletin of the Institute for Worship and Religious Architecture*. University of Birmingham, 81–92.

1989   "A Short History of the Basel Mission." *Texts and Documents* 10, (May): 2–25. (Irregular publication of the Basel mission.)

Jochim, Christian.
1986   *Chinese Religions: A Cultural Perspective.* Englewood Cliffs, New Jersey: Prentice Hall.

Johnson, Elizabeth L.
1975   "Women and Childbearing in Kwan Mun Hau Village: A Study of Social Change." In *Women in Chinese Society.* Margery Wolf and Roxane Witke, eds. Stanford: Stanford University Press, 215–42.

1976a   " 'Patterned Bands' in the New Territories of Hong Kong." *Journal of the Hong Kong Branch of the Royal Asiatic Society* 16:81–91.

1976b   *Households and Lineages in an Urban Chinese Village.* Ph.D. diss., Cornell University.

1984   "Great Aunt Yeung: A Hakka Wage Laborer." In *Lives: Chinese Working Women.* Mary Sheridan and Janet W. Salaff, eds. Bloomington: Indiana University Press, 76–91.

1988   "Grieving for the Dead, Grieving for the Living: Funeral Laments of Hakka Women." In *Death Ritual in Late Imperial and Modern China.* James L. Watson and Evelyn S. Rawski, eds. Berkeley: University of California Press, 135–63.

1992   "We Guest People: Hakka Identity in Hong Kong." In *Guest People: Studies of Hakka Chinese Identity.* Nicole Constable, ed. Unpublished typescript.

Johnson, Graham E.
1971   *Natives, Migrants and Voluntary Associations in a Colonial Chinese Setting.* Ph.D. diss., Cornell University.

Juergensmeyer, Mark.
1982   *Religion as Social Vision: The Movement Against Untouchability in 20th Century Punjab.* Berkeley: University of California Press.

Keyes, Charles.
1976   "Towards a New Formulation of the Concept of Ethnic Group." *Ethnicity* 3:202–13.

1981   "The Dialectics of Ethnic Change." In *Ethnic Change.* Charles F. Keyes, ed. Seattle: University of Washington Press, 3–30.

Knapp, Ronald G.
1977   "The Changing Landscape of the Chinese Cemetery." *The China Geographer* 8 (Fall): 1–14.

1986   *China's Traditional Rural Architecture: A Cultural Geography of the Common House.* Honolulu: University of Hawaii Press.

Kuhn, Philip A.
1977   "Origins of the Taiping Vision: Cross-Cultural Dimensions of a Chinese Rebellion." *Comparative Studies in Society and History* 19, no. 3:350–66.

1978   "The Taiping Rebellion." In *Late Ch'ing, 1800–1911.* Vol. 10 of *The Cambridge History of China.* John K. Fairbank, ed. Cambridge: Cambridge University Press, pt. 1, 264–317.

Laai, Yi-faai.
    1950   *The Part Played by the Pirates of Kwangdung and Kwangsi Province in the Taiping Insurrection.* Ph.D. diss., University of California, Berkeley.
Lai, David Chuen-Yan.
    1974   "A *Feng-shui* Model as a Location Index." *Annals of the Association of American Geographers* 64, no. 4:506–13.
Lamley, Harry J.
    1981   "Sub-Ethnic Rivalry in the Ch'ing Period." In *The Anthropology of Taiwanese Society.* Emily Martin Ahern and Hill Gates, eds. Stanford: Stanford University Press, 282–318.
Lanternari, Vittorio.
    1963   *The Religions of the Oppressed: A Study of Modern Messianic Cults.* New York: Alfred A. Knopf.
    1974   "Nativistic and Socio-Religious Movements: A Reconsideration." *Comparative Studies in Society and History* 16, no. 4:483–503.
Law, Gail.
    1982   *Chinese Churches Handbook.* Hong Kong: Chinese Coordination Centre of World Evangelism.
Law, Joan, and Barbara E. Ward.
    1982   *Chinese Festivals in Hong Kong.* Hong Kong: South China Morning Post.
Lechler, Rudolf.
    1878   "The Hakka Chinese." *The Chinese Recorder and Missionary Journal* 9:352–59.
Leong, S. T.
    1980   "The Hakka Chinese: Ethnicity and Migrations in Late Imperial China." Paper prepared for the 1980 Association of Asian Studies Conference.
    1985   "The Hakka Chinese of Lingnan: Ethnicity and Social Change in Modern Times." In *Ideal and Reality: Social and Political Change in Modern China, 1860–1949.* David Pong and Edmund S. K. Fung, eds. Lanham, Maryland: University Press of America, 287–326.
Liao, David C. E.
    1972   *The Unresponsive: Resistant or Neglected? The Hakka Chinese in Taiwan Illustrate a Common Missions Problem.* Chicago: Moody Press.
Linebarger, Paul.
    [1925] 1969 *Sun Yat Sen and the Chinese Republic.* New York: AMS Press.
Lin[g] D. Y.
    1951   Report of a Trial Survey of the Economic Conditions of Sixty Families in the New Territories of Hong Kong. Hong Kong: Chinese University of Hong Kong Library. Unpublished typescript.
    1974   "Pianduan huiyi" (Memories). In *Jidujiao Xianggang Chongzhenhui shilue* (History of the Christian Tsung Tsin mission, Hong Kong). Hong Kong: Tsung Tsin Mission, 75–76.
Lip, Evelyn.
    1979   *Chinese Geomancy.* Singapore: Times Books International.

Liu, Kwang-Ching.
1990   "Introduction: Orthodoxy in Chinese Society." In *Orthodoxy in Late Imperial China*. Kwang Ching Liu, ed. Berkeley: University of California Press, 27–52.

Lo, Wan.
1965   "Communal Strife in Mid-Nineteenth-Century Kwangtung: The Establishment of Ch'ih-Ch'i." In *Papers on China*. Harvard University, East Asian Research Center 19:85–119.

Loercher, F. G.
1879   Register of Names to the Map of the Province of Canton Hong Kong. Noronha and Sons.

Lun Ng, Alice Ngai-ha.
1984   "Village Education in the New Territories Region Under the Ch'ing." In *From Village to City: Studies in the Traditional Roots of Hong Kong Society*. David Faure, James Hayes, and Alan Birch, eds. Hong Kong: Centre of Asian Studies, University of Hong Kong, 106–18.

Luo Xianglin.
1933   *Kejia yanjiu daolun* (Introduction to the study of the Hakkas in its ethnic, historical, and cultural aspects). Xingning, Guangdong: Xishan Library.
1950   "Kejia yuanliukao" (Investigation of the origin and movements of the Hakka)." In *Xianggang Chongzheng conghui sanshih zhounian jinian tekan* (Hong Kong Tsung Tsin Association thirtieth anniversary special publication). Hong Kong: Tsung Tsin Association, iii–iv, 1–106.
1965   *Kejia shiliao huipian* (Historical sources for the study of the Hakka). Hong Kong: Institute of Chinese Culture, Ling Nam Printing Company.
1974   "Fenling Chongqiantang jianshi" (Brief history of Shung Him Church in Fanling). In *Jidujiao Xianggang Chongzhenhui shilue* (History of the Christian Tsung Tsin mission, Hong Kong). Hong Kong: Tsung Tsin Mission, 71–74.

MacGillivray, Donald.
[1907] 1979 *A Century of Protestant Missions in China, 1807–1907: Being the Centenary Conference Historical Volume*. San Francisco: Chinese Materials Center.

Malinowski, Bronislaw.
1922   *Argonauts of the Western Pacific*. New York: E. P. Dutton and Co.

Marcus, George E., and Michael M. J. Fischer.
1986   *Anthropology as Cultural Critique: An Experimental Moment in the Human Sciences*. Chicago: University of Chicago Press.

Martin, Howard, J.
1992   "The Hakka Ethnic Movement on Taiwan, 1986–1991." In *Guest People: Studies of Hakka Chinese Identity*, Nicole Constable, ed. Unpublished typescript.

Michael, Franz.
1966   *The Taiping Rebellion: History and Documents*. Vol. 1. Seattle: University of Washington Press.
1971   *The Taiping Rebellion: History and Documents*. Vol. 2. Seattle: University of Washington Press.

Moser, Leo J.
1985   *The Chinese Mosaic: The Peoples and Provinces of China.* Boulder: West-
              view Press.
Nagata, Judith.
1981   "In Defense of Ethnic Boundaries: The Changing Myths and Char-
              ters of Malay Identity." In *Ethnic Change.* Charles F. Keyes, ed. Seat-
              tle: University of Washington Press, 87–116.
Nakagawa, Manabu.
1975   "Studies on the History of the Hakkas: Reconsidered." *The Devel-
              oping Economies* (Tokyo) 13, no. 2:208–23.
Naquin, Susan, and Evelyn S. Rawski.
1987   *Chinese Society in the Eighteenth Century.* New Haven: Yale University
              Press.
Nash, June.
1979   *We Eat the Mines and the Mines Eat Us: Dependency and Exploitation in
              Bolivian Tin Mines.* New York: Columbia University Press.
Nelson, H. G. H.
1974   "Ancestor Worship and Burial Practices." In *Religion and Ritual in Chi-
              nese Society.* Arthur P. Wolf, ed. Stanford: Stanford University Press,
              251–77.
Newbern, William C.
1953   *The Taiping Rebellion, 1850–1865: A Messianic Movement in China.*
              M.A. thesis, University of California at Berkeley.
Ng, Ronald.
1968   "Culture and Society of a Hakka Community on Lantau Island, Hong
              Kong." In *Hong Kong: A Society in Transition, Contributions to the Study
              of Hong Kong Society.* Ian C. Jarvie and Joseph Agassi, eds. New York:
              Frederick A. Praeger, 53–63.
Norman, Jerry.
1988   *Chinese.* New York: Cambridge University Press.
Oehler, Wilhelm.
1922   "Christian Work Among the Hakka." In *The Christian Occupation of
              China.* Milton T. Stauffer, ed. Shanghai: China Continuation Com-
              mittee, 351–53.
Ortner, Sherry B.
1973   "On Key Symbols." *American Anthropologist* 75, no. 5:1338–46.
Oxfeld, Ellen (see also Ellen Oxfeld Basu).
1993   *Blood, Sweat and Mahjong: Family and Enterprise in an Overseas Chinese
              Community.* Ithaca: Cornell University Press.
Pang Lok Sam.
1934   *Xianggang Xinjie Longyuetou Chongqiantang cunzhi* (History of Shung
              Him Tong village, Lung Yeuk Tau, New Territories, Hong Kong).
              Mimeographed manuscript. Hong Kong University Library.
Pasternak, Burton.
1972   *Kinship and Community in Two Chinese Villages.* Stanford: Stanford
              University Press.
1983   *Guests in the Dragon: Social Demography of a Chinese District, 1895–
              1946.* New York: Columbia University Press.

Piton, Charles.
1873   "On the Origin and History of the Hakkas." *China Review* 2, no. 4:222–26.
Potter, Jack M.
1968   *Capitalism and the Chinese Peasant: Social and Economic Change in a Hong Kong Village.* Berkeley: University of California Press.
Pratt, Jean.
1960   "Emigration and Unilineal Descent Groups: A Study of Marriage in a Hakka Village in the New Territories, Hong Kong." *Eastern Anthropologist* 13, no. 4:147–58.
Rabinow, Paul.
1977   *Reflections on Fieldwork in Morocco.* Berkeley: University of California Press.
Ramsey, S. Robert.
1987   *The Languages of China.* Princeton, New Jersey: Princeton University Press.
Rosaldo, Renato.
1986   "From the Door of His Tent: The Fieldworker and the Inquisitor." In *Writing Culture: The Poetics and Politics of Culture: A School of American Research Advanced Seminar.* James Clifford and George E. Marcus, eds. Berkeley: University of California Press, 77–97.
Rossbach, Sarah.
1983   *Feng Shui: The Chinese Art of Placement.* New York: E. P. Dutton.
Sagart, Laurent.
1982   *Phonologie du Dialecte Hakka de Sung Him Tong* (Phonology of the Hakka dialect of Shung Him Tong). Paris: Centre de Recherches Linguistiques Sur L'Asie Orientale.
Schlatter, Wilhelm.
1916   *Geschichte der Basler Mission, 1815–1915.* (History of the Basel mission, 1815–1915). Vol. 2. Basel: Verlag der Basler Missionsbuchhandlung.
Schultze, Otto.
1916   "Lutheran Group: Evangelische Missionsgesellschaft Zu Basel." *China Mission Year Book* 7:83–86.
Shack, William A.
1973   "Urban Ethnicity and the Cultural Process of Urbanization." In *Urban Anthropology: Cross Cultural Studies of Urbanization.* Aidan Southall, ed. New York: Oxford University Press, 251–86.
Shih, Vincent Yu-chung.
1967   *The Taiping Ideology: Its Sources, Interpretations, and Influences.* Seattle: University of Washington Press.
Siu, Anthony Kwok-kin.
1984   "The Hong Kong Region Before and After the Coastal Evacuation in the Early Ch'ing Dynasty." In *From Village to City: Studies in the Traditional Roots of Hong Kong Society.* David Faure, James Hayes, and Alan Birch, eds. Hong Kong: Centre of Asian Studies, University of Hong Kong, 1–9.

Skinner, G. William.

1976   "Mobility Strategies in Late Imperial China: Regional Systems Analysis." In *Economic Systems*. Vol. 1 of *Regional Analysis*. Carol A. Smith, ed. New York: Academic Press, 327–64.

1977   "Regional Systems in Late Imperial China." Paper prepared for the Second Annual Meeting of the Social Science and History Association, Ann Arbor, Michigan.

Smith, Carl T.

1976   "Notes on Friends and Relatives of Taiping Leaders." *Journal of the Hong Kong Branch of the Royal Asiatic Society* 16:117–34.

1985   *Chinese Christians: Elites, Middlemen, and the Church in Hong Kong*. New York: Oxford University Press.

Sparks, Douglas W.

1976a   "The Teochiu: Ethnicity in Urban Hong Kong." *Journal of the Hong Kong Branch of the Royal Asiatic Society* 16:25–56.

1976b   "Interethnic Interaction—A Matter of Definition: Ethnicity in a Housing Estate in Hong Kong." *Journal of the Hong Kong Branch of the Royal Asiatic Society* 16:57–80.

Strauch, Judith.

1984   "Middle Peasants and Market Gardeners, the Social Context of the 'Vegetable Revolution' in a Small Agricultural Community in the New Territories, Hong Kong." In *From Village to City: Studies in the Traditional Roots of Hong Kong Society*. David Faure, James Hayes, and Alan Birch, eds. Hong Kong: Centre of Asian Studies, University of Hong Kong, 191–205.

Sung Hok-P'ang.

1973   "Legends and Stories of the New Territories: Kam T'in." *Journal of the Hong Kong Branch of the Royal Asiatic Society* 13:111–32.

1974   "Legends and Stories of the New Territories: Kam T'in." *Journal of the Hong Kong Branch of the Royal Asiatic Society* 14:160–85.

Tan Bian.

1963   "Sun Zhongshan jiashi yuanliu jiqi shangdai jingji zhuangkuang xinzheng" (New evidence on Sun Yat-sen's ancestry and his ancestor's economic situation). *Xueshu yanjiu* 3:32–38.

Teng, Ssu Yu.

1962   *Historiography of the Taiping Rebellion*. Cambridge, Massachusetts: Harvard University Press.

1971   *The Taiping Rebellion and the Western Powers: A Comprehensive Study*. Oxford: Clarendon Press.

Thompson, Stuart E.

1988   "Death, Food, and Fertility." In *Death Ritual in Late Imperial and Modern China*. James L. Watson and Evelyn S. Rawski, eds. Berkeley: University of California Press, 71–108.

Topley, Marjorie.

1964   "Capital, Savings and Credit Among Indigenous Rice Farmers in Hong Kong's New Territories." *Capital, Savings and Credit in Peasant Societies: Studies from Asia, Oceania, the Caribbean and Middle America*. Raymond Firth and B. S. Yamey, eds. Chicago: Aldine Publishing Company, 157–86.

1974   "Cosmic Antagonisms: A Mother-Child Syndrome." In *Religion and Ritual in Chinese Society*. Arthur P. Wolf, ed. Stanford: Stanford University Press, 233–49.

Trosper, Ronald L.
1981   "American Indian Nationalism and Frontier Expansion." In *Ethnic Change*. Charles F. Keyes, ed. Seattle: University of Washington Press, 246–70.

Tsang, Kwok Fu, ed.
1983   "Centenary Magazine, 1882–1982." Basel Christian Church of Malaysia. Hong Kong: Tat To Printing Company.

Voskamp, C. J.
1914   "The Work of German Missions in China." *China Mission Yearbook* 5:371–76.

Wagner, Rudolf G.
1982   *Reenacting the Heavenly Vision: The Role of Religion in the Taiping Rebellion*. Institute of East Asian Studies, University of California, Berkeley: China Research Monographs.

Wang, Sung-hsing.
1974   "Taiwanese Architecture and the Supernatural." In *Religion and Ritual in Chinese Society*. Arthur P. Wolf, ed. Stanford: Stanford University Press, 183–92.

Ward, Barbara E.
1965   "Varieties of the Conscious Model: The Fishermen of South China." In *The Relevance of Models for Social Anthropology*. Michael Banton, ed. New York: Frederick Preager, ASA Monographs no. 1, 113–38.
1966   "Sociological Self-Awareness: Some Uses of the Conscious Models." *Man* 1, no. 2:201–7.

Watson, James L.
1975   *Emigration and the Chinese Lineage: The Mans in Hong Kong and London*. Berkeley: University of California Press.
1983   "Rural Society: Hong Kong's New Territories." *China Quarterly* 95:480–90.
1988   "The Structure of Chinese Funerary Rites: Elementary Forms, Ritual Sequence, and the Primacy of Performance." In *Death Ritual in Late Imperial and Modern China*. James L. Watson and Evelyn S. Rawski, eds. Berkeley: University of California Press, 3–19.

Watson, Rubie S.
1982   "The Creation of a Chinese Lineage: The Teng of Ha Tsuen, 1669–1751." *Modern Asian Studies* 16, no. 1:69–100.
1985   *Inequality Among Brothers: Class and Kinship in South China*. Cambridge: Cambridge University Press.
1986   "The Named and the Nameless: Gender and Person in Chinese Society." *American Ethnologist* 13, no. 4:619–31.
1988   "Remembering the Dead: Graves and Politics in Southeastern China." In *Death Ritual in Late Imperial and Modern China*. James L. Watson and Evelyn S. Rawski, eds. Berkeley: University of California Press, 203–27.

Weber, Max.
    [1930] 1958   *The Protestant Ethic and the Spirit of Capitalism.* Trans. Talcott Parsons. New York: Charles Scribner's Sons.

Weller, Robert P.
    1987   *Unities and Diversities in Chinese Religion.* Seattle: University of Washington Press.

Whyte, Martin K.
    1988   "Death in the People's Republic of China." In *Death Ritual in Late Imperial and Modern China.* James L. Watson and Evelyn S. Rawski, eds. Berkeley: University of California Press, 289–316.

Witschi, H.
    1965   *Geschichte der Basler Mission, 1914–1919* (History of the Basel mission, 1914–1919). Vol. 4. Basel: Verlag der Basler Missionsbuchhandlung.
    1970   *Geschichte der Basler Mission, 1920–1940* (History of the Basel mission, 1920–1940). Vol. 5. Basel: Verlag der Basler Missionsbuchhandlung.

Wolf, Arthur P.
    1970   "Chinese Kinship and Mourning Dress." In *Family and Kinship in Chinese Society.* Maurice Freedman, ed. Stanford: Stanford University Press, 189–207.
    1974a   "Introduction." In *Religion and Ritual in Chinese Society.* Arthur P. Wolf, ed. Stanford: Stanford University Press, 1–18.
    1974b   "Gods, Ghosts and Ancestors." In *Religion and Ritual in Chinese Society.* Arthur P. Wolf, ed. Stanford: Stanford University Press, 131–82.

Wolf, Margery.
    1968   *The House of Lim: A Study of a Chinese Farm Family.* Englewood Cliffs, New Jersey: Prentice Hall, Inc.

Worsley, Peter.
    1968   *The Trumpet Shall Sound: A Study of 'Cargo' Cults in Melanesia.* New York: Schocken Books.

Yang, C. K.
    1961   *Religion in Chinese Society: A Study of Contemporary Social Functions of Religion and Some of Their Historical Factors.* Berkeley: University of California Press.

Yang, Paul S. J.
    1967   "Elements of Hakka Dialectology." *Monumenta Serica* 26:305–51.

Young, Crawford.
    1983   "The Temple of Ethnicity." *World Politics* 35, no. 4:652–62.

Yu Wai Hong.
    1987   "Chongzhenhui yibaisishinian laiwen gongzuo, yingxiang yu zhanwang" (Work, influence, and prospects of the Tsung Tsin mission in the past hundred and forty years). In *Xianggang Chongzhenhui lihui yibaisishi zhounian jinian tekan, 1847–1987* (Hong Kong Tsung Tsin mission one hundred and fortieth anniversary special publication, 1847–1987). Hong Kong: Tsung Tsin Mission, 55–70.

Index

Adoption, 96; posthumous, 96, 148
Africa: churches in, 16, 185n. 4, 189n. 13; immigration to, 11
Ahern, Emily M., 106, 111, 192n. 6, 193nn. 10, 14
Aijmer, Goran, 136
All Saints' Day, 193n. 11
All Souls' Day, 112
Alliances, Hakka, 21, 59, 133; with non-Christians, 4; with non-Hakka, 4. *See also* United Hakka Association
Alter, Joseph S., 7–8
American Baptist mission, 31
Anagnost, Ann, 136
Ancestral halls, 112, 147, 163, 182
Ancestor tablets, 100, 147
Ancestors: burial of, 98, 102; care of, 98, 101, 126; commemoration of, 101, 109, 126, 147; offerings to, 97, 109, 112, 116; worship of, 97, 109, 126, 147, 164, 186n. 2
Anderson, Benedict, 20, 21
Anderson, Eugene N., 13, 107, 115, 128
Anderson, Marja L., 115
Anhui province, 26
Anthropology, connotations of, 6

Architecture, Hakka, 12, 13
Arkush, R. David, 131
Assemblies of God Church, 76, 77
Assimilation to Cantonese, 10, 12, 13, 41
Associations, Hakka, 10, 13, 17, 21–22, 25, 26, 36–37, 60, 148, 150, 156, 157, 186n. 3, 194n. 2; establishment of, 21, 37, 60; persistence of, 14; publications, 25; 130, 133, 147; rhetoric of, 21. *See also* God Worshipers, Society of; Luen On Tong; Luen Wo Tong; Tsung Tsin mission
Australia, immigration to, 26
Austria, Basel mission affiliation with, 16
Aw Boon Haw, 133

Baainihn, 116, 117
Baaisahn, 116. *See also* "Idol worship"
Baker, Hugh, 10, 41, 46, 118n. 3, 189n. 12, 194n. 4
Balfour, S. F., 40, 41
Banquets: Christmas, 113–14; funeral, 107, 108; marriage, 121; New Year, 115, 116; 140th

Catholics: attempts to convert, 98; as Hakka "skeptics," 150–51, 159; as "non-Christians," 85, 191n. 5; and Protestants, 191n. 17; in Shung Him Tong, 85; as successful Hakka, 150
Cemetery, public, 102, 109
Cemetery, Shung Him, 52–54, 101–5, 126, 192n. 7, plate 7; at Ching Ming, 109; crowding of, 105, 192n. 6; *feng-shui* of, 122–23; as genealogy, 126, 147; as historical text, 103–4, 147; and Luo Xianglin, 103; at New Year, 117; and Pang Lok Sam, 102; preferred locations, 104; rules of, 103; and social structure, 104. *See also* Burial; Ching Ming; Graves
Chan Cheong Wo, 181–82
Chan Kwai Choi, 49
Chan Yuk Choi, 49
Chang, Chung-li, 190n. 14
Changle. *See* Wuhua
Chaozhou, 188n. 4; Basel mission work among, 16, 141; economic success of, 128, 150; Hakka speakers, 69, 157, 158; in Hong Kong, 1; as honorary Hakka, 69; and Hungry Ghost festival, 112; origins, 11; restaurants, 13; stereotypes of, 128; wood-carvers, 121
Char, Tin Yuke. *See* Hsieh Ting-yu
Charity, 87
Cheuk Hing Ko, 49, 180–81
Cheung Fuk Hing, 149, 169, 170
Cheung Hing Tong, earlier name of Shung Him Tong, 51
Cheung Sui Wing, 47, 53, 177
Cheung Wo Ban, 49, 53, 55, 56, 60, 179–80
Childbirth, 119
Children. *See* Youth

Chinese Christian Organization for World Evangelism, 75, 156
Chinese Evangelical Church in Fanling, 76
Chinese festivals. *See* Chinese New Year; Ching Ming; Chung Yeung; Hungry Ghost festival; Midautumn festival
Chinese identity, 20, 163, 164; and Christianity, 4, 18, 126; and concept of *zu*, 23; and culture, 100; and religion, 100; and ritual, 18, 100, 191n. 3, 192n. 5; in Shung Him Tong, 125. *See also* Hakka identity; Han Chinese
Chinese language groups, 186n. 6. *See also* Cantonese language; Hakka language; Hokkien; Language
Chinese New Year, 114–19, 163; banquet, 115–16; church attendance at, 98, 116; clothes, 116; couplets 115, 117–18; decorations, 114–15, 116; gifts, 133; greetings, 117; house cleaning, 115; kitchen god, 115; lucky papers, 115, 117, 118, 164; practices, 98; preparations, 114–15; in Shung Him Tong, 115–16; "superstitions," 163; visits, 4, 116–17
Chinese orthodoxy, 101, 163
Chinese religion, 97–99; 118, 186n. 2; almanacs, 97; altars, 97; astrology, 97; and Christianity, 100, 118, 125; deities, 79, 97, 109, 115, 117, 166, 168, 170; secularized, 98–99, 100–101, 108, 112, 125–26; temples, 97. *See also* Ancestors, worship of; Buddhism; Chinese New Year; *Feng-shui*; Taoism
Chinese stereotypes. *See* Stereotypes, Chinese